The Construction
of Personality

An Introduction

Introductions to Modern Psychology

General Editor: Max Coltheart, Birkbeck College,
University of London

The Construction of Personality: An Introduction, Sarah Hampson
Clinical Psychopathology: An Introduction, E.M. Coles
Consistency in Cognitive Social Behaviour: An Introduction to Social Psychology, Camilla Mower White

The Construction of Personality

An Introduction

Sarah E. Hampson

Department of Psychology
Birkbeck College
University of London

Routledge & Kegan Paul
London, Boston and Henley

First published in 1982
by Routledge & Kegan Paul Ltd
39 Store Street, London WC1E 7DD,
9 Park Street, Boston, Mass. 02108, USA and
Broadway House, Newton Road,
Henley-on-Thames, Oxon RG9 1EN

Set in Baskerville by
Hope Services, Abingdon, Oxon
and printed in Great Britain by
Redwood Burn Ltd, Trowbridge, Wiltshire

Library of Congress Cataloging in Publication Data

Hampson, Sarah E., 1951–
The construction of personality.
(Introductions to modern psychology)
Bibliography.
Includes index.
1. Personality.   2. Personality–Research.   I. Title.
II. Series. [DNLM: 1. Personality.   2. Psychological
theory.   BF 698 H231c]
BF698.H333   155.2   81–12033
ISBN 0-7100-0872-4   AACR2
ISBN 0-7100-0873-2 (pbk)

Contents

	Acknowledgments	vii
1	The Concept of Personality	1
2	The Personality Theorist's Perspective: Single-Trait Theories	7
3	The Personality Theorist's Perspective: Multi-Trait Theories	33
4	The Issue of Consistency and the Personality Theorist's Perspective	63
5	The Lay Perspective	97
6	The Lay Perspective and Reality	135
7	The Self Perspective	172
8	Personality over the Life-Span	206
9	Criminal Personality	246
10	The Construction of Personality	279
	Bibliography	287
	Index	311

Acknowledgments

A number of people have read some or all of this book at different stages in its preparation and their reactions have been invaluable. I am especially indebted to Max Coltheart for his help with the entire manuscript and to Camilla Mower White who also commented on all the chapters. In particular, I would like to thank Paul Harris for his candid comments. I am also grateful to Mary Boyle, Gordon Craig, Peter Dowrick, Daphne Loasby, Angus McLachlan and the third and fourth year Birkbeck Psychology undergraduates in 1979-80 for their evaluations of various chapters, and I would like to thank Carol Machen and Patricia Caple for their assistance with typing.

The figure from *Dimensions of Personality*, edited by H. London and J.E. Exner (1978), is adapted on p. 13 with kind permission of John Wiley & Sons.

1 The Concept of Personality

A Definition of Personality

This is a book about the psychological study of personality, and therefore the first step is to provide a definition of this overworked term. In the past, it has had different meanings for theologians, philosophers and sociologists; and within psychology it has been defined in many ways (Allport, 1937). Rather than give examples of the diversity of definitions, which tends to be confusing rather than illuminating, we will begin by considering just one definition of personality considered acceptable by many psychologists today (Block, Weiss and Thorne, 1979): personality refers to *'More or less stable internal factors that make one person's behaviour consistent from one time to another, and different from the behaviour other people would manifest in comparable situations'* (I.L. Child, 1968, p.83).

In a few words, this definition manages to encompass all the important elements of a generally accepted definition of the concept of personality. However, the definition will not be given wholesale acceptance here, but instead used as a means of introducing the major issues that frequently arise as points of disagreement in the study of personality. These issues are found in the form of underlying assumptions which may be exposed beneath the deceptively straightforward exterior of Child's definition. The assumptions are revealed by the use of certain key words: *stable, internal, consistent* and *different*.

Stability
The definition begins with the assumption of stability by stating that personality is *more or less* stable. It is not assumed that personality is *entirely* stable; the assumption is that it can, to a limited extent, undergo changes. Such a view allows for the possibility of long-term personality growth and change over the life-span and short-term fluctuations in personality from day to day. Nevertheless, these instabilities are regarded as relatively superficial when compared with the underlying core of continuity implied by the personality concept. The assumption of stability corresponds to our everyday experience: friends and acquaintances do not present radically different personalities on every fresh meeting, but instead are likely to be approximately the same from occasion to occasion. Even when we are taken by surprise by an old friend's dramatic new image, we are usually able to fit the new and old selves into a coherent whole, and to reassure ourselves that deep down the person is still the same.

Internality
The next assumption in the definition is that personality is *internal*: personality is located inside the individual. A corollary of this assumption is that personality is not available for direct observation. It can only be measured indirectly by making observations of that which is available externally. Thus on the basis of personality tests a psychologist will infer the presence of underlying personality traits which determine that person's test performance. Similarly, we make inferences about the personalities of our friends and acquaintances on the basis of observations of their behaviour.

Consistency
The definition goes on to state that personality *make[s] one person's behaviour consistent from one time to another*. The assumption that behaviour is consistent is one of the most controversial issues in personality. Consistency over time refers to the similarity between a person's behaviour on two different occasions. Everyday life is full of examples of consistency, from trivial daily routines such as the order in which you brush your teeth to more weighty matters such as which

way you vote in a general election. Personality is assumed to explain behavioural consistency because it is assumed to be a major determinant of behaviour and, since personality remains relatively stable, the behaviour it determines will be consistent.

Individual differences
Finally, the definition states that personality makes a person's behaviour *different from the behaviour other people would manifest in comparable situations.* It is a major assumption underlying the personality concept that there are individual differences in behaviour which are large enough to warrant investigation: people respond to the same situation in different ways. For example in even such a constrained situation as a lecture, students' behaviour will vary from sleep to furiously energetic note-taking. Individual differences in response to the same situation are assumed to be the product of variations in personality.

The definition of personality has been pulled apart to reveal four underlying assumptions, and it would probably be possible to unearth some more. It is important to remember that these assumptions are just that: they are assumptions rather than undisputed facts. For example, it may be quite wrong to assume that personality is essentially stable; it may be nearer the truth to regard personality as continually changing. It may be wrong to assume that personality is located within the individual; perhaps, like beauty, it resides in the eye of the beholder. Behavioural consistency and individual differences are assumed; but how far are people consistent from one occasion to another, and to what extent do they behave differently from one another in the same situation? If no empirical support for these assumptions can be found, a radical reappraisal of what psychologists mean by the term personality will be required. These issues will provide discussion points throughout this book although the weight given to each issue will vary according to the subject-matter of particular chapters.

Perspectives on Personality

This book is organised around three different perspectives on personality. In the present context, perspective is not being used metaphorically to mean theoretical point of view, but more literally to mean the standpoint from which personality is being observed and investigated. There are three perspectives from which personality has been studied: the perspective of psychologists studying other people, which has yielded psychological theories of personality; the perspective of non-psychologists, producing lay theories of personality; and the perspective from the standpoint of the self, which is concerned with the theories people have about their *own* personalities.

The personality theorist's perspective
From observations of other people, psychologists have studied personality, and developed formal theories to account for their findings; hence this will be referred to as the personality theorist's perspective. Personality theories typically consist of propositions concerned with three main areas: the structure, dynamics and development of personality (Hall and Lindzey, 1978). Propositions about personality structure are meant to specify more precisely the nature of the internal factors making up personality; the study of personality dynamics is concerned with what drives the structure to result in behaviour; and personality development has to do with the origins of the mature structure and its dynamics.

These three elements may be briefly illustrated by reference to Freud's theory of personality (which is dealt with in more detail in Chapter 8). First, the id, ego and the superego are the three interrelated systems which make up the structure of personality. Second, they are regarded as being in constant competition for control of psychic energy, which is the basis of the Freudian account of dynamics. Finally, Freud proposed that personality develops predominantly as a sequence of three stages, a sequence which is completed around the age of five years. These three stages are the oral, anal and phallic stages, their names deriving from the part of the body assumed to provide the major source of gratification during the particular stage. Other personality theories, such as Eysenck's and Cattell's, are based on more objective observations of normal populations. The personality theorist's perspective is presented in Chapters 2 and 3 and is criticised in Chapter 4.

The lay perspective
The lay perspective refers to the widely shared set of beliefs about personality which are not generally made explicit, but which remain implicit and form the basis of lay or everyday theories of personality, theories which we all use in an informal and often unconscious way (Bruner and Tagiuri, 1954). Lay theories have become embodied in the language of personality description, e.g. we might be telling friends about a person we had recently met and describe this new person as 'warm' and 'friendly'. Our friends would have no difficulty in understanding this description and would probably infer that were they also to meet this person it would be easy to strike up a conversation, since the person would be likely to be 'sociable' as well. In short, we tend to believe that certain personality characteristics like 'warm', 'friendly' and 'sociable' go together, and we use these beliefs to make additional inferences about personality on the basis of limited information. These beliefs help us to simplify and organise our social world by enabling us to categorise people in terms of their personality characteristics in ways which then allow us to make predictions about their future behaviour. Lay personality theory is a form of general knowledge comparable to our knowledge about other aspects of the animate and inanimate environment. One does not need to be a biologist to know that dogs can bite, or a chemist to know that paper dissolves in water.

General knowledge about personality is of interest to psychologists for at least two reasons: first, in order to understand social behaviour it is necessary to understand the informal personality theories people use to categorise one another and to make predictions about additional characteristics and behaviour; second, the existence of the lay perspective raises the question of how it relates to the personality theorist's perspective. They are both perspectives on the same subject matter but how far are they the same? These issues will be considered in Chapters 5 and 6.

The self perspective

The final perspective to be considered is the self perspective. Psychologists have been concerned with the origins of our self-awareness (Mead, 1934), and the form in which our self perceptions are structured (Rogers, 1959). One of the most interesting issues raised in connection with the concept of the self perspective is the extent to which our self perceptions are accurate. While we may think that no one knows us better than we do ourselves, there is evidence to suggest that this self knowledge is not as accurate as we would like to believe. The self perspective is discussed in Chapter 7.

These three perspectives are not the only standpoints from which observations about personality can be made; sociologists, philosophers and theologians all have their own perspectives from which to think about and study personality. However, the three perspectives described here incorporate the main areas of psychological research into personality. Traditionally, these three perspectives have not been given equal weight in personality text books. Lay theories of personality and the self perspective are more commonly found in social psychology texts, but it is the intention here to show that the understanding of personality is enhanced by a consideration of all three perspectives and their inter-relations. In Chapter 8 the discussion of personality over the life-span will try to show how these differing perspectives work together to produce the impression of an enduring personality. In Chapter 9 we shall see how these perspectives contribute to the concept of a deviant personality.

2 The Personality Theorist's Perspective: Single-Trait Theories

From the personality theorist's perspective personality is typically regarded as internal and hence not directly accessible. It is made manifest in a person's behaviour and appearance; these provide the outward signs from which the internal elements of personality may be inferred. This inference process is not always accurate; for example, the nineteenth-century criminologist Lombroso believed that the criminal personality could be inferred from a variety of physical characteristics such as long arms and flat noses. The long arms were not for reaching into pockets, nor were the flat noses a consequence of such behaviour; both were regarded as inherited features indicative of a reversion to animals lower down the evolutionary scale such as the apes. However, Lombroso's outward signs of criminality turned out to be nothing more than the physical concomitants of severely subnormal intelligence. Another example of the inferring of personality from behaviour is Freud's view that relatively trivial and usual behaviour like slips of the tongue or forgetting people's names reveal volumes about a person's underlying conflicts; but while Freud's interpretations of everyday behaviours may be fascinating, they are virtually impossible to put to the test.

Despite the dangers, the assumption that outward signs may be used for the inference and assessment of personality remains the hallmark of the personality theorist's perspective (Wiggins, 1973). It is assumed that carefully selected samples of behaviour may be used to measure a person's position on the underlying personality dimensions believed to give rise to the overt behaviour.

Interest in personality measurement developed as a result of successful attempts to measure another dimension of individual variation: intelligence. Since personality measurement started out with many of the assumptions and techniques which had proved successful in mental testing, it is worth mentioning these briefly here before moving on to personality proper.

Origins of Personality Measurement

Measurement of intelligence
Mental testing was first introduced at the beginning of this century by Binet in France. His goals were pragmatic: to find tests that would discriminate between children in schools in Paris, so that the duller ones could be identified and sent for special education (Herrnstein, 1973). He was not primarily concerned with the nature of intelligence but instead with producing ways of testing it that were sensitive to the range of individual differences in ability. If he did not understand the nature of intelligence, how could he be sure that his tests were measuring it? His approach relied on the fact that it is generally agreed that as children grow older they become more intelligent and within each age-group some children are more precocious than others. Binet used these two sources of information about intelligence as the yardstick against which to measure the success of his tests: they had to be able to sort out the younger children from the older ones and within one age-group they had to sort out the ones the teachers thought were bright from the ones regarded as dull.

Although Binet's approach to intelligence testing was pragmatic, subsequent researchers were not content to let the nature of intelligence remain an enigma. They noticed that intelligence appeared to be composed of a number of different abilities, such that a person might be more able in some areas than others. By studying the intercorrelations between subtests that make up an intelligence test it is possible to pick out separate groups of subtests in such a way that all the subtests within a particular group seem to be measuring the same ability, whilst the different groups of tests are measuring different abilities.

The statistical technique for isolating separate groups of subtests is factor analysis (Harman, 1967) which will be described in more detail in the next chapter. The pioneers of factor analysis in mental testing were Spearman and Thurstone. Spearman (1927) argued that intelligence involves two kinds of factors: a *general factor* (which enters into all subtests) and a *specific factor* (restricted to the particular ability being measured by the subtest). Thurstone (1947) proposed several general factors which enter into the correlations between subtests, and he developed a more sophisticated form of factor analysis to demonstrate the plurality of general factors.

Similarities between measuring intelligence and measuring personality

Personality testing has the same aims as intelligence testing: to distinguish between individuals and to make predictions about their performance in other settings. One of the major problems for personality testing is the lack of an obvious yardstick or criterion against which to assess the ability of the test to measure what it claims to be measuring. There are hundreds of ways of discriminating between people from their body weight to their taste in light reading and the problem is to decide which of these outward signs may be taken as an index of personality. Unfortunately the natural yardstick of age which is appropriate for intelligence testing is not relevant so far as personality testing is concerned.

While personality probably does change with age, it does not appear to do so in any straightforward way. We cannot say that 7-year-olds are 'less' extraverted than 9-year-olds. Nor is there an obvious group of experts, such as teachers, who might agree on a rank ordering of people in terms of personality characteristics. Instead, other less satisfactory criteria have to be used, as we shall see later in the chapter.

Personality testing inherited the technique of factor analysis for unravelling the structure of personality and thus also inherited the propensity to produce several fiercely disputed solutions to the puzzle; for factor analysis can be used in a variety of ways, and the final solution looks different depending on, for example, the choice of items put into the analysis and the level in the hierarchy of factors with which the researcher chooses to work. These issues will be examined more closely when the work of Eysenck and Cattell is considered.

To summarise, personality and intelligence have a number of features in common. They are both psychological components of the individual which can be measured to reveal individual differences. Factor analysis has been used to investigate the structure of the psychological components assessed by intelligence and personality tests. Intelligence is fortunate in having both a natural criterion (age changes) and teachers' expert opinions against which to validate its tests; but those interested in measuring personality are not so lucky.

Single-Trait Theories

Single-trait theories are concerned with the role played by one particular part of the personality structure in the determination of behaviour. The most influential single-trait theories have been those which describe traits that enter into a wide variety of behaviours. Some well-known examples of such traits are Authoritarianism (Adorno, Frenkel-Brunswick, Levinson and Sanford, 1950), the Achievement Motive (McClelland, Atkinson, Clark and Lowell, 1953), and Repression versus Sensitisation (Byrne, 1964). The ambitions of a single-trait investigator studying one aspect of personality are far more humble than those of the multi-trait investigator, who hopes to describe personality in its entirety; multi-trait theories such as those of Eysenck and Cattell are described in the next chapter.

When discussing the personality theorist's perspective, the terms 'trait' and 'dimension' will be used interchangeably to refer to an internal characteristic which is capable of distinguishing between individuals in the sense that it is believed to be present to a greater extent in some people than in others. The two single-trait theories and their associated measures to be presented here involve the traits of Field Dependence-Independence (FD–I) and Locus of Control respectively. These particular theories have been chosen because of the vast amount of research they have generated (approximately three thousand studies between them — ample testimony to their popularity and influence). Reviews of these and other single-trait theories are to be found in Blass (1977) and in London and Exner (1978).

Field Dependence–Independence

FD–I is a dimension of individual variation which characterises an aspect of information processing. The relatively field dependent person is readily influenced by the environment and tends to incorporate information non-selectively. In contrast, the field independent person relies more on internally generated cues and is more discriminating in the selection of environmental information. FD–I has been the subject of extensive investigation by Witkin and his colleagues (Witkin, Lewis, Hertzman, Machover, Meissner and Wapner, 1972; Witkin, Dyk, Faterson, Goodenough and Karp, 1974). It forms part of Witkin's general theory of the development of perception and cognition in which he proposes that development involves the gradual shift away from the interpretation of the environment in a relatively global, unstructured manner towards a more complex interpretation in which the environment is perceived as consisting of many independent elements forming a detailed organisation. FD–I is sometimes referred to as a 'cognitive style' variable, since it is concerned with individual differences in information processing; but this does not mean that its relevance is limited to tasks we typically regard as cognitive, such as remembering telephone numbers or problem solving. The environment is also rich in *social* information, and this too requires selective attention and processing. It is thus not surprising that FD–I has been investigated in relation both to the more cognitive kinds of behaviours and to social behaviours.

Origins of the concept of FD–I
It is helpful to look into the historical origins of the FD–I dimension in order to understand the nature of this ubiquitous trait. It shares, along with penicillin and North America, the distinction of having been discovered by accident.

Originally, Witkin and his co-workers were investigating the factors involved in the perception of verticality in visual stimuli. In particular, they were studying the relative importance of external cues about verticality (such as the presence of other vertical lines in the environment) and internal cues about verticality (cues made available by the mechanisms of balance in the body). They devised several ingenious tests by which they could separate the influences of these external and internal cues: the rod and frame test, the rotating room test, and the embedded figures test.

In the rod and frame test (RFT), the cues available in the external environment are distorted by having the subject sit in a darkened room and adjust a luminous rod set in a luminous frame. Nothing can be seen but the rod and frame. The frame can be tilted so that if the subject, when asked to set the rod to vertical, relies on external cues, then the rod will be lined up parallel with the frame since that is the only external information available. If the subject relies on internal cues then the rod will be set vertically, and hence at an angle to the frame. Subjects who behave in the former way may be described as field dependent; those who behave in the latter way may be described as field independent.

The RFT holds internal cues constant and manipulates external cues. A more elaborate testing apparatus, the rotating room test (RRT), was devised to study the effects of varying internal cues independently of external cues. In the RRT the subject's task is to set his or her own body position so that it is upright. The subject is seated in a boxlike room which is suspended from an arm onto a circular track. The room is then spun round on the horizontal track, causing its occupant to be subjected to gravitational and centrifugal forces which distort the mechanisms of balance inside the body. The chair in which the subject is seated is adjustable and while the room is being spun round the subject is asked to adjust the chair, and thus him or herself, to the upright. Reliance on internal cues in this situation would result in error since these cues are distorted by the forces resulting from the motion of the room.

Although, with an inventive battery of these and other tests, Witkin was able to separate the effects of internal and external cues in perceiving the vertical, his hope of discovering which of the two was more important was never realised because the results were swamped with individual differences. Some people consistently relied on internal cues while others relied on external cues. These individual differences were so marked that Witkin decided to explore them further and therefore abandoned his research on the perception of the visual vertical. Instead, he and his colleagues set about investigating the generality of these individual differences and testing hypotheses about their underlying psychological basis. One of their first discoveries was that a test of a person's ability to differentiate within the visual field, the embedded figures test (EFT), was highly correlated with the RFT and RRT. The EFT requires the subject to locate a simple geometric shape within a complex pattern (see Figure 2.1).

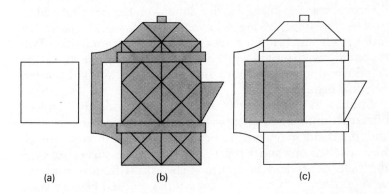

(a)   (b)   (c)

Figure 2.1. *An example of an item of the type used in the Embedded Figures Test (adapted from Goodenough, 1978, p. 175). The task is to find the square (a) within the coffee pot (b). The solution is shown in (c)*

In addition to providing results confirming that Witkin and his colleagues were studying a general perceptual dimension, the EFT also provided a paper-and-pencil measure of FD–I which is more convenient to administer than the RFT or RRT. Several reliable individual and group forms of the EFT for use with adults and with children have been developed

(Jackson, Messick and Myers, 1964). Some tests purporting to measure FD-I such as the Hidden Picture Test have low reliability and validity (Karp, 1977), so the FD-I researcher must take care in choosing a sound test.

Differences between FD and FI individuals
The development of measures of FD-I has been helped by the existence of objective criteria in the form of the original tests by which it was first observed. Any subsequent measure had to correlate with the original tests to demonstrate it was measuring the same variable and, in this way, the early perceptual tests formed the keystones around which the dimension has been built. Armed with reliable measures FD-I researchers have ventured into a wide range of territories looking for differences between field dependent and independent people. These explorations have led them into extremely diverse areas; for example, the dimension has been related to problem solving, driving skills, attitude change, facial recognition, self disclosure, career choice and criminality. Two representative studies will be described here, one from the cognitive domain and the other from the study of interpersonal behaviour.

Studies in the cognitive domain have typically involved different kinds of problem-solving tasks (Witkin *et al.*, 1974) and the field independent person usually, although not always (Nebelkopf and Dreyer, 1973), is more successful than the field dependent person in such tasks. Effective problem solving often requires that a person has reached Piaget's stage of formal operations which permits abstract, scientific thinking. Possibly as many as 50 per cent of adolescents and adults fail to achieve the stage of formal operations, and Lawson (1976) hypothesised that these people would be field dependent. To test his hypothesis he gave twenty-five 10- to 12-year-olds the EFT and two Piagetian tasks requiring attainment of formal operations for successful completion. When performances on the two Piagetian tasks were correlated with the EFT, a significant positive relationship between field independence and success on each task was demonstrated. The study showed that, for these young subjects at least, the attainment of formal operations and field independence co-occur.

Studies in the social domain have tested the hypothesis that field dependent people are more responsive to the social stimuli provided by others in the environment than are field independent people. Clearly, such sensitivity could either be advantageous or disadvantageous, depending on the situation: when sitting an examination, sensitivity to the appearance of the other candidates would be distracting rather than helpful, whereas when one is conducting a job interview the behaviour and appearance of the candidate is of prime importance. Witkin and Goodenough (1977) reviewed a wide range of studies on field dependence and interpersonal relations, and concluded that field dependent people make use of information provided by others in the environment only under certain conditions: when the situation is ambiguous and the source of information is regarded as helpful. Under the same conditions, field independent people do not make use of the social information.

The attention to social stimuli characteristic of field dependence can be measured in terms of the amount of time spent looking at others. In a study by Ruble and Nakamura (1972), looking at the experimenter was compared in field dependent and independent children aged around 8 years. There were two tasks. In the first task, the child had to assemble a puzzle, and in one condition on the first trial the experimenter also assembled the puzzle in front of the child. Field dependent children were found to look at the experimenter's face more than field independent children. However, looking at the experimenter did not improve their performance on the next trial. Presumably, watching how the experimenter solved the problem would have been helpful in this situation rather than looking at her face. In the second task the field dependent children's tendency to look at the experimenter worked to their advantage. It was a concept formation task in which, on each trial, the child had to select the correct instance out of a choice of three. In one condition, the experimenter provided social cues as to which was the correct instance (she looked at it and leaned slightly towards it). Field dependent children did better than field independent children in this condition, where looking at the experimenter's face did provide relevant social cues.

From the extensive research into the characteristics of relatively field dependent and independent adults and children, separate portraits of the two extremes can be drawn. Field independent people emerge as possessing the necessary qualities to be effective in the cognitive domain: they possess a clear view of the distinction between self and other, and an ability to analyse the environment into its components and make use of this information selectively. According to Witkin and Goodenough (1977) such individuals are not particularly popular and are described by others as ambitious, inconsiderate and opportunistic. They tend to be found in occupations such as engineering, architecture, experimental psychology, and science teaching (Goodenough, 1978). In contrast, field dependent people possess qualities resulting in superior effectiveness in interpersonal relations. They are sensitive to others in the environment and are regarded by others as popular, friendly, considerate and warm (Witkin and Goodenough, 1977). They tend to be found in occupations such as social work, clinical psychology and elementary school teaching (Goodenough, 1978).

Studies of FD-I demonstrate how the two extremes of the dimension are favoured differentially in different contexts within the same culture. It has also been observed that similar effects occur on a wider scale: it has been hypothesised that some cultures would favour field independence while others would favour field dependence. More specifically, it has been suggested that 'loose' societies of hunters and gatherers where autonomous action is encouraged would be more field independent than 'tight' societies of farmers and herders which depend on a close-knit, highly ordered social structure (Witkin and Berry, 1975). Two contrasting societies were selected by Berry (1966) for study: the Eskimos of Baffin Island and the Temne of Sierra Leone. The Eskimos are hunters and live in family groups, they encourage independence in their children, and are relatively lax over discipline; this is a 'loose' society. The Temne are farmers, place a strong emphasis on their rule-governed society and bring up their children strictly, encouraging them to be dependent; this is a 'tight' society. Using the RFT and the EFT, Berry (1966) found that the Eskimo people were more field independent than the Temne, as predicted.

Distinguishing between FD-I and intelligence

Some investigators, notably Vernon (1972), have claimed that FD-I is indistinguishable from intelligence. Since certain performance subtests of the Wechsler intelligence scales do correlate with FD-I, it can be argued that FD-I is not a dimension in its own right, but merely a spatial aspect of intelligence. Developmental studies have shown that between the ages of 8 and 17 years there is a steady increase in field independence as measured by the RFT (Witkin, Goodenough and Karp, 1967), and these changes are found cross-culturally. Such findings support the view that FD-I is indistinguishable from intelligence, since intelligence also increases with age.

However, work on sex differences in FD-I conflicts with the intelligence hypothesis. Women tend to perform less well than men on spatial tasks (Maccoby and Jacklin, 1974) and, since performance on spatial tasks is correlated with FD-I (Vernon, 1972), it is reasonable to expect sex differences in FD-I; and such differences have been found. On the EFT, females from 12 years upwards are more field dependent than males (Maccoby and Jacklin, 1974), although interestingly there is some evidence that under 12 years girls are more field independent than boys (Coates, 1972; Immergluck and Mearini, 1969). On the RFT, the majority of studies show females as more field dependent than males. Since there is probably no sex difference in intelligence the findings suggesting, if anything, a trend towards higher IQ in females (Jensen, 1971; Maccoby and Jacklin, 1974), then the association between females and field dependence goes against the hypothesis that FD-I is merely measuring intelligence.

Why, then, does field independence increase with age, if it is not because of the increase in intelligence with age? Witkin considers FD-I to be one aspect of a more general concept of cognitive differentiation, and he considers that cognitive differentiation increases with age; as we mature, we become more able to differentiate between aspects of the environment, and hence more field independent. Witkin's view is supported by the findings that although certain cultures have been found to be relatively field dependent, (e.g. the Temne), the age change towards greater field independence is found universally. It seems that maturation is accompanied by an increase in psychological differentiation (i.e. field independence), although some cultures foster more differentiation than others.

However, there is an alternative explanation of the apparently universal age trend towards greater differentiation and hence field independence. In intelligence tests and in the RFT and RRT, the better and more sophisticated strategy is typically the field independent strategy. It could be argued that, as children get older, what they learn is to adopt the better strategy, and hence they only appear to be growing more field independent. If appropriate tests were to be devised where being field *dependent* were the better strategy, then developmental changes towards increasing field dependence might also be observed. Such tests should not prove too difficult to construct since we already know of certain contexts (such as interpersonal relations) where the relatively field dependent person performs better. In the cross-cultural work, FD–I was measured using tests where the better strategy is to be field independent. Although age changes towards greater field independence were generally observed, some societies (e.g. the Temne), were found to be less field independent than others (e.g. the Eskimos). It could be argued that the Temne have more experience with problems where the better strategy is to be field dependent than is the case for the Eskimos, or Western Societies. Therefore the Temne are less knowledgeable about situations where the field independent strategy is more successful, and so perform less well on tests requiring the field independent strategy. Nevertheless they are not entirely ignorant of the field independent strategy and their ability to apply it correctly does improve, as is indicated by the developmental change towards increased field independence, even though it is less marked than in other cultures.

If tests favouring the hypothesised developmental change towards increased field dependence were to be used in cultures such as the Temne, changes towards greater field dependence might be observed. Witkin has argued that development involves increasing psychological differentiation which results in increasing field independence. The alternative argument is that development involves the acquisition of knowledge about good strategies, and these may be either field independent or dependent. The alternative interpretation does not succeed in making a clear distinction between FD–I and intelligence since the ability to acquire and apply knowledge about good strategies is presumably an aspect of what is meant by intelligence.

Summary
FD–I contrasts two approaches to the processing of information: field dependence, which emphasises the role of external cues and the non-selective intake of information, versus field independence which emphasises the role of internal cues and a more discriminating processing of input. Although it is generally found that people become more field independent as they mature, it is possible to distinguish between relatively field dependent and field independent individuals in both children and adults. Behavioural differences between such groups have been demonstrated for a wide variety of social and cognitive tasks. In the main, field dependent people function more effectively in the former, whereas field independent people are more successful in the latter.

The main criticism of the concept of FD–I is that it is so similar to intelligence that there is nothing to be gained by studying it in addition to intelligence. To counter this criticism, there is evidence that there are groups that can be distinguished on the basis of FD–I but not in terms of intelligence (e.g. women are more field dependent than men but no less intelligent). Such evidence indicates that FD–I is worthy of study in its own right as an aspect of personality. Indeed, FD–I has been one of the most extensively studied personality traits and it has been implicated in a diversity of behaviours. The next section discusses another extensively studied trait: internal versus external locus of control.

Internal versus External Locus of Control (I–E)

Theoretical background
Consider the following situation: imagine you have been learning to drive and your driving test is due shortly. Would you approach the test with the attitude that passing or failing

is primarily dependent on how well you have prepared for the test? Or, instead, would you regard passing or failing as being very little to do with how much preparation you had put in and far more to do with factors beyond your control, such as how heavy the traffic is on the day, or whether the examiner is in a good mood?

If you regard a driving test as primarily dependent on your own effort, then you see the locus of control in the situation (control over whether you pass or fail) as being with you. If you regard passing or failing as being predominantly out of your hands, then you see the locus of control depending upon chance or fate (e.g. how heavy the traffic is) or upon powerful others beyond your influence (the driving examiner). The former point of view would be typical of someone with *internal* locus of control, the latter of someone with *external* locus of control.

The concept of I–E was first proposed by Rotter (1966) and it forms a relatively small part of a more extensive personality theory incorporating many of the principles established in the psychology of learning; this theory is known as *social learning theory* (Rotter, 1954; Rotter, Chance and Phares, 1972). Rotter proposed that the degree to which people believe their lives to be under their own control is an important dimension of individual variation. People who are relatively internal believe they are responsible for their destiny, whereas people who are relatively external believe that the good and the bad things that happen to them are determined by luck, chance or powerful others. In Rotter's social learning theory I–E is regarded as a characteristic attitude towards the world, referred to as a *generalised expectancy*. The expectancy about the locus of control over rewards and punishment generated by a person's position on the I–E dimension will influence the way that person perceives most situations, and hence will partially determine how the person will behave.

Rotter regards generalised expectancies as only one of the factors which determine the way a person behaves in a particular situation. Since he is a social learning theorist, he believes that behaviour is a function of reinforcement, but generalised expectancies have important modifying effects on the expected relation between behaviour and reinforcement. First, people have to believe that they have the capability to perform the necessary behaviour to earn the reinforcement, and also to regard the reward as worth the effort before they will act. Second, and even more important, they have to expect that when they behave appropriately they will actually receive the desired reward. Whether or not a behaviour occurs depends on these three conditions being met: a person must have the capacity to produce the behaviour, must regard the reward as desirable, and must expect that the reward will be received if the behaviour is produced.

Rotter and his colleagues investigated the role of expectancy in the laboratory (Phares, 1957; James and Rotter, 1958; Rotter, Liverant and Crowne, 1961) and their findings confirmed that subjects are influenced by reinforcement only to the extent that they perceive it as contingent on their own behaviour. Given the empirical evidence confirming the importance of expectancy, it seemed reasonable to hypothesise that individuals might differ in their generalised expectancy about the locus of control of reinforcement and Rotter (1966) developed the first scale to measure the I–E dimension.

Measurement of I–E
Rotter's (1966) I–E scale consists of twenty-nine items each comprising a pair of statements lettered *a* or *b*. The respondent is asked to choose the statement from each pair which he or she believes in more strongly. Twenty-three of the items measure I–E while the remaining six are fillers consisting of statements unrelated to locus of control. The filler items are included to make the dimension being measured by the test less obvious to the respondent. Two examples of the sort of items appearing in the test are:

I more strongly believe that:
1*a* Whether I make a success of my life is entirely up to me;
1*b* Success is a matter of being lucky enough to be in the right place at the right time.
2*a* Pressure groups can influence government decisions;
2*b* The government is beyond the influence of the ordinary person.

These items do not appear in the actual test and were composed for illustrative purposes only. 1*a* and 2*a* are intended as examples of typical internal statements; 1*b* and 2*b* are intended as examples of typical external statements. Producing a questionnaire is not simply a matter of sitting down and writing out a series of items that appear to relate to the dimension the investigator is studying. If this were all the investigator did, then it would be highly likely that the resulting test would measure nothing much, least of all the dimension which the investigator had in mind. Test construction is a technical subject described in detail in more specialised texts (e.g. Anastasi, 1976). To give an introduction to the process of constructing a personality questionnaire, the steps involved in the development of Rotter's I–E scale will be described.

The first stage in questionnaire construction is to write a pool of items that by guesswork and from previous research would seem likely to measure the dimension. The next stage is to give these items to a representative sample of people for whom the test is intended and carry out a detailed analysis of their responses. First, each item has to be checked to see by what percentage of the sample it was endorsed. Items with which everyone agrees, and those with which everyone disagrees, are useless, since they do not distinguish between respondents (which, after all, is the aim of the questionnaire). In developing the I–E scale, Rotter discarded every item with which more than 85 per cent or less than 15 per cent of the sample agreed.

The next stage in developing a questionnaire is to make sure that the test is internally consistent. The internal consistency of a scale refers to the extent to which *each* individual item is measuring the same dimension as is measured by the scale as a whole. At this stage, the investigator is concerned with constructing a test that measures reliably, and internal consistency is one requirement for a reliable test. Internal consistency may be measured in a number of ways but the general principle is that the responses to individual items should correlate reasonably highly with the total scale score. While internal consistency should be high, it is unlikely that measures of internal consistency will yield correlations of 1.0. A scale consisting of the same item repeated twenty times would produce perfect internal consistency (unless the respondents were playing games which well they might given such a dull scale); but personality dimensions are expressed in a variety of behaviours so scales usually have a corresponding variety of items. Hence internal consistency does not have to be extremely high for the scale to be acceptably reliable. Rotter (1966) cites reliability coefficients ranging from 0.65 to 0.79 for the I–E scale which is acceptable for a scale purporting to measure a dimension entering into a wide range of behaviour.

Having produced an internally consistent set of items, the scale constructor's worries are far from over. The next task is to check for the influence of response biases (Berg, 1967). There are two of particular importance: *acquiescence response set* and *social desirability*.

Acquiescence response set refers to the tendency for respondents to agree with a relatively large proportion of the items ('Yeasayers') or to reject a relatively large proportion ('Naysayers') (Couch and Keniston, 1960). It can be overcome by writing items which require a 'yes' or 'no' answer in such a way that the maximum total scale score on the whole scale consists of 'yes' responses to half the items (positively keyed items) and 'no' responses to the other half (negatively keyed items). The intention is that respondents will be forced to consider each item carefully: to some respond 'yes' and to others respond 'no'. Yeasayers and naysayers who did not pay attention to the wording of the items would be recognised because they would have total scale scores of zero, as a result of the positively and negatively keyed items cancelling each other out. Since Rotter's I–E scale is composed of items in which a forced choice between alternative statements is required, it avoids the acquiescence problem. However, a similar response set could crop up with respondents adopting a strategy of always endorsing either the *a* or the *b* statement. As a control for this, the response corresponding to external locus of control is the endorsement of the *a* part of the item for exactly half of the items.

Social desirability response bias refers to the tendency to agree with items referring to positively-evaluated behaviour or beliefs and to reject those which are negatively-evaluated, regardless of whether the respondents really are the paragons of virtue they make themselves out to be (Edwards, 1957). The tendency to make socially desirable responses is so pervasive that psychologists have studied it as a personality dimension in its own right (Millham and Jacobson, 1978): some individuals are particularly prone to this bias while others are comparatively immune. There are several questionnaires for measuring this, one of the most popular being the Marlowe-Crowne Social Desirability Scale (Crowne and Marlowe, 1960). Using such a scale it is possible to measure the extent to which a person tends to make the socially desirable response when answering questionnaires. By giving subjects both the personality scale under construction *and* the Marlowe-Crowne scale, and then correlating scores on each of the items of the personality scale with the total scores on the social desirability scale, it is possible to determine the extent to which responses on the personality scale are being influenced by social desirability. Rotter (1966) selectively rejected individual items with high social desirability correlations. However, the scale as a whole has been criticised on the ground that there is a substantial correlation with social desirability (Nowicki and Duke, 1974). The results of Nowicki and Duke suggest that the internal response is recognised as the desirable one. In the driving test example given at the beginning of this section, the internal response (the belief that passing is dependent on the testee's own efforts through adequate preparation) certainly has a socially desirable ring to it.

Rotter (1975) has countered this criticism with the point that social desirability is not a property inherent in a questionnaire, but is rather the product of the total testing situation. It is possible to devise test situations in which the socially desirable response on the I–E scale would be to endorse the external items: for example, if it was the selection test for entry into the higher echelons of an occult society. In more down-to-earth circumstances, there are ways of reducing the likelihood of contamination from social desirability by adjusting aspects of the test situation (such as not requiring subjects to give their names). However, this may encourage the respondents to contaminate their responses in other ways; for example, subjects are more likely to submit spoiled response sheets under conditions of anonymity. The best the test constructor can do is to ensure that each item has a reasonably low correlation with social desirability and pass the problem on to the tester, who must use ingenuity to make the test situation evaluatively neutral.

Having constructed a scale which was internally consistent and relatively free from response bias, Rotter then had to demonstrate a further aspect of its reliability: test-retest reliability. If a person completes the same test on two separate occasions, the two sets of responses should be highly correlated. Correlations for I-E scores obtained from the same subjects on two different occasions range from being as high as 0.84 to as low as 0.26 (Phares, 1978). Low test-retest reliability can be explained as being the result of experiences of relevance to I-E during the test-retest interval. However, there is a limit to which a score on a dimension can vary from one occasion to another beyond which it becomes meaningless to regard the dimension as a more or less stable aspect of personality; therefore consistently low test-retest correlations are a cause for concern. Fortunately, with correlations as high as 0.83, the I-E scale is acceptably reliable.

Having established that a test is a reliable measure, it is next necessary to demonstrate that it is valid. Test validity refers to the degree to which the test actually measures what it claims it does. It is determined in studies which seek behavioural differences between groups selected on the basis of their test scores. Unlike intelligence with its objective, age-related criterion, the I-E scale has to demonstrate that it measures what it claims to measure by showing that predicted behavioural differences between internals and externals do in fact occur. We shall be considering a limited selection of the hundreds of studies which have a bearing on the I-E scale's validity in the next section.

Since Rotter's original I-E scale, a number of alternative measures have been developed. A commonly used I-E measure for children is the Intellectual Achievement Responsibility Questionnaire (Crandall, Katkovsky and Crandall, 1965). A measure for non-college adults, which is easier to read and is claimed to have a lower correlation with social desirability than Rotter's I-E scale, is the Adult Nowicki-Strickland Internal External Scale (Nowicki and Duke, 1974).

The investigation of I-E
Research into locus of control can be divided into three categories: the study of different components of I-E; the characteristics of relatively internal and relatively external people; and investigations of the interplay between I-E and other determinants of behaviour. Much of this research involves making comparisons between subjects identified by measures of I-E as tending to believe that the locus of control is internal and those tending to believe the locus of control is external. As a shorthand these two groups will be referred to here as 'internals' and 'externals', but it should be remembered that I-E is a continuum and there are no internal or external *types*, but rather degrees of internality and externality.

Rotter's original scale was designed to measure a generalised expectancy relevant to a wide variety of situations. The items refer to different types of situation, and it is likely that if they were studied individually, they would reveal components of I-E interesting in their own right. One example of such a subdivision of the concept of I-E is the suggestion that beliefs in an internal locus of control may be broken down into two kinds: people may be internal in so far as they believe in the principle that mankind in general has only itself to blame for the good and bad things that happen, whilst at the same time, when it comes to beliefs about their own personal control over events in their lives, being sceptical about the power they in particular have (Mirels, 1970). For example, while you may believe in democracy because it gives everyone a share in the power and responsibility of government, you may feel personally powerless over events directly concerning you, such as finding a rewarding job or a decent place to live.

In a study of I-E in black college students in the southern USA, Gurin, Gurin, Lao and Beattie (1969) found a marked distinction between beliefs about personal locus of control and more depersonalised beliefs about the degree of control experienced by others. Students who felt themselves personally to be powerless nevertheless held the general belief that most people were in control of their own destinies. Students with personalised beliefs in internal locus of control had higher aspirations about their own lives than students with beliefs in internal locus of control for the culture generally. In addition to the I-E scale, the students were also given a questionnaire on the causes of the conditions of the black population. Their responses indicated that they tended to blame either themselves as individuals or the 'system'. Those who blamed the system were more likely to have taken part in civil rights activities than those who blamed themselves.

The relationship between I-E and political activism remains unclear. In the study by Gurin *et al.* there was no relationship between individual versus system blame and I-E scores. Phares (1976) reported that some studies have related internality to activism whereas others have related externality to activism. At first sight it would appear that internals, believing in their own power to change things, would be more likely to take part in political activities. However, if internals believe in the power of the individual, then what need is there to take part in action to change the system? Perhaps externals, who believe that people in positions of power can exert considerable control over individuals, are more likely to become involved in politics. As Phares (1978) points out, it is probably an oversimplification to make predictions on the basis of I-E scores alone. In Rotter's original theory, reinforcement value plays a large part in the determination of behaviour and it is likely that, in many cases, the social rewards of joining in group activities or the importance of the cause are more significant determinants than generalised expectancy (I-E).

A second example of subdivision of the concept of I-E is in terms of the type of outcome the expectancy refers to. People may believe in internal locus of control for successful outcomes and external locus of control for failures. The significance of this distinction has been investigated in children using the Intellectual Achievement Responsibility Questionnaire (Crandall, Katkovsky and Crandall, 1965) which contains two subscales: one measuring the strength of belief that success is contingent on one's own efforts, the other that failure is due to one's lack of effort. Morris and Messer (1978) used these scales in their study of children's academic task persistence.

Highly internal and highly external children were allocated in a two by two design to either a self-reward or an external-reward condition on a teaching machine task. Under conditions of self-reward the children decided how many points to give themselves for a right answer whereas in the external-reward condition the children were allotted points by the experimenter. Morris and Messer predicted that under conditions of self-reward the internals would work harder, whereas under conditions of external reward the externals would work harder. However, the predicted interaction between locus of control and type of reinforcement did not occur. The subjects were then reclassified so that the internal group consisted only of those children who scored highly on both internal subscales: they believed they controlled the positive as well as the negative events in their lives, and the external children had low scores on both scales. When the data were analysed with the subjects classified in this way the predicted interaction was obtained. When the distinction between the subscales was ignored in the original analysis no significant results were obtained, because the high scorers would have included some subjects with internal beliefs with respect to either success or failure, but not both.

The characteristics of internal and external people have been explored in a large number of studies; for reviews see Phares (1976, 1978) and Strickland (1977). Investigations reported by Phares (1978) into the relationships between I–E and demographic variables suggest that there are no sex differences in I–E, that whites tend to be more internal than blacks, and that middle-class subjects tend to be more internal than working-class subjects. Phares also reports that there is no substantial relationship between intelligence and I–E.

From the research summarised by Phares (1978) relating I–E to a wide variety of behaviours, a distinct picture of the internal as compared with the external person emerges. The internal person is more likely to be receptive to aspects of health care such as weight-watching, giving up smoking, taking exercise and carrying out prophylactic measures such as going to the dentist regularly. In part, this behaviour is a result of the internals' superior knowledge about such things, since internals are characterised by their effort to seek out information which enables them to exert greater control over their environment. Their desire for self-determination is reflected in their greater resistance to social influence and attempted attitude change. In the area of mental health, internals are generally found to be better adjusted and less anxious than externals, and external beliefs are symptomatic of a number of psychiatric disorders such as depression and schizophrenia. In short, the internal individual, in contrast to the external, is independent, achieving and masterful.

The internal person conforms to the American ideal (Sampson, 1977). Sampson describes the prevailing cultural ethos in the USA as one of 'self-contained individualism' by which he means that people are encouraged to be independent as opposed to interdependent, and focus on self-enhancement and self-sufficiency instead of surrendering individuality in the pursuit of the wider goals of the community.

Sampson draws attention to the danger of mistaking products of the prevailing cultural ethos for fundamental principles. For example, the concept of psychological androgyny (S.L. Bem, 1974) is currently a popular research topic. Androgynous people are those characterised by both typically feminine and typically masculine behaviours and beliefs. In a culture such as ours, where self-contained individualism is highly valued, psychological androgyny is desirable since it avoids dependence on members of the opposite sex. However, in cultures where interdependence is highly valued, androgyny would not be regarded as a psychological concept of fundamental interest.

The same argument applies to locus of control. Internal locus of control is necessary for successful self-contained individualism and hence, in our culture, locus of control is regarded as being an important psychological concept. However, it may be quite irrelevant in other societies. Of course, the possibility that a phenomenon is culture-specific does not automatically render it unworthy of study, but investigators need to be cautious in the sort of claims they may make about the significance and generalisability of their findings.

It is a disappointing feature of studies of the characteristics of internal and external people that they are so mundane from a theoretical point of view. Elaborating the network of correlations between a personality dimension and a range of behaviours smacks of butterfly collecting. More interesting are those studies which have sought to investigate the role of I-E within the context of Rotter's formulation for the prediction of social behaviour.

In just such an investigation, Karabenick and Srull (1978) studied the relations between I-E, situational variables, and cheating, with college student subjects. They were interested in the effects of expectancy on reinforcement value. The experimental task consisted of solving a series of line puzzles. The subject was required to trace a line figure onto a blank piece of paper without lifting the pencil from the paper or re-tracing over any of the lines. There were twelve such figures, only two of which were possible to trace in accordance with the rules, the remainder being unsolvable. The subjects were not informed that only two of the puzzles could be solved. They were told to mark their successful attempts with an X, therefore the number of unsolvable figures marked in this fashion provided an index of cheating. They were allowed as many goes at each figure as they liked.

The subjects (half of whom were female and half male) were preselected on the basis of their I-E scores in such a way that half the group were highly internal and half were highly external. Some of the subjects were told that the task was a measure of intelligence and involved skill, and some were told that performance on the task was entirely unrelated to ability. Cheating was measured by totalling the number of unsolvable figures marked with an X. The experiment thus involved three factors, each at two levels: sex, I-E, and skill versus chance instructions. The experiment manipulated locus of control of the subjects' beliefs and also the locus of control in the situation; this permitted a comparison of the effects of congruence versus incongruence between these two variables. Congruent conditions were those in which externals were told the task was one of chance and internals were told it was one of skill; incongruent conditions were the reverse. The dependent variable was frequency of cheating, which provided an index of the reinforcement value of success.

The analysis of cheating frequency showed a marked congruence effect. Internals cheated more under skill conditions and externals cheated more under chance conditions (see Table 2.1).

Table 2.1 Mean frequency of cheating (out of a maximum of 12) for the two locus of control groups under the two task conditions (Karabenick and Srull, 1978)

Group	Task condition	
	Skill	Chance
Internal	1.3	0.4
External	0.3	1.6

Reinforcement value (indexed by cheating) was a function of I-E and task conditions with congruence between I-E and task conditions resulting in higher reinforcement value. Karabenick and Srull offered the following interpretation of the congruence effect: internals cheat to conform to their status on the internal dimension of ability, whereas externals cheat to maintain their belief in their status as fortunate individuals.

At the beginning of this chapter, in discussing the applications of techniques developed in measuring intelligence to personality, two problems were raised: the question of an appropriate criterion against which to validate a personality measure and the problem of how best to conceptualise the trait, i.e. how many components are involved. For I-E, there is no longer any doubt about its validity in the light of the sheer bulk of favourable studies where predicted differences between internal and external people have been found. Research into I-E can afford now to branch out beyond the stage of collecting a convincing set of behavioural correlations and investigate how I-E, in the context of social learning theory, can help in the understanding and prediction of behaviour.

The issue of the components of I-E still remains. Should it be divided into subscales such as personalised internality versus a generalised internal ideology, or locus of control for success versus failure? The issue here is a familiar one in personality measurement: if a scale measures a broadly conceived dimension applicable to a wide variety of situations, its powers of prediction are less than if its relevance is narrowed down to a more limited range. If one achieves better prediction by narrowing down the scope of a scale, on the other hand, one may end up with an entirely trivial scale.

Rotter argued that I–E is a generalised expectancy that remains invariant across situations. The development of subscales detracts from its generalisability, although they may enhance prediction in specific situations. The more generalisable I–E scale and the more context-specific subscales each have their own part to play in different types of research.

Conclusions

To conclude this chapter on single-trait theories, some of the advantages and disadvantages of this approach to personality will be considered. Given the complexity of personality, it is a sensible strategy to restrict research to one aspect at a time as the single-trait approach is doing. However, such a piecemeal approach is inevitably unsatisfactory, since no one single-trait theory can provide a complete explanation of behaviour. Despite the vast amount of data each theory has generated, no single-trait theory can be said to have had anywhere near the impact on psychology that, say, Freud's much more general personality theory can claim.

Why are single-trait theories flourishing? One explanation lies not in the intrinsic merits of the dimensions themselves, but in the change in emphasis of current personality research. As we shall see in Chapter 4, there is a growing interest in investigating the joint effects of personality and situational variables in efforts to understand and predict behaviour. Single-trait theories provide measures of discrete aspects of personality which can be varied relatively easily, whereas the more general multi-trait approaches to personality, to be considered in the next chapter, make the manipulation of personality variables much more difficult.

3 The Personality Theorist's Perspective: Multi-Trait Theories

Introduction

Multi-trait theories are designed to describe the entire personality. Their purpose is to locate the constellation of traits that make up the structure of personality and to devise appropriate measures of each of these traits. This approach assumes we all share the same personality structure, although people differ from each other because we are each characterised by our own particular combination of trait scores. Hence the multi-trait approach captures both the underlying similarity between human beings and the surface differences or, to use Allport's terminology, it is able to make both nomothetic and idiographic statements about personality (Allport, 1937). It is surprising that, although the subject-matter of the various multi-trait theorists has been the same (they have all been studying personality), they have nevertheless produced different models of personality structure. These differences, and the possible reasons for them, will be one of the main discussion points of this chapter.

This discussion will be restricted to the two best-known multi-trait theories, those of Eysenck and Cattell, although there are a number of such theories, others being represented by, for example, Guilford and Zimmerman (1956) and Comrey (1970). Since the personality tests devised by Eysenck and Cattell are some of the most widely used tests today it is important to understand something of the theories behind them. Also, their approaches to the study of personality differ from each other in a number of interesting ways.

The most obvious difference is that Eysenck regards the structure of personality as being best described by three traits, whereas Cattell insists on at least sixteen.

The multi-trait approach, in contrast to single-trait approaches, has a characteristic methodology which remains fundamentally the same from theorist to theorist. Multi-trait theories are all attempts to represent the whole personality, they all originate from similar data bases, and they all use the same method of statistical analysis.

The data base for multi-trait theories
Personality is inferred from behaviour, and multi-trait theorists have developed three techniques of data collection each of which measures a different form of behaviour: questionnaires, ratings and objective tests.

Probably the best-known technique is the questionnaire. The rationale behind the use of questionnaires is that the best way to find out about an individual's personality is to ask that person. Respondents are required to answer questions about their behaviours, feelings, thoughts and opinions. These responses provide the investigator with a limited sample of people's behaviour, namely their self-observations. These data are prey to distortions resulting from the respondent's inaccurate self-observations, which may be deliberate, or may be due to genuine ignorance or misunderstanding of the meaning of the items, or to people's misperceptions of themselves. We have already seen how a great deal of care is taken in the construction of reliable questionnaires to attempt to overcome these problems. Nevertheless, the basic limitation of the questionnaire is unavoidable: it only measures the respondents' views of themselves.

The second technique for collecting personality data is by observers' ratings of other people's behaviour. A group of observers is given a list of items describing various behaviours such as 'keeps their room neat and tidy' or 'takes the lead in group discussion' and they rate their allotted ratees on these items. Ratings avoid the problem of self-distortion encountered in questionnaire data, but have their own inherent sources of bias and error. Raters are not mechanical recording devices, but human beings; hence they are subject to distortions and inaccuracies. The main problem with ratings is that the items are difficult to frame in an unambiguous way. Thus different raters will have different personal standards of neatness and tidiness and while one rater might consider the ratee's room obsessionally immaculate, another might only consider it moderately tidy. What exactly is meant by 'takes the lead' in discussion? Would a ratee who did most of the talking count as taking the lead, or one who made occasional but effective comments which redirected the conversation? Raters may only see one side of the ratees' personality: for example, they may be scrupulously tidy at home (perhaps because they know they are being rated) while their desk at work is a disaster area; they may be vociferous in group discussions but, when left alone with someone of the opposite sex, be reduced to speechlessness. Would it be correct to rate such people as 'tidy' and 'dominant'? Designers of ratings scales are aware of these problems and are often as skilful as questionnaire constructors in their efforts to overcome them. Nevertheless, the problems of the idiosyncrasies of raters and their limited exposure to ratees are, ultimately, unavoidable.

Aware of the inherent inaccuracies in questionnaire and rating data, some investigators (notably Cattell) have turned their attention to the third technique of data collection: the use of objective tests. These are samples of behaviour obtained under laboratory-type conditions which make it impossible for the subjects to know exactly what is being assessed and thus have any distorting influence on their responses. The behaviours measured in this way may be physiological; for example, Eysenck has developed a lemon-drop test which discriminates between introverts and extraverts in terms of the amount of saliva they produce when lemon juice is placed in their mouths: introverts generally produce more saliva than extraverts (S.B.G. Eysenck and H.J. Eysenck, 1967). Alternatively, the behaviours may be cognitive: for example, solving puzzles or making up captions for cartoons. Another alternative is a test of visual motor co-ordination, such as the pursuit rota. Although objective tests overcome the problems of distortion encountered in the other two types of personality data, they confront the investigator with a set of new problems. In practical terms, they may be inconvenient to transport and administer, requiring elaborate apparatus; but more important, it may be difficult to demonstrate precisely what aspect of personality they are measuring.

Whatever technique or techniques are used to collect data about personality, the next step is to try to make sense of the material. The most commonly used method for doing this is a statistical technique known as factor analysis.

Factor analysis
Factor analysis can be applied in the same way to any of the three forms of personality data. It will be discussed here as it is applied to rating data.

Let us imagine that an investigator was interested in personality in the classroom, and collected ratings on twenty items of behaviour (A–T) on fifty ratees. The ratees were schoolchildren and the items were classroom behaviours such as asking questions (item A), volunteering for jobs (item B), whispering to friends (item C), getting on with studying (item D), and so on down to item T. The observers' ratings of these behaviours form the raw data, which can be set out in a table in which the twenty columns are the rated behaviours and the fifty rows are the ratees (see Figure 3.1a). The numbers in the body of the table would be the average of the ratings given to each child by the observers on each of the twenty items.

The first step in factor analysis is to produce a correlation matrix. This is done by correlating each item with every other. A correlation measures the degree to which items covary: thus there will be a large positive correlation between items A and C if the children who were rated highly on A were also rated highly on C, and the children who had low ratings on A also had low ratings on C. For example, the children who asked lots of questions (A) were probably the ones who whispered to their friends (C), whereas the ones who got on with studying (D) neither asked questions nor whispered. So there will be a high correlation between A and C, but not between A and D nor between C and D.

The correlations are arranged in a matrix in which both the

(a) Raw data

	Items
Ratees	A B C D ... T
1	
2	
3	
4	
.	
.	
.	
50	

(b) The correlation matrix

	Items
Items	A B C D ... T
A	
B	
C	
D	
.	
.	
.	
T	

(c) Results of factor analysis showing positive high loading items

Factor I	*Factor II*
A	B
C	D
E	F

(d) Results of factor analysis showing positive and negative high loading items

Factor I	*Factor II*
A+	B+
C+	D+
E+	F+
G−	H−
I−	J−
K−	L−

Figure 3.1 *The stages involved in factor-analysing rating data*

columns and the rows are the item names and the body of the matrix contains the correlation coefficients, which can vary between +1.0 through 0 to −1.0 (see Figure 3.1b). The correlation matrix is the clay from which the mathematical procedures of factor analysis will mould a representation of personality.

Factor analysis is a mathematical technique for extracting the underlying dimensions ('factors') of the correlation matrix, but it is not necessary to understand mathematics in order to appreciate, in general terms, what factor analysis does with the correlation matrix. (For a simple explanation of the mathematical technique involved see Child, 1970.) The procedure discovers how best to reduce the large number of correlations (in our example it would be 190) to a much smaller number of factors by picking out the clusters of items which, as indicated by the correlations, are closely related and therefore measuring the same underlying characteristic. These clusters are composed of items which are intercorrelated. For example, items A, C, E and G in our example might be intercorrelated in the sense that each correlates strongly with every other: A correlates with C, and C with E, and E with G, and A with E, etc. Given this pattern of intercorrelations between items A, C, E and G, one could infer that these four items were measuring basically the same thing (the same 'factor') and hence one has reduced four different measures to a single underlying dimension.

When the calculations are complete, the results consist of a number of basic factors which represent the clusters of similar items. Let us assume there are only two factors in our example (see Figure 3.1c). In addition to determining the number of factors, the analysis also calculates the degree to which the items are related to the factors. Every item's relationship to each factor is calculated in the form of a correlation known technically as a 'factor loading'.

The identification and naming of factors is based on inspection of the factor loadings and figuring out what the high loading items have in common. In our example, Factor I has high loadings from items A (asking questions), C (whispering to friends) and E (participates in group games). These items all appear to be measuring an outgoing approach to the child's relationships with his or her peers and so we could identify this factor as 'sociability'. The high loading items on Factor II are B (volunteering for jobs), D (getting on with studying) and F (tidy desk) so this factor could be identified as 'conscientiousness'.

Since factor loadings consist of correlations they can be positive or negative. A high negative factor loading is just as informative as a high positive factor loading. In our example, the items strongly related to the factors were assumed to have high positive loadings. However, what if some of the

items had high negative loadings? Let us assume that three
further items have high negative loadings on Factor I and
these are G (plays on own during break), I (blushes and
stammers when answering the teacher's questions), and K
(participates in individual as opposed to team sports). Such
a pattern came about because all those children with high
ratings on A, C and E had low ratings on G, I and K and
vice versa. In this case, Factor I would be identified as a
bipolar factor and named 'sociable-withdrawn' (see Figure
3.1d).

Similarly, Factor II would be identified as a bipolar factor
and named 'conscientious-slapdash' if there were items with
high negative loadings such as H (spills ink), J (loses pens and
pencils) and L (late returning library books).

From our hypothetical examples, the investigator would
conclude that the broad spectrum of classroom behaviour is
characterised by two underlying dimensions: 'sociability'
and 'conscientiousness'. While the basic techniques of factor
analysis remain constant there are certain variations favoured
by some users but not others, and these are often the cause
of dispute. As we shall see in the following sections, the
different variations favoured by Eysenck and Cattell have
resulted in two rather different representations of personality.

H.J. Eysenck's Personality Theory

Eysenck's application of factor analysis to personality data
has led him to propose that personality is adequately described by three factors: extraversion-introversion, neuroticism and psychoticism. He arrived at this tripartite view of
the structure of personality as a result of a series of factor
analytic studies in which he tested hypotheses about the
nature of personality.

The structure and measurement of personality
On the basis of extensive psychological and philosophical
reading, Eysenck observed that similar descriptions of particular human personality types kept cropping up (H.J.
Eysenck, 1953). From the days of Greek philosophy to

twentieth-century psychiatry, there has been a tendency to categorise people. The Greeks used four categories: melancholic, choleric, sanguine and phlegmatic. These were 'types' in the sense that people were pigeonholed into one of them; a person could not be described as having a bit of each.

Another way to conceptualise the differences between people is in terms of dimensions. The concept of dimension differs from the concept of type in that people can be located at any point along a dimension, whereas whether one belongs to a certain type is an all-or-none matter. Eysenck was influenced by Kretschmer's theory of the psychoses (Kretschmer, 1948) in which it is proposed that normal and abnormal people can be arranged along a dimension or continuum of psychosis ranging from schizophrenia at one extreme to manic depression at the other. Schizophrenics and manic depressive patients would be placed at these extremes and normal people would be placed at the mid-point of the dimension.

Eysenck was also influenced by Jung's theory of personality (Jung, 1921). Jung proposed that people tend either towards extraversion, directing their energies outwards, or to introversion, directing their energies towards their inner mental state. Jung applied this conceptualisation to neurotic disorders and proposed that neurotics liable to hysterical symptoms were extraverted whereas neurotics liable to anxiety were introverted.

Eysenck's theory of the structure of personality manages to encompass all these views (see Figure 3.2). He favours a dimensional as opposed to a typological approach. Initially (Eysenck, 1953), he hypothesised that two dimensions only would suffice to describe the variation in human personality: introversion–extraversion and neuroticism–stability. More recently (H.J. Eysenck and S.B.G. Eysenck, 1976) he has proposed the addition of a third dimension, psychoticism.

The two dimensions introversion–extraversion and neuroticism–stability yield four quadrants which correspond to the four Greek types. Kretschmer's dimension was regarded by Eysenck as corresponding to the introversion–extraversion dimension. Jung's two varieties of neuroses, anxiety and hysteria, correspond to neurotic introversion and neurotic

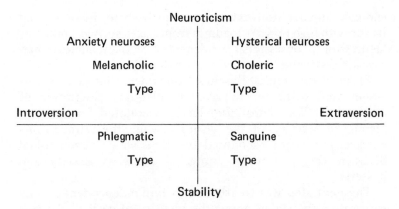

Figure 3.2 *Hypothesised human personality dimensions encompassing earlier conceptualisations*

extraversion or the Greek types of melancholic and choleric. In his early studies Eysenck set out to test this hypothetical two-dimensional structure using rating data obtained from an abnormal population. Eysenck (1944) tested the hypothesis that neurotic patients could be conceptualised in terms of these two dimensions such that hysterical patients would be highly extravert and neurotic, whereas anxious patients would be highly introvert and neurotic. He collected psychiatrists' ratings of seven hundred patients in a military hospital, suffering from various forms and degrees of neurotic disorders, on thirty-nine rating scales covering present behaviour and past life history. Some examples of the scales are: 'dependent', 'sex anomalies', 'headaches', 'married', 'degraded work history' and 'narrow interests'. The scales were intercorrelated and factor analysed.

The factor analysis resulted in two main factors with high loadings from two different subsets of the thirty-nine scales. Eysenck's hunch that two dimensions would be adequate to describe the data was confirmed; and consideration of the scales most strongly associated with each of the factors led to the identification of one factor as neuroticism and the other as introversion–extroversion. All the high loadings on the neuroticism factor were positive and included scales such as 'badly organised personality', 'dependent' and 'little energy'. Introversion–extraversion proved to be a bipolar factor with high positive loadings from scales such as 'anxiety', 'depression', 'obsessional tendencies', 'sex anomalies', 'narrow interests' and 'degraded work history'.

From these results Eysenck concluded that two factors alone were sufficient to give an adequate description of personality. The neuroticism factor accounted for items referring to severity of the disorder while the introversion-extraversion factor accounted for items which distinguished between the two major forms of neurosis: anxiety and hysteria.

The next step was to attempt to find independent criteria to support the claims about the identity of each of the two personality factors (Eysenck, 1947). We have already discussed the problem that the natural criterion of age changes used in the validation of intelligence tests is not available in personality. The other criterion for intelligence was teachers' expert opinion, and Eysenck made use of this type of criterion in his personality study.

Eysenck obtained expert psychiatric opinion as to what type of neurosis each of his subjects was suffering from, and validated his dimensions against these opinions. By locating the high loading scales on each factor and working back to each subject's score on these scales, he could classify them according to his dimensions as neurotic introverts or neurotic extraverts. Eysenck predicted that neurotic introverts would include subjects diagnosed as anxious, obsessional or depressed, whereas neurotic extraverts would include subjects diagnosed as hysterical or psychopathic. This is what he found. The technique of comparing the results of factor analysis with an independent classification is known as criterion analysis. Since the dimensions agreed with the criterion, Eysenck could be confident that they were a meaningful way of classifying people. Further studies, involving literally thousands of normal and abnormal people, have subsequently shown that these two factors emerge repeatedly when different samples are tested, they are normally distributed throughout the population, and there are important behavioural differences between introverts and extraverts and neurotic and stable individuals selected on the basis of these dimensions.

The typical high scorer on extraversion is a sociable person who thrives on human company and seeks out exciting activities. He or she is restless, impulsive and optimistic. In contrast, the low scoring introverted person prefers the company of books to people and is orderly, restrained and serious. The high scorer on neuroticism is characterised by a variety of somatic and interpersonal difficulties reflecting tension and anxiety while the low scorer, the normal person, does not possess these difficulties.

Eysenck's initial studies used rating data: later he and his colleagues, notably S.B.G. Eysenck, investigated the factor structure of questionnaire data, and devised a series of questionnaires to measure extraversion–introversion and neuroticism. The current version is the Eysenck Personality Inventory (EPI) (H.J. Eysenck and S.B.G. Eysenck, 1964).

Recently Eysenck has expanded his conceptualisation of personality structure to include a third factor, psychoticism (H.J. Eysenck and S.B.G. Eysenck, 1968; S.B.G. Eysenck and H.J. Eysenck, 1968; H.J. Eysenck and S.B.G. Eysenck, 1976). Psychoticism is claimed to measure an aspect of personality not subsumed by the extraversion and neuroticism dimensions and may be summarised as the individual's predisposition to psychotic breakdown. There is now a questionnaire, the Eysenck Personality Questionnaire (EPQ) to measure all three personality factors: extraversion, neuroticism and psychoticism (H.J. Eysenck and S.B.G. Eysenck, 1975).

Some of the items measuring psychoticism are 'Do you enjoy hurting people you love?', 'Do you worry a lot about catching diseases?' and 'Would it upset you a lot to see a child or animal suffer?' (S.B.G. Eysenck and H.J. Eysenck, 1968). High scorers on this dimension have not necessarily experienced a psychotic breakdown; Eysenck considers both neurotic and psychotic disorders to be the result of predisposing personality characteristics and precipitating environmental events. However, studies of criterion groups indicate that criminals and schizophrenics have high psychoticism scores. Although there is some evidence of a low, positive correlation between neuroticism and psychoticism (S.B.G. Eysenck and H.J. Eysenck, 1968), the three factors are relatively independent, and therefore it is possible for a given individual to have any combination of high or low scores on the three factors.

The hierarchical nature of personality
According to Eysenck, the structure of personality may be described with only three factors. But how can three scores adequately summarise all the complexities that go into making up a person's individuality? Eysenck's chief critic, Cattell, argues that this conceptualisation is far from adequate. Adopting a non-critical frame of mind for the moment, let us consider Eysenck's theoretical account of how human personality reduces to just three factors (Eysenck, 1947). This is achieved by adopting a hierarchical model (see Figure 3.3).

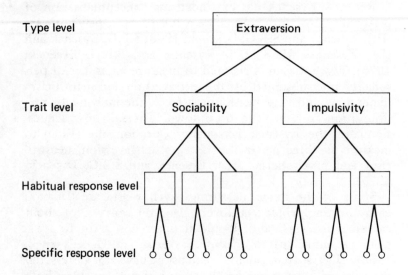

Figure 3.3 *Eysenck's hierarchical model of personality* (*adapted from Eysenck, 1947*)

At the lowest level are specific responses. These refer to particular pieces of behaviour such as talking to the person in front of you in the bus queue or reading a book on the train. At the next level are habitual responses. These are composed of clusters of specific responses. The third level consists of traits. These are characteristics inferred from observable behaviour. A number of different habitual responses may all be explained by a single underlying trait. For example, in Figure 3.3, 'sociability' subsumes 'being friendly to strangers', 'going to parties' and 'participating in team games'. Above the trait level, at the top of the hierarchy, comes the type level. Types consist of clusters of related traits: thus extraversion has several subcomponents, sociability and impulsivity being the two major ones (S.B.G. Eysenck and H.J. Eysenck, 1963). Although Eysenck refers to the top of the hierarchy as the type level, extraversion, neuroticism and psychoticism are dimensions, not types, and hence everyone possesses all three to varying degrees.

By knowing a person's score on one of the three dimensions at the type level it is possible to predict the extent to which he or she will be characterised by the traits, habitual responses and specific responses which the dimension subsumes, but prediction is less reliable at the lower levels of the hierarchy. For example, measures of the subcomponents of extraversion will result in more accurate prediction of behaviour in specific situations. A measure of sociability would probably predict a person's behaviour at a party more accurately than the more general measure of extraversion. The issue of generality versus specificity has already been encountered in the discussion of the subcomponents of locus of control (see Chapter 2). Eysenck, like Rotter, prefers working with the broader, more widely-applicable level of measurement to relying on subcomponents.

The hierarchical model corresponds to the processes involved in factor analysis. Questionnaires and ratings consist of items drawn from the habitual and specific response levels. When these items are intercorrelated and factor analysed they yield factors corresponding to the trait and type levels. The factors that emerge from analysing the intercorrelations between items are called first-order factors. These may then be intercorrelated and factor analysed to form second-order factors. It is tempting, but wrong, to equate the trait level with first-order factors and the type level with second-order factors. In Eysenck's analyses, extraversion, neuroticism and psychoticism all emerge from the factor analysis of *items* and therefore are first-order factors. As we shall see later on, Cattell has argued that the way Eysenck uses factor analysis has led him mistakenly to regard these three dimensions as first-order factors when actually they are second-order factors.

The physiological basis of personality

So far we have seen how Eysenck's conceptualisation of personality consists of underlying dimensions inferred from observations of behaviour (rating data) or self-report (questionnaires). As such, these dimensions have the status of hypothetical constructs. That is to say, the dimensions are not directly observable but are implied by the data and have been validated by criterion analysis and proved useful in explaining and predicting behaviour. However, Eysenck has developed a theory of the physiological basis of personality which gives the dimensions a physical reality (H.J. Eysenck, 1967). He has proposed that the extraversion–introversion dimension is related to the activity of a particular part of the brain, the ascending reticular activating system (ARAS). The level of activity in the ARAS determines the arousal level in the higher brain centres which, in turn, influences the amount of cortical control exerted over the lower brain centres. The extravert is one whose level of arousal is low, whilst the introvert is continuously over-aroused. Hence the extravert's desire to seek, and the introvert's desire to avoid, additional (arousing) stimulation.

The hypothesised physiological basis of neuroticism is the autonomic nervous system (ANS). The neurotic is believed to possess a changeable or labile ANS which is highly sensitive to stimulation. The subjective experience of fear and anxiety has a number of familiar, unpleasant autonomic components such as butterflies in the stomach, increased heart-rate and sweating. A neurotic person with a sensitive ANS is more prone to such autonomic reactions than is the normal individual. These reactions can become association with neutral stimuli through the process of conditioning and Eysenck claims that the neurotic person is liable to accumulate an excess of unnecessary conditioned emotional reactions. (For further physiological details, see Green (in press.)

The psychophysiological structures implicated in extraversion and neuroticism are said to explain most of the observed differences between introverts, extraverts, neurotic and stable individuals. As yet a physiological basis for psychotism has not been proposed. Eysenck claims that one of the most significant psychological differences between introverts and extraverts is the relative ease or difficulty with which they acquire conditioned responses. This difference was demonstrated in an early study by Franks (1956, 1957) who studied eye-blink conditioning.

The experiment was a classical conditioning paradigm, in which a puff of air to the eyeball (the unconditioned stimulus) causing the eye to blink (the unconditioned response) was paired with a buzzer (the conditioned stimulus). After repeated pairings, subjects blinked on hearing the buzzer in the absence of the puff of air. This blink is a conditioned response. It was found that introverts acquired the conditioned response after fewer pairings of buzzer and air-puff than did extraverts; and also that introverts required more trials to extinguish the response than extraverts. The psychophysiological explanation for these observed differences in conditionability is that since introverts are at a higher level of arousal than extraverts, their nervous systems are more ready to form the necessary associations.

The psychophysiologically-based differences in conditionability are believed to explain why neurotic introverts acquire a surplus of conditioned anxiety responses; Eysenck regards this surplus as being the basis of neurotic anxiety, obsessional and depressive neuroses. The conditionability differences are also proposed as an explanation for neurotic extraverts being deficient in certain learned characteristics: such deficiencies are in turn used to explain hysteria and psychopathy. For example, one such learned characteristic, Eysenck argues, is the conscience (H.J. Eysenck, 1977).

Psychopaths are people who do not feel guilt or remorse for their antisocial behaviour. Eysenck claims that psychopaths are highly neurotic, extravert and psychotic and their behaviour is antisocial because they have failed to acquire (via conditioning) the constraints of a conscience. The conscience is seen as a product of socialisation and is composed of conditioned anxiety responses to antisocial acts. Psychopaths, since they are extraverts and hence under-aroused are constitutionally inferior in their ability to acquire the constraints of a conscience. The neuroticism dimension also plays a part since when the level of neuroticism is extremely high it can interfere with learning because of the excessive fear and anxiety provoked by the learning experience. Therefore psychopaths, who are highly neurotic, are particularly difficult to condition. However, attempts to test Eysenck's theory using criminal populations have failed to find convincing evidence that offenders are more extraverted than non-offenders although there is some evidence that they are more neurotic and psychotic (see Chapter 9).

If it is the case that Eysenck's personality dimensions are the product of distinct psychophysiological structures, then there should be a significant genetic factor in personality. With the aid of colleagues expert in genetical analysis, Eysenck has been determining the relative contributions of heredity and environment to extraversion (Eaves and Eysenck, 1975). A popular method is to correlate the trait scores within pairs of identical and fraternal twins (Loehlin, 1977). In a review of the twin study data, Shields (1976) concluded that extraversion scores for identical twins correlated around 0.5 whereas for fraternal twins the correlation can be as low as 0.2. Hence there is evidence for a considerable genetic component in extraversion. However, the validity of the assumption made in this research, that genetics and environment act independently, is now seriously questioned, and techniques for investigating heredity and environment correlation and interaction are being developed (Loehlin, 1977) which may alter the picture.

Eysenck's theory of the psychophysiological structures underlying extraversion and neuroticism is highly speculative and it has received only mixed support (Claridge, 1967). For example, the theory predicts that extraverts will differ from introverts on the classic measure of cortical arousal, the electroencephalogram (EEG). However, numerous studies have failed to yield consistent differences between introverts' and extraverts' EEGs (Gale, 1973). There remain many conceptual problems which have not been adequately dealt with

— for example, what are the precise mechanisms by which cortical arousal and autonomic lability affect conditioning? Are these the same or different for operant versus classical conditioning? A revised statement is needed incorporating recent developments in physiological psychology and learning theory.

This need has been partially met in a modification of the theory proposed by Gray (1970, 1972). He proposed that the diffuse arousal functions of the ARAS should be replaced with two separate physiological systems in the brain, one connected with punishment, the other with reward. Gray reviewed the evidence for a general factor of conditionability and observed that introverts are only found to condition better than extraverts under certain situations. Introverts are the more susceptible to conditioning where punishment and frustrative non-reward are involved, whilst extraverts are the more susceptible to conditioning when rewards are positive. To accommodate these differences in conditioning Gray proposed that introverts have the more sensitive punishment system and extraverts have the more sensitive reward system. Neuroticism may involve both systems, with highly neurotic people being sensitive to both reward and punishment.

A recent study by Nagpal and Gupta (1979) supported Gray's hypothesis. Subjects were selected on the basis of their extraversion and neuroticism scores to form four groups consisting of those scoring high on both dimensions, low on both dimensions, high on extraversion but low on neuroticism, and low on extraversion but high on neuroticism. They were assigned at random to either a punishment condition (electric shock for errors) or reward condition (verbal praise for correct responses) in a verbal operant conditioning task. The analysis of the conditioning scores showed that the neurotic extraverts conditioned more readily than the three groups in the reward condition, whereas the neurotic introverts conditioned more readily than the other groups in the punishment condition.

Gray's conceptualisation of the physiological basis of conditioning is superior to Eysenck's on two counts. First, it takes into account recent physiological findings. Second, it utilises a more sophisticated view of conditioning in line with recent developments in learning theory (Mackintosh, 1974), where conditioning is regarded as a process of learning about relations between events rather than the automatic strengthening of stimulus-response relations through reinforcement. (For more detail on this point, see Boakes in this series.)

When Eysenck embarked on his investigations, he studied the ways in which people, throughout the ages, had classified one another. He believed that these classification systems, although developed in a non-scientific way, would nevertheless reflect an accumulated wisdom based on observation and experience, and would therefore provide sound hypotheses for a scientific study of personality. He then set out to test this hypothetical picture of the major dimensions by which peoples' personalities could be distinguished from one another. From his investigations he concluded that personality may be described by three broad dimensions and he postulated their biological basis.

In contrast, Cattell's investigations began in an entirely different way, and at first sight, it looks as though the two theories have come up with two entirely different personality structures. The next section discusses how this came about and then presents a reconciliation of the two views.

Cattell's Personality Theory

Cattell differs from Eysenck both in his approach to the study of personality and in his findings. Methodologically, Cattell favours an atheoretical approach in which factor analysis is used in an exploratory way to discover personality factors. Eysenck, on the other hand, used factor analysis to test previously formulated hypotheses about likely personality factors. The end result of the extensive work of Cattell and his colleagues in several different countries is a complex personality structure involving at least twenty traits and a massive supporting personality theory embracing areas often ignored by other personality theorists (such as ability, motivation, emotion and learning). As in the discussion of Eysenck's theory, the intention here is to outline Cattell's approach and summarise the main findings. A more detailed account and a comparison between Cattell and several other multi-trait theorists is available in Cattell and Kline (1977).

The structure and measurement of personality
The first stage in Cattell's methodology was to devise a technique whereby every possible aspect of personality would be included in the investigation, with the eventual aim of reducing this mass of non-selective material to more manageable proportions. For his starting-point Cattell chose the English vocabulary of personality description. His rationale was that all the significant dimensions of variation in human personality would have found their way into the language, and therefore the complete set of adjectives used to describe personality, known as personality traits, would encompass the whole personality or, as Cattell terms it, the 'personality sphere'.

By ensuring that the entire personality sphere was represented at the beginning of the investigation, there was no possibility that the personality structure that would eventually emerge would be based on an incomplete data base and therefore be deficient in any respect. Note that by taking the ordinary language of personality description as a starting-point, Cattell made the assumption that language bears a direct correspondence to reality and, for our present purposes, we shall accept this view. However, when we come to examine the language of personality description more closely in Chapter 6 we shall be forced to reconsider this assumption.

The English vocabulary of personality description has been identified by Allport and Odbert (1936). From their survey of a standard English dictionary, they found eighteen thousand words which could be used to describe personality and around four and a half thousand which they regarded as specifically for personality description. Cattell's first task was to reduce this huge number of adjectives to a more workable size by removing all the synonyms. By this process, the list was reduced to one hundred and sixty traits to which were added eleven traits from the psychological literature. Cattell regarded these one hundred and seventy-one traits, or personality variables, as representing the personality sphere. The complete list is given in Cattell (1946).

The list was still too large to form the basis for a rating study, so Cattell surveyed the findings from previous rating studies which had used some or all of the variables from this list to discover which traits were typically found to covary. As a result of pooling the results of fourteen such studies he was able to locate clusters of traits which tended to covary and he selected a single variable to represent each cluster. These variables, thirty-five in all, were used as the scales in his rating study.

Cattell calls rating data L data (life data) and, in his early studies, it was collected in the following manner (Hammond, 1977). Groups of up to sixteen people, often college students, who had known each other for at least six months would rate each other on the scales (thus each person was both a rater and a ratee). To control for the fact that individuals differ from one another in their propensity to use extreme versus middle-of-the-road judgments, Cattell required each rater to use the various points of the rating scale in a fixed proportion. For example, the mid-point of each scale could be used 30 per cent of the time. The ratings across raters were summed so that each ratee's score on a scale was the total of the fifteen raters' ratings. These ratings were then subjected to factor analysis to discover the number and identity of the underlying dimensions. Cattell and his colleagues carried out several such investigations and concluded that around fifteen factors were necessary to describe personality as revealed by these data (Cattell, 1957).

Why is it that Cattell's rating studies resulted in around fifteen underlying dimensions whereas Eysenck's initial rating studies only resulted in two? The reason for this discrepancy lies in the contrasting ways Cattell and Eysenck use factor analysis (Cattell, 1966). There are two stages in the calculation of a factor analysis at which the investigator has to make a decision. The first decision concerns the number of factors to be extracted from the correlation matrix; and the second concerns the particular technique for arriving at the final solution. Eysenck and Cattell disagree on procedure at both these decision points thus producing different results.

In deciding how many factors should be extracted, the investigator tries to avoid erring on the side of too many or too few: too many factors will leave nearly as complicated a picture as was given by the original correlation matrix and too few means that some important dimensions may have been lost by being subsumed under a more general dimension. To use a simple analogy, the Left–Right dimension fails to capture all the variations between the political parties to be found in, for example, the European Assembly. On the other hand, to have as many dimensions as there are parties would not be helpful in trying to understand the major dimensions of political belief. The aim of factor analysis is to achieve a midway position which results in a manageable number of factors locating dimensions of psychological interest. Although there are various tests that can be applied to the data to indicate, in an objective way, the appropriate number of factors to extract (Harman, 1967), there is still room for the subjective element to enter into the decision; and Cattell, who regards the structure of personality as a complex edifice, favours working with more factors than other investigators generally do.

The second decision point concerns the choice of technique used to achieve the final calculation of the factor loadings (the correlations between the items and each factor from which the psychological identity of the factor is inferred). The final solution is achieved via a set of procedures known as rotation and factor analysts become extremely heated in their arguments over the best methods of rotation. Their arguments are highly technical and will not be gone into in any detail here (see Cattell and Kline, 1977, for a more thorough discussion). For the present purposes, rotation may be seen as a form of fine tuning in which factors are delicately adjusted in order to ensure that they have located as accurately as possible the clusters of intercorrelations in the original correlation matrix. The different techniques of rotation break down into two kinds: orthogonal or oblique.

In orthogonal rotations, the factors produced will be independent of each other. For example, in his work on the dimensions of political belief, Eysenck (1954) has discovered that there is a tender-minded (liberal) versus tough-minded (authoritarian) dimension which is independent in the sense that knowing a person's position on one does not necessarily indicate where their position will be on the other: for example, authoritarians may be either radical (communist) or conservative (fascist).

Eysenck has generally favoured orthogonal solutions, although more recently he has begun opting for oblique factors (H.J. Eysenck and S.B.G. Eysenck, 1969), which has meant that extraversion, neuroticism and psychoticism are treated as independent factors referring to separate areas of personality: knowing a person's score on one of them does not enable you to predict their score on the others. Cattell, on the other hand, has favoured oblique solutions where the factors are correlated, i.e. they are not entirely independent of one another but refer to related areas of personality. Cattell prefers oblique solutions because he believes in the interconnectedness of personality.

Factors are rotated either orthogonally or obliquely until they have been located in the optimal position as defined by the principles of simple structure which correspond to the principles of parsimony. Simple structure has been achieved when the number of zero factor loadings has been maximised. A solution in which each factor's loadings are either high or near to zero means that only a few of the factors are involved in accounting for the variance associated with each variable. Such a solution is more parsimonious than a solution in which all the factors are implicated in every variable. Cattell argues that simple structure can only be achieved through using oblique rotation and advocates that the final adjustment of the factors be done by visual inspection of the solution rather than by mathematical procedures alone.

Having located the factors present in rating data, Cattell and his colleagues went on to investigate the personality structure revealed by the two other sources of data: questionnaires and objective tests. Cattell (1957) discussed the relative merits of rating, questionnaire and objective test data, which he called L, Q and T data respectively. He assumed that all three data bases would tap the same underlying personality structure, although there might be some minor variations, since some aspects of personality may only be expressed in one kind of data; for example, a person's hopes and aspirations could be measured in a self-report questionnaire but would be much harder to infer from observing their overt, day-to-day behaviour (L data). Also, the techniques for measuring the different data have their particular distortions (called 'instrument factors') which may influence the appearance of the structure revealed in each domain. For example, a person's tendency to give the socially desirable response (to 'fake good') may distort Q data, and a rater's idiosyncratic definition of the item being rated may distort L data. As it turns out, there is considerable agreement between the factor structure found in L and Q data, but T data appears to be tapping a rather different aspect of personality, as we shall see below.

As a result of extensive investigation of questionnaire data (involving several thousand subjects), sixteen factors, including an intelligence factor, have been found repeatedly. These well-substantiated Q factors are set out in Table 3.1 which also shows which of these Q factors are the same as the factors in L data.

A glance at Table 3.1 shows that Cattell has invented the words used to label many of the factors and, although other words have been used in addition to these inventions, the preponderance of words like threctia, harria and zeppia create something of a barrier between Cattell and his students. The rationale for these invented names is that the factors refer to what Cattell calls source traits and these are dimensions underlying the surface traits and it is the surface traits which we refer to with our large vocabulary of trait language. Since source traits had not been discovered before Cattell's investigations, there were no appropriate names for them in the language; hence he had to invent them.

Cattell has developed a widely used questionnaire for measuring Q factors; it is called the Sixteen Personality Factor questionnaire (16PF) (Cattell, Eber and Tatsuoka, 1970). There is a supplement to the 16PF (Cattell, 1973) for the assessment of the Q factors only discovered recently (shown as Q+ factors in Table 3.1). Versions of the 16PF

Table 3.1 Factors found in L and Q data (adapted from Cattell and Kline, 1977, pp. 112-19)

Factor	Description			
A	Sizia (reserved) *v*. Affectia (outgoing)	L	Q	
B	Intelligence	L	Q	
C	Dissatisfied emotionality *v*. Ego strength	L	Q	
D	Excitability	L	–	Q+
E	Submissiveness *v*. Dominance	L	Q	
F	Desurgency *v*. Surgency	L	Q	
G	Superego	L	Q	
H	Threctia (shy) *v*. Parmia (adventurous)	L	Q	
I	Harria (tough-minded) *v*. Premsia (tender-minded)	L	Q	
J	Zeppia (zestful) *v*. Coasthemia (individualistic)	L	–	Q+
K	Boorishness *v*. Mature socialisation	L	–	Q+
L	Alexia (trusting) *v*. Protension (suspicional)	L	Q	
M	Praxernia (practical) *v*. Autia (unconventional)	L	Q	
N	Natural forthrightness *v*. Shrewdness	L	Q	
O	Self-confident *v*. Guilt-prone	L	Q	
P	Sanguine casualness	–	–	Q+
Q1	Conservatism *v*. Radicalism	–	Q	
Q2	Group dependency *v*. Self-sufficiency	–	Q	
Q3	Strength of self-sentiment	–	Q	
Q4	Ergic tension	–	Q	
Q5	Group dedication with sensed inadequacy	–	–	Q+
Q6	Social panache	–	–	Q+
Q7	Explicit self-expression	–	–	Q+

have been developed to study the structure of children's personality and tests for all ages ranging from the pre-school child to the adolescent are now available (Dreger, 1977). All these questionnaires are suitable for use on normal populations. In contrast to Eysenck, Cattell regards the abnormal personality as being qualitatively different from the normal personality (Cattell, 1973). Although the 16PF is able to discriminate between neurotics and normals, additional factors are needed for the discrimination of psychotics who are regarded as possessing personality traits not present in normal and neurotic populations. Cattell and Kline (1977) present twelve abnormal factors, seven of which are related to depression.

So far we have only considered two sources of information about personality: behaviour ratings (L data) and self-report questionnaires (Q data). Cattell and his colleagues have also devoted a great deal of research effort to the investigation of personality via objective tests (T data). An objective test, as defined at the beginning of the chapter, is one in which a person is required to respond to a miniature life situation which is presented in such a way that the person is unaware of what the test is actually measuring and therefore cannot 'fake good'. The rationale behind objective tests lies in the assumption that all behaviour is potential personality data, from handwriting to nose blowing. The choice of miniature life situations is restricted only by practical limitations of portability and administration time and the ingenuity of the researcher. There are now over four hundred objective tests in regular use and over two thousand different measures may be derived from them (Cattell and Warburton, 1967). Several objective tests are usually administered in one session, making up what is termed an objective test battery. Some instances of the more zany objective tests, selected from the examples given by Cattell and Kline, are: blowing up a balloon (which identifies timid, inhibited people), reading backwards (which is difficult for rigid people) and selecting the funnier of two jokes (which reveals a person's repressed impulses). There are also more familiar tests, such as physiological measures and reaction times.

Theoretically, T data are regarded as tapping the same personality sphere as L and Q data. Therefore the same personality structure should emerge when T data are factor analysed. Minor differences are to be expected due to instrument factors but the same essential structure should be there. The results so far have been less clear than had been predicted. Twenty factors have been located and replicated, but the correspondence between these factors and those found in L and Q data is yet to be fully established.

Motivation

For Cattell, the structure and measurement of personality does not stop at describing temperament and ability but also includes dynamics or motivation: personality is composed of both the way we do things (temperament and ability) and why we do things (motivation). Motivation is regarded as having two aspects requiring separate investigation and measurement: its strength and the goals involved (Cattell and Child, 1975).

Motivational strength refers to the degree of interest a person displays in particular activities. For example, some people regard cooking as an unavoidable chore while others find it a never-ending delight. Cattell was interested in discovering if a person's strength of interest in an activity could be broken down into various components. Some interests may be equally strong and yet reflect different aspects of motivation. Thus the person who is keen on cooking may also be an enthusiastic worker for a charity. These two different interests, the former tending towards hedonism the latter towards selflessness, suggest that motivation is multi-dimensional.

Cattell studied motivational strength using objective tests. When the scores were factor analysed, three main dimensions of motivational strength emerged. They corresponded approximately to the Freudian concepts of id, ego and superego. For example, imagine a person buying a house. Their strength of interest in the purchase could be impulsive: they see a charming house and desire to own it. In this case the id component is predominant. Alternatively, the house may fulfil all the criteria of the appropriate choice for that person: it is the right size, in the right area and the price is reasonable. Interest in the purchase in this case is predominantly ego-based. A third possibility is that the house represents a sound investment and the buyer knows that buying property is a sensible hedge against inflation and is something one ought to do, even though it is much less trouble to rent a place. Here, the superego component is at work. Usually, house-buying involves all three components to varying degrees. In brief, motivation consists of three components: id interest (I want), ego interest (I choose to want) and superego interest (I ought to want).

So much for motivational strength, but what about the goals of motivation? Cattell calls the ultimate goals of motivated behaviour the ergs. These are roughly comparable to instincts, e.g. food-seeking, sex, gregariousness. While ergs are culturally universal because of their biological origins, the means by which ergs can be satisfied will vary from culture to culture. In our society areas such as sport, occupations, religion and the home are all mediums for erg satisfaction. These culture-specific activities through which ergs are satisfied are called sentiments by Cattell. A single sentiment such as a sport may be involved in the satisfaction of a number of different ergs such as gregariousness, pugnacity and possibly even sex if one of the aims of taking physical exercise is to develop an attractive physique. The complex connections between all the different sentiments and the ergs to which they are related are termed the dynamic lattice, a much simplified version of which is shown in Figure 3.4. Such a lattice can be constructed for a particular culture or, more specifically, for a particular individual. It will tell the investigator what a person's interests are and what basic ergs these interests are satisfying.

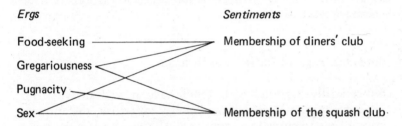

Figure 3.4 *A simplified representation of a part of a dynamic lattice*

Temperament, ability and motivation factors make up the key elements of Cattell's theory of the structure of personality; they form what may be regarded as its relatively fixed base. However, people change from day to day and year by year, and a complete personality theory needs to be able to accommodate these short- and long-term fluctuations. Cattell has studied relatively short-term moods and states and concludes that anxiety in particular is the most important aspect of these transient conditions (Cattell and Scheier, 1961). More permanent changes in personality structure are the result of maturation and learning experiences, and Cattell has begun to develop an account of how learning affects the relatively fixed elements of the personality structure to bring about enduring changes.

We have now seen how Cattell's conceptualisation of personality describes the basic structure of personality, its dynamics, and the temporary and more permanent changes it can undergo. Cattell attempts to draw together all these separate influences bearing on behaviour in a single equation. The behaviour specification equation sets out the components of a particular behaviour specifying the level of involvement of traits, ergs, states, learning factors and situational variables. What began as a simple formula has expanded over the years, in pace with the theory, to an unwieldy and impractical series of algebraic terms, some of which refer to concepts as yet unmeasurable. The specification equation is no longer a succinct and useful description of behaviour and perhaps the same is true of Cattell's theory as a whole. In an effort to be all-embracing it has itself become too vast to encompass.

An Integration of Cattell and Eysenck

Superficially, Cattell and Eysenck have arrived at two different conceptualisations of personality structure, the former's comprising twenty-three traits and the latter's a mere three. Since both have been investigating the same subject-matter it would appear that one of them must be wrong. However, happily for them both, it can be shown that the two conceptualisations are not irreconcilable.

The issue can be resolved by a closer examination of the different ways the two theorists have used factor analysis. The factors obtained in the initial analysis of personality data are called first-order factors. As has already been described, Cattell favours oblique factors. Because they are correlated, the twenty-three oblique factors resulting from Cattell's analyses can themselves be inter-correlated and factor analysed. As a result of this process, a smaller number of so-called second-order factors may be obtained. When this is done with Cattell's twenty-three first-order factors several second-order factors emerge but the two most important are Exvia–Invia and Anxiety. Second-order factors can be identified by their high loadings on first-order factors which the Exvia–Invia are sociable (A), surgent (F), adventurous (H) and dependent (Q2), and for Anxiety are weak ego strength (C), timid (H), suspicious (L), guilt prone (O), low self sentiment (Q3) and tense (Q4) (Cattell and Kline, 1977).

Cattell (1973) argues that Eysenck's factors of Extraversion and Neuroticism are not true first-order factors but appeared as such because of Eysenck's improper use of factor analysis. Eysenck is regarded as having underfactored his data and the resulting factors of Extraversion, Neuroticism and Psychoticism are pseudosecondaries, i.e. they are first-order factors which have positioned themselves roughly in line with true second-order factors. As a result, Extraversion–Introversion is highly similar to Cattell's second-order factor Exvia–Invia, and Neuroticism is similar to Anxiety. Psychoticism is regarded as probably a first-order approximation of Cattell's second-order general psychoticism factor, but is insufficient for describing the abnormal domain because it bears no relation to the other second-order factor of general depression (Cattell and Kline, 1977).

Thus the structures proposed by Cattell and Eysenck do not turn out to be fundamentally different. Eysenck prefers to keep things simple and work with a broad, three-dimensional picture, while Cattell believes that by turning the power of the microscope up and working with a larger number of traits a more accurate picture is obtained. Despite these preferences, it is recognised that their conceptualisations are essentially the same.

As we have seen, both Eysenck's and Cattell's theories of personality rely heavily on factor analysis as the chief tool for determining the structure of personality. The validity of these theories is therefore dependent on the validity of factor analysis. In comparing Eysenck and Cattell's different preferences regarding the details of factor analytic methods, it was clear that there is considerable room for subjective judgment to play a part in what is often claimed to be an objective technique. The user must make decisions concerning how many factors to rotate, what method of rotation to adopt (orthogonal or oblique) and when the best solution in terms of the principles of simple structure has been achieved. All these decisions will have significant effects on the appearance of the final solution.

Factor analysis is also open to a number of other criticisms. Factors are identified by the inspection of the high loading items and this process is vulnerable to bias by the investigator's pre-existing beliefs. It is often difficult to assess if a factor has been replicated across studies where identical variables have not been used. A well-known cliché with regard to factor analysis is that you only get out what you put in, which implies that the results will tell you nothing you did not know already and will not be generalisable. However, like most clichés this is a glib comment which does not withstand close inspection. The work of Eysenck and Cattell has told us a great deal about personality and repeated studies have confirmed the generality of at least some of the findings.

The final criticism of factor analysis is of particular interest in the light of more recent developments in personality research to be described in the next chapter. Factor analysis assumes that factors contribute additively to the explanation of behaviour. For example, Cattell's specification equation states that a certain behaviour, e.g. helping a blind person across the road, is the result of the addition of several contributing factors, e.g. G (Superego), K (Mature socialisation) and O (Self-confidence). In the last decade there has been an upsurge of evidence to suggest that behaviour is the product of *interactive*, as opposed to *additive*, effects which suggests that factor analysis may be an inappropriate technique for capturing the full complexities of the determinants of behaviour.

4 The Issue of Consistency and the Personality Theorist's

Consistency is an integral part of the standard definition of personality given at the beginning of this book: personality consists of the 'More or less stable internal factors *that make one person's behaviour consistent from one time to another,* and different from the behaviour other people would manifest in comparable situations' (I.L. Child, 1968, p.83, emphasis added). The personality theorist's perspective sets out to explain why an individual's behaviour is consistent by postulating stable, internal factors which determine behaviour. It also aims to provide assessment techniques which permit the prediction of behaviour, and these too rely on the assumption that behaviour is consistent.

The most damaging criticisms of the personality theorist's perspective are those which undermine its basis in consistency. Indeed, the consistency issue may be seen as the personality theorist's Achilles' heel. In this chapter, the evidence against the postulate of consistency is reviewed and, in view of the strength of this evidence, modifications to the personality theorist's perspective are proposed.

The Meaning of Consistency

In the above definition of personality, consistency is taken to mean the similarity in a person's behaviour across two different points in time. This definition is brief to the point of being obscure: it is not stated whether the situations in which the behaviour is compared from one time to another are the same or different, and it is not stated whether the behaviours are the same or different. Presumably, the person who drives to work with the radio at full volume and spends the lunch break with colleagues in a noisy restaurant is exhibiting consistency in the sense that both behaviours demonstrate a need for high levels of stimulation, but comparison here involves not only two points in time but also two different situations and two different behaviours. In contrast, the person who drives to work every morning on exactly the same route is also being consistent and in this case the situations and the behaviours being compared across time are the same. These two examples suggest that consistency, in the context of personality, is a complex concept. When personality theorists claim to have demonstrated consistency and their critics claim to have demonstrated inconsistency, there are several different meanings of the concept to which they may be referring, and it is useful to have a framework within which to sort these meanings out.

The four types of consistency

To clarify the different meanings of consistency it is possible to represent them by means of a two-by-two table (see Figure 4.1). Demonstrating consistency always involves comparing two different time points, but either the same or different behaviours can be compared in either the same or different situations.

		Situation	
		Same	Different
Behaviour	Same	Type A	Type B
	Different	Type C	Type D

Figure 4.1 *The four types of consistency*

The four types of consistency: A, B, C and D, in Figure 4.1 are obtained by combining the two possible cases for the situations (same or different) with the two possible cases for the behaviours (same or different). Strictly speaking, no two behaviours or situations occurring at different times may be considered identical; however, such logical niceties are generally ignored by personality researchers once every effort has been made to ensure that the behaviours and situations are as similar as possible.

In type A consistency, the behaviours and situations being compared across time points are the same. When a person takes the same personality questionnaire under identical test conditions (the same room, supervisor, time of day, etc.) on two separate occasions, then type A consistency is being investigated. Studies of test re-test reliability are concerned with type A consistency.

Type B consistency requires that the same behaviour be compared across different situations. For example, in an investigation into altruism, subjects' helping behaviour might be compared across two different situations where a person was in distress: one where there were several bystanders and one where the subject was alone. If altruism is a stable personality characteristic, then subjects should be consistently altruistic in both situations. If it is determined by situational factors, then the difference between several bystanders and none may result in inconsistencies in helping behaviour in the two situations. In both types A and B, consistency is demonstrated by the same behaviour occurring at each time point, either in the same or different situations.

Type C consistency requires that the behaviours be different but the situations the same. At first glance, type C consistency seems something of a contradiction. How can it be consistent for a person to behave in different ways in repetitions of the same situations? Type D consistency appears even more contradictory: if a person behaves differently in a different situation then this is being consistent. The resolution of this contradiction is achieved through the personality concept. There are far fewer personality factors than overt behaviours, hence each factor is involved in the determination of a number of different behaviours, a subset of behaviours. The performance of one behaviour in a particular situation allows for the prediction of the occurrence of other behaviours from the same subset either in a repetition of the same situation (type C consistency) or even in a different situation (type D consistency). In types C and D consistency, although the overt behaviours may be extremely different, they share an underlying similarity because they are determined by the same personality factor.

Type C consistency may be illustrated by the study of group interaction, where it is commonly found that people adopt characteristic styles, the two best known being task-orientated and socio-emotional (Bales, 1951). Over a series of group discussions, or during the course of one session, it may be found that the person who asks questions also re-directs the conversation back to the discussion topic (task-orientated) and that the person who tells jokes also makes supportive comments (socio-emotional). Here the situation remains the same but the group members exhibit different behaviours from one time point to the next and these different behaviours may be regarded as demonstrating consistency because they are drawn from mutually exclusive subsets.

An example of type D consistency would be an investigation into the validity of a personality test. Thus if a person scored highly on a questionnaire measure of extraversion it would be consistent if this person behaved in typically extraverted ways at a party later on in the day. Responding to a personality questionnaire and having a good time at a party are different behaviours in different situations; but, to the extent that they are both determined by the same underlying factor (extraversion) and knowledge of the factor permits prediction of the behaviour, the occurrence of these different behaviours is evidence of type D consistency.

When consistency is discussed in the context of personality it is not usually specified which of these four types of consistency is meant. However, by examining the behaviours and situations used to assess consistency and using the classification system described above, the identification of the different forms of consistency becomes straightforward. Armed with a framework for identifying the different types of consistency, it is possible to be more precise about the sorts of consistency upon which the personality theorist's perspective is based and which the critics have sought to undermine.

The personality concept and its basis in consistency
Both single-trait and multi-trait personality theories rely on
the existence of all four types of consistency. The first three,
A, B and C, are the phenomena which the theories set out to
explain, and the last, D, provides the rationale for the prediction of behaviour on the basis of personality assessment.

The personality theorist's perspective explains types A, B
and C consistency by proposing that underlying internal
personality factors are the major cause of behaviour, and that
situational variables, (although often important) generally
play a lesser role. Locus of control is a good example of a
dimension which explains types A and B consistency. Rotter
and his colleagues observed that some people behaved in a
consistently internal fashion while others behaved externally
both in repetitions of the same situation and when confronted
with new situations. Rotter's personality theory is particularly
sensitive to the importance of the role of situational variables
in the determination of behaviour; nevertheless he believed it
was necessary to develop the I–E dimension to account for
the fact that people approach situations with a characteristic
internal or external approach which is a more powerful determinant of their behaviour than the variables specific to the
situation.

Type C consistency is best explained by Eysenck and
Cattell's multi-trait theories. Take the trait of sociability
recognised by both theories (as a component of extraversion
in Eysenck's theory and factor A in Cattell's theory). Sociability is presumed to underlie a variety of behaviours found
to co-occur in the same people, although not necessarily
simultaneously, e.g. talkativeness, preference for the company of others, frankness, etc.

A person who exhibits some of these sociable behaviours
on one occasion is expected to exhibit other sociable behaviours on other, similar occasions. It would be inconsistent
if on one occasion a person's behaviour appeared to be determined by their underlying sociability and on another by their
underlying reserve. By postulating underlying personality
factors which determine a variety of behaviours, personality
theorists can explain and predict type C consistency.

Personality theorists also explain type D consistency in

terms of underlying personality factors, and such explanations form the rationale for personality assessment. Techniques of assessment involve obtaining a small sample of a person's behavioural repertoire, a sample which is regarded as an index of the person's position on an underlying dimension. On the basis of this index it is possible to make wide-ranging predictions about the person's subsequent behaviour. To take an extreme example, the lemon juice test is claimed to discriminate between introverts and extraverts. Therefore, on the basis of the amount of saliva a person produces to a drop of lemon juice, the Eysenckian personality theorist is prepared to predict how that person will behave at a party — because both the party behaviour and the degree of salivation reflect the person's position on the extraversion dimension.

In sum, the personality theorist's perspective, whether exemplified in single-trait or multi-trait theories, is based on the existence of all four types of consistency, and these are all explained by the concept of underlying personality factors, which are regarded as responsible for observed behavioural consistency. The personality theorist regards personality as a major determinant of behaviour. Most theories do acknowledge that situational variables play a part (for example, Cattell's specification equation contains situational variables), but the essence of the personality concept is that a great deal of behavioural consistency is best explained by stable, internal personality factors.

As is now apparent, the most telling criticism of the personality theorist's perspective would be the failure to find behavioural consistency in all its forms. In that event, personality theorists would lose both the phenomena they set out to explain plus any claim to utility, since their supposed ability to predict behaviour on the basis of personality assessment would be discredited. Even a failure to find evidence for just one form of consistency would be serious, since the same explanation (underlying personality factors) is proposed for all forms.

Mischel's Attack on the Personality Theorist's Perspective

In 1968 Mischel published a book called *Personality and*

Assessment, in which he set out a powerful argument against the personality theorist's perspective backed with an impressive array of evidence. At the very least, this book has demonstrated that personality theorists have overstated the case for behavioural consistency and Mischel goes so far as to argue that the personality concept is invalid, and the process of explaining and predicting behaviour would be better off without it.

Mischel did not restrict his attack to any one theory but aimed it at two influential groups of theories: psychodynamic theories, such as that of Freud, and trait theories. The key features shared by the two types of theories he defined as follows:

> Both dynamic (state) and trait theories focus on responses as signs (indirect or direct) of pervasive underlying mental structures; both assume that these underlying inferred dispositions (whether called traits, states, processes, dynamics, motives or labeled in other ways) exert generalized and enduring causal effects on behavior; and both have been devoted to a search for signs that serve as reliable indicators of these hypothesized underlying dimensions. (Mischel, 1968, p. 8)

Mischel's definition of personality is very close to the one adopted here (see the beginning of this chapter) and he also recognises that consistency is the key issue:

> Data that demonstrate strong generality in the behavior of the same person across many situations are critical for trait and state personality theories; the construct of personality itself rests on the belief that individual behavioral consistencies exist widely and account for much of the variance in behavior. (Mischel, 1968, p. 13)

Mischel does not discuss the different forms of consistency, and in the above quotation he seems to be referring to what is described here as type B consistency (same behaviour, different situation). However, in his presentation of evidence of relevance to the consistency assumption it is clear that he is concerned with all types.

The evidence for and against consistency
Mischel examined the evidence for behavioural consistency
from a variety of areas: not only personality, but also intelligence and cognitive style. He was justified in widening
the circle of the debate in this way because the arguments
for psychological constructs such as intelligence and cognitive style are similar to those for personality: they all rely
on the concept of underlying factors to explain behavioural
consistency.

Beginning with type A, there is plenty of evidence for
consistency in all three domains: intelligence, cognitive style
and personality. All studies of test-retest reliability are investigations of type A consistency: subjects perform the
same test-taking behaviour under the same situational conditions. Measures in all three domains are expected to achieve
a high level of test-retest reliability and many of them do.
One of the problems with these studies is that on retesting
subjects may remember how they answered the test on the
first occasion and hence the similarity between the two sets
of answers reflects the subjects' good memories rather than
their behavioural consistency. A common way round this
problem is to use two different versions of the test which
have previously been shown to be equivalent. For example,
the Eysenck Personality Inventory is available in two adult
versions and these are regarded as equivalent tests although
the wording of the items is different.

Test-retest reliability studies compare repeated performances of highly specific and contrived behaviours. In more
everyday experience type A consistency may not be so easy
to demonstrate. One of the reasons for this is that it is easier
to replicate situations faithfully in the laboratory than it is
in real life. However, Mischel was satisfied that type A
consistency had been satisfactorily demonstrated.

The evidence for type B consistency was also satisfactory
but only so far as intelligence and cognitive styles were concerned. For example, Mischel discussed the concept of field
dependence–independence which, as we saw in Chapter 2,
can be measured with a variety of techniques such as the
RFT and EFT. These different tests may be regarded as
different situations, and the required behaviour, separating

figure from ground, is essentially the same in all of them. The correlations between different measures of FD-I are reasonably high; this is a demonstration of type B consistency.

When Mischel examined the evidence for type B consistency in more personality-related behaviour the findings, from the personality theorist's perspective, were disappointing. Mischel placed considerable emphasis on the classic studies of moral behaviour by Hartshorne and May (Hartshorne and May, 1928, 1929; Hartshorne, May and Shuttleworth, 1930). The aim of their investigations was to test the validity of the concept of a trait of honesty, a trait considered to determine people's moral behaviour in a variety of situations. It is generally believed that someone who is basically honest will behave with honesty in all kinds of situations, regardless of situational incentives to be either honest or dishonest. However, Hartshorne and May's studies showed that honesty was influenced by situational factors. Several thousand children participated in these studies and over a hundred different situations were devised where there was an opportunity for the children to behave dishonestly and, apparently, avoid detection. However, all dishonest behaviour was, in fact, monitored. For example, while consistency was high between self-report questionnaires about moral behaviour filled out by the same children on different occasions in the classroom (type A consistency), consistency between behaviours such as cheating on a test by copying compared with cheating by adjusting the final score was poor (type B consistency). Mischel agreed with Hartshorne and May's interpretation of their findings: that honesty is primarily a function of situational factors and is not a consistent behaviour determined by an underlying personality characteristic.

Hartshorne and May's studies have been the subject of much discussion and reanalysis over the fifty years since they were carried out, in an attempt to establish whether the original interpretation was correct (e.g. Burton, 1963); but no definitive conclusions have emerged. One of the most telling comments on this work is that it used children as subjects, and evidence on the development of children's moral thinking obtained more recently (Kohlberg, 1976) suggests that a trans-situational moral code resulting in consistent moral behaviour does not develop at least until adolescence. It is therefore not surprising that Hartshorne and May's child subjects failed to demonstrate type B consistency. Thus an experiment using adult subjects would be more appropriate.

On the basis of the honesty study, and several other similar investigations, Mischel concluded that the evidence for type B consistency in the personality domain was far from convincing. His conclusion has not gone unchallenged. Block (1977a) has commented adversely on the quality of the studies cited by Mischel as evidence of inconsistency. While this criticism is fair in many cases, there is a danger with this type of argument that findings of inconsistent behaviours will always be dismissed by personality theorists as evidence that the study was badly designed, thus rendering the postulate of type B consistency irrefutable. Mischel and his opponents can exchange evidence for and against type B consistency without advancing the argument one jot. People cannot always be relied upon to behave similarly in different situations; inconsistent behaviour is the result of situational variables exerting a stronger determining influence than personality factors, and it is always possible to contrive situations where this will be the case. Will the pacifist be consistent when faced with a madman attacking his wife and children? Even the most dedicated dieter occasionally succumbs to a really tempting dessert. Mischel has argued convincingly that type B consistency is not as pervasive a phenomenon as personality theorists would wish, but this fact alone does not constitute a major threat to the personality concept so long as personality theorists are prepared to accept that some, but not all, behaviours are explained more parsimoniously by situational determinants than by personality factors.

For evidence concerning type C consistency (different behaviour, same situation) Mischel drew on studies of the validity of personality ratings. Both Eysenck and Cattell used rating data in their early studies of personality: observers rated their subjects' behaviour on a series of scales which were then intercorrelated and factor analysed. The results of these analyses were assumed to describe the personality structure of the ratees. Subsequent studies, however, questioned the validity of this assumption, claiming that observers' ratings reveal the constructs used by the observer in categorising another's behaviour rather than the personality structure of the person being rated (D'Andrade, 1965; Mulaik, 1964; Passini and Norman, 1966). These studies are concerned with type C consistency in the sense that the rating scales constitute measures of different behaviours and these are observed by the rater in the same or similar situations. Type C consistency is demonstrated when clusters of behaviour are found to co-occur in the same people in the same situation (e.g. talkativeness, frankness, adventurousness and sociability) and hence constitute a factor (e.g. extraversion).

The validity of personality ratings was questioned because these studies found that the same factor structure emerged in analyses of ratings made by raters with varying degrees of acquaintance with their ratees ranging from three years to fifteen minutes (Passini and Norman, 1966). In addition, when no ratees were involved and subjects simply rated the scales in terms of how similar in meaning each one was to every other, the same factor structure emerged (D'Andrade, 1965; Mulaik, 1964). These findings suggest that the trait categories used by raters for classifying behaviour exist independently of the ratees' actual behaviour. It is these conceptual categories which emerge when ratings are factor analysed, rather than the personality traits characterising the ratees.

On the basis of such findings, Mischel has argued that type C consistency has not been demonstrated: analysis of personality ratings tells us more about the rater than the ratee. This is a grave indictment of personality ratings; but there is one important point Mischel has overlooked. Demonstrating a correspondence between the factor structure or ratings of actual behaviour and raters' conceptual categories could mean one of two things: if the raters' conceptual categories do not correspond with reality, Mischel's interpretation that personality ratings are invalid is correct; but if raters' conceptual categories do correspond with reality then the similarity between these categories and the factor structure of personality ratings may be accepted as accurate. The extent to which raters' conceptual categories are an accurate reflection of which kinds of behaviour do actually co-occur in real life is an empirical question which has been investigated since Mischel's 1968 critique. This work will be discussed in full in Chapter 6.

Finally, Mischel considered the evidence for type D consistency. Personality theorists claim that behaviour in one situation can serve as a sign for how the person will behave in another situation, and the utility of the personality theorist's perspective depends on the success of this claim. Mischel reviewed the research on the correlations between personality test scores and actual behaviour (comparing the test-taking situation with other situations where other behaviours were sampled) and arrived at his now famous 'personality coefficient':

> Indeed, the phrase 'personality coefficient' might be coined to describe the correlation between .20 and .30 which is found persistently when virtually any personality dimension inferred from a questionnaire is related to almost any conceivable external criterion involving responses sampled in a different *medium* — that is, not by another questionnaire. (Mischel, 1968, p. 78, original emphasis)

An example of a failure to establish type D consistency is Cattell's work on objective test data. The personality factors found in analyses of objective test data do not match up with the factors found in questionnaire and rating data — which means that questionnaire scores do not predict objective test performance.

The low level of consistency between scores on personality tests and actual behaviour in different situations naturally raises serious doubts as to the utility of the personality theorist's perspective. Mischel proposed that more reliable prediction could be achieved by estimating future behaviour on the basis of how a person has behaved in similar situations in the past. In effect, he proposed that type A consistency, of which we can be reasonably confident, should form the basis of prediction rather than type D. In so doing, he abandoned the personality concept, in the sense that he was advocating that behaviour be regarded as merely predictive of itself and not as a sign of an underlying personality factor and hence predictive of a variety of other behaviours.

Mischel's attack on the personality theorist's perspective was aimed at its most vulnerable point – consistency – and the attack was partially successful. While type A consistency survived relatively unscathed, type B consistency was shown not to exist as generally as personality theorists have tended to assume. Although Mischel regarded type C consistency as a figment of raters' imaginations, the validity of their imaginations has yet to be disproved and so the status of type C consistency remains unclear. Type D consistency has certainly been exaggerated by personality theorists. Since Mischel can only claim partial success in his assault, the personality concept (and hence the personality theorist's perspective) still has a role to play. However, the perspective has had to be modified to accommodate situational factors which Mischel's critique of consistency has shown do sometimes play a more important role than personality in the determination of behaviour.

Situationism

After 1968 it soon became apparent that Mischel's book had re-awakened interest in the longstanding debate in psychology over the relative importance for the determination of behaviour of what the person brings to bear upon the situation versus what the situation brings to bear upon the person. This debate is by no means new; the issues were articulated as long ago as 1935 by Kurt Lewin who proposed the compromise that behaviour is a function of both the person and the environment; and it is doubtful whether the debate has progressed conceptually much further since his statement. (The history of this debate is described by Ekehammar, 1974.)

Mischel's approach to the explanation and prediction of behaviour, an approach which advocated abandoning the personality concept in favour of situational variables, became known as 'situationism' (Bowers, 1973). Although Mischel did not in fact succeed in entirely discrediting personality and its assessment, he himself was so convinced by his arguments that he proposed an alternative to personality theory, an alternative which he called social learning theory. It is similar to Rotter's theory in that it is based on the principle of learning discovered in laboratory experiments and is applied to the full range of normal and abnormal social behaviour. It is a behaviouristic position in so far as it eschews the concept of any internal personality factors. Instead, behaviour is seen as being determined solely by environmental factors. The weaknesses of pure situationism were revealed early on by Mischel's most erudite critic, Kenneth Bowers. In an outstanding critique of the situationist position, Bowers (1973) illuminated the methodological weaknesses of this rival to trait psychology.

Bowers argued that situationism is the product of the experimental method and therefore incorporates several biasing features, one of the most important being that the experimental method is primarily concerned with demonstrating the circumstances under which behaviour changes, as opposed to investigating behavioural stability. In an attempt to demonstrate the relation between a behaviour and its presumed controlling variables, the experimenter seeks rejection of the null hypothesis which asserts that the behaviour will be insensitive to situational manipulation. The operation of situational variables is inferred from changes in behaviour. If such changes do occur, the experimenter concludes that situational variables determined the behaviour and the null hypothesis is rejected. However, if the behaviour does not change, the experimenter is unwilling to concede that the null hypothesis may not be rejected. More likely, further experiments will be conducted to try to sort out why the situational manipulations 'failed to work'. Of course such a strategy goes against the fundamental principle of the scientific method, to which situationism (like many other psychological theories) is committed, namely that of falsifiability (Popper, 1959). As Bowers (1973, p.317) said: 'Now, if one wants to argue that behaviour is situation specific, then it must be possible to conclude that it is *not* situation specific; otherwise the assertion that behaviour is situation specific is non-falsifiable.' Bowers' point here is that experimental methods for studying personality are biased to seek out behavioural changes and ignore stability and so, since the former supports the situationist position and the latter the trait position, there is likely to be a spurious imbalance of evidence in favour of situationism.

Having criticised pure situationism, Bowers went on to argue that it is wrong to seek the causes of behaviour in traits or situations. The absurdity of such a search is demonstrated by the ease with which it is possible to think up experiments to 'prove' either position. For example, London's traffic provides constant proof of the superiority of situation over person variables: virtually everyone obeys the traffic lights. Conversely, motorway driving demonstrates the role of person variables. Not everyone chooses to drive at the maximum permitted speed; instead, drivers adopt the cruising speed which they personally prefer. In this case, the situation exerts less control over the individual who is then free to behave more idiosyncratically. The pitting of traits against situations is an unhelpful exercise, and Bowers recommends it be abandoned in favour of an interactionist approach which takes both into account.

In his recent work Mischel has adopted a position more in sympathy with Bowers' arguments. One of the problems for the situationist is to account for individual differences: why do we not all respond in the same way when placed in the same situation? Social learning theory explains individual differences with the argument that everyone goes through a unique set of learning experiences which result in situational variables exerting different influences depending on the person's past experiences. Such differences are most marked in the abnormal domain. For example, a person who has a phobia about being in a crowded shopping area as a result of adverse past experience will show all the symptoms of an anxiety attack (e.g. trembling, sweating, feeling faint and panic-stricken) when placed in this situation, whereas the other shoppers will go about their business more or less happily. Mischel has proposed that past experience affects the individual's information processing strategies, which govern the way situational variables are perceived, and hence their effects on behaviour (Mischel, 1973, 1977a, b). His theory has become a cognitive social learning theory. As a result of past experience, people approach situations with characteristic modes of information processing which will determine the unique meaning of that situation for that person.

A cognitive social learning theory begins to sound suspiciously similar to the traditional concept of personality: instead of personality traits, individuals are characterised by trans-situational cognitive processes which determine how the situation is perceived and responded to. These idiosyncrasies in cognitive development sound like acceptable candidates for the role of 'stable internal factors' referred to in the definition of personality. They also account for individual differences. The major difference between cognitive social learning theory and traditional personality theory is that the former does not depend on consistency to the same degree as the latter, because it recognises that these cognitive person factors operate in conjunction with situational factors to determine behaviour.

Interactionism

In the aftermath of Mischel's critique of traits many personality researchers advocated the adoption of an approach in which both personality and situational factors are taken into account in the explanation of behaviour (Alker, 1972; Argyle and Little, 1972; Averill, 1973; Bem, 1972; Bowers, 1973; Endler, 1973; Endler and Edwards, 1978; Endler and Magnusson, 1976; Magnusson and Endler, 1977). This approach has been termed 'interactionism'.

Interactionism has been advocated as applying to topics as diverse as child development, altruism, education and stress, in addition to personality (Pervin and Lewis, 1978). The task set by an interactionist approach, as described by Pervin and Lewis (p. 20), is one of defining 'the critical variables internal to the organism and those external to it, and then studying the processes through which the effects of one are tied to the operations of the other'. There are various ways of translating this task into an experiment, but in the personality domain this has typically been done by using analysis of variance designs.

Analysis of variance

The simplest experimental design involves only one independent variable or factor. Let us take as a hypothetical example an experiment on the relative efficacy of two different problem-solving conditions, an experiment in which children of the same intellectual ability worked on a maths problem either alone or in pairs. The independent variable or factor here is problem-solving condition (alone or paired) and the dependent variable is the time taken to reach a correct solution. The imaginary results of this experiment are shown in Figure 4.2. The mean solution time for the subjects working on their own was significantly faster than for subjects working in pairs.

The experiment appears to show that working on a problem alone is more efficient than working with another person. But it was limited by the fact that only the effects of one factor on problem solving was investigated, and it could be that there are other factors that play an important part whose effects were ignored. For example, perhaps there is a personality dimension which influences speed of problem solving. Let us extend the above experiment by introducing a second independent variable, the personality dimension of introversion–extraversion. Now, instead of two groups of subjects (alone or paired) we would have to test four groups: introverts alone or paired and extraverts alone or paired. The resulting data would then be suitable for analysis using a two-way analysis of variance which would yield three pieces of information about the statistical significance of the differences between these groups: first, whether the problem-solving condition had any effect; second, if the personality dimension had any effect; and third, if there was a significant interaction between these two factors. An interaction occurs when one variable is sensitive to the effects of another. The imaginary data for the second experiment are shown in Figure 4.3.

It can be seen that the pattern of results is different for introverts and extraverts. Let us assume that the results of the analysis of variance were as follows. First, as in the first experiment, there was a significant effect for problem-solving condition: subjects in the alone condition solved the problem

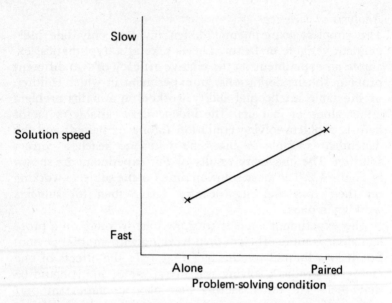

Figure 4.2 *Mean solution speed for the alone and paired groups*

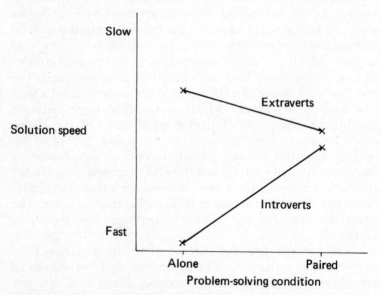

Figure 4.3 *Mean solution speeds for the introvert alone and paired groups and the extravert alone and paired groups*

faster than subjects in the paired condition. Second, there was a significant effect of personality type: introverts performed faster than extraverts. Third, the interaction between problem-solving condition and personality type was significant. To understand what this interaction means it is necessary to study the graph carefully. Taking the line representing the introverts first, it can be seen that they performed faster in the alone condition than in the paired condition and that they were generally faster than the extraverts. The extraverts, although generally slower than the introverts, showed a different pattern to the introverts in their responses to the problem-solving condition. Instead of performing even more slowly in the paired condition, they showed an improvement relative to their performance in the alone condition.

In this hypothetical experiment, a situational variable and a personality variable had separate effects on problem solving and together they had an interactive effect: extraverts reacted in a different way to introverts when the situational variable was altered. It is always possible to spot when variables interact by examining their graphical representation, as in Figure 4.3. The lines in this graph converge; if there had been no interaction between the two variables, then the lines would have been parallel. Occasionally, the lines converge to such an extent that they actually cross over. If there had been a cross-over interaction in this experiment, then the introverts would have been faster than the extraverts in the alone condition and the extraverts would have been faster than the introverts in the paired condition.

In the above experiment there were two groups representing the person factor: introverts and extraverts. It is unlikely that each of the subjects in the two groups would have possessed identical introversion or extraversion scores and, with a fine enough measuring instrument, it would have been possible to extend the person factor to, say, four levels: high and low introverts and high and low extraverts. Logically, the process of extension could continue to the point where each subject formed a discrete 'group' representing a particular level of the introversion–extraversion factor. In this case, the number of levels of the person factor would equal the number of subjects in the study.

Person by situation interactions

The early interactionist studies of personality, reviewed by Bowers (1973), used the type of analysis of variance design where individual subjects were treated as separate levels of the person factor. These studies assessed the relative importance of the person versus the situation in what amounted to a direct test of type B consistency (same behaviour, different situation). One of these early studies (Moos, 1969) used psychiatric patients as subjects. A variety of their behaviours, such as talking and smoking, was observed in different hospital settings such as at lunch or during therapy. If type B consistency was present, then the person factor should prove significant. From the calculations involved in an analysis of variance it is possible to work out the proportion of variance attributable to each of the factors and to their interaction. The results were mixed, with some behaviours showing consistency (e.g. smoking), while others showed situational specificity (e.g. talking); but the main finding was that when the results of the separate analyses for all the different behaviours were put together, the person by situation interaction accounted for more of the variance than either factor independently.

The same was true of the other ten studies reviewed by Bowers: by combining the results of all eleven studies he was able to calculate the mean percentage variance attributable to person factors (12.71 per cent), to situational factors (10.17 per cent) and to the person by situation interactions (20.77 per cent). The numerical supremacy of the percentage of variance accounted for by interactions over persons and situations was taken as evidence against both a pure trait position and a pure situationist position; hence this was considered to be a demonstration of the importance of taking both factors into account, i.e. of adopting an interactionist model.

However, the validity of using relative contributions to total variance as evidence of the superiority of interactionism over the trait position or situationism has been challenged (e.g. Olweus, 1977). First, at the empirical level, the actual size of these percentage variances is essentially arbitrary since the relative contributions to the total variance from the person factor, the situation factor and their interaction will vary depending on the range of persons and situations sampled; the narrower the range, the lower the percentage. Averaging percentage variances from several studies sampling widely differing ranges on the person and situation factors further reduces their informativeness.

Second, at the theoretical level, percentage variances do not provide an unambiguous test between interactionism, a trait position and situationism. For example, a particular trait theory may place considerable emphasis on situational factors and hence not be invalidated by the superiority of interactions over main effects. The type of study reviewed by Bowers is too crude a test of the different theoretical positions to warrant the blanket recommendation of an interactionist position.

However, there are other more sophisticated studies to support interactionism. The studies cited in Bowers (1973) did not investigate the effects of specific personality dimensions, but not all interactionist studies have been of this type and there are many studies similar in design to the hypothetical example given earlier where the levels of the person factor are groups of subjects differing on a personality dimension. Three areas investigated in this way are reviewed by Endler and Edwards (1978): anxiety, locus of control and conformity.

Anxiety is generally thought of as primarily a function of the person, but the research shows that it does interact with situational variables (e.g. Endler, 1975). Anxiety is a multi-dimensional personality trait consisting of several components such as physical harm anxiety and ego-threat anxiety. High scorers on one of these components, say physical harm anxiety, will become anxious only in congruent situations, i.e. where there is a threat of physical harm, and will not be anxious in, say, an ego-threat situation. High scorers on ego-threat anxiety would show the reverse pattern.

Locus of control can be characteristic of the person or of the situation. Studies have generally found a congruence effect such as in the Karabenick and Srull (1978) study described in Chapter 2. They obtained a crossover interaction: internals cheated more than externals under skill conditions, whereas externals cheated more than internals under chance conditions (see Table 2.1).

Conformity is usually regarded as determined more by the situation (e.g. social influence) than the person, as the classic Asch studies demonstrated (Asch, 1956). However, more recent studies have produced person by situation interactions. For example, Mausner and Graham (1970) compared the conformity of either field dependent or independent subjects' judgments of the flicker rate of a flashing light in relation to a confederate's judgments. Prior to the experiment, the subjects had been led to believe that they were either more or less competent than the confederate. It was found that field independents' judgments were unaffected by this prior experience whereas field dependents conformed more with confederates whom they had been led to believe were more competent than themselves.

All these studies demonstrated person by situation interactions: in each case groups differentiated in terms of a personality dimension responded in different ways to the situational manipulation. When one variable acts on another in this manner it is sometimes called a 'moderator variable', and the results it produces 'moderator effects' (Bem, 1972; Kogan and Wallach, 1964). Thus, whenever an interaction is obtained each factor may be said to be having a moderating effect on the other, and either a person or a situation factor may be the moderator variable.

An Evaluation of Interactionism

When interactionism was advocated as an alternative to the pure trait or pure situationist position, it was heralded by some as a new paradigm for personality research (e.g. Alker, 1972). Has it proved the panacea it was claimed to be? Unfortunately, the answer is no. While it has cleared away some of the old problems, it has also brought along with it several new ones which leave us with a novel but similarly unsatisfactory picture.

Criticisms of interactionist research

The impact of person by situation research using analysis of variance designs has been reduced considerably by a pertinent statistical observation by Golding (1975). His criticism applies wherever the interaction obtained is *not* a crossover interaction, or where main effects only occur. It is easiest to illustrate in relation to studies of the type reviewed by Bowers (1973).

Golding pointed out that the computations involved in estimating the amount of variance accounted for by each factor ignores an important feature of the data. The personality theorist's perspective assumes type B consistency (same behaviour, different situations), and one of the ways it may be demonstrated is by showing that although individuals may not maintain the same level of trait expression across different situations, they will maintain the same rank order relative to others. Thus a very friendly person will behave in a more friendly way in both an encounter group and a job interview than a less friendly person, although the level of friendly behaviour will be higher for both people in the encounter group than in a job interview. This effect is shown graphically in Figure 4.4, where person F is the most friendly of a group of six people whose different levels of friendliness in the two situations are plotted. Although the total amount of friendly behaviour was greater in the encounter group the people maintained the same rank order in both situations which demonstrates they behaved consistently relative to one another. A statistical analysis of such a study should therefore be sensitive to rank order so that the significance of the person factor is located.

Golding demonstrated how percentage variance fails to pick up this important aspect of the data whereas another statistic, the coefficient of generalisability, is responsive to rank order effects. He presented some hypothetical data similar to those shown in Figure 4.4, in which the rank order of the group's scores remained identical although in absolute terms the scores varied from situation to situation. Using analysis of variance, he found that most of the variance was attributable to persons (62 per cent) although a substantial amount went to situations and none to the person by situation

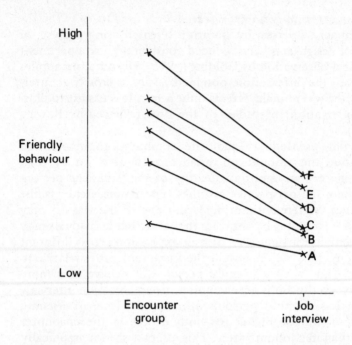

Figure 4.4 *Mean friendly behaviour for six people in two situations*

interaction. Thus the analysis suggested that situations had a considerable influence, a conclusion detracting from the importance of person variables despite the fact that rank order of persons remained identical across the situations. When the same data were analysed using coefficients of generalisability a perfect coefficient of 1.00 for persons was obtained, reflecting the fact that knowing the rank order for the group in one situation permits perfect prediction about the group's rank order in another situation. Information concerning rank order is lost in variance percentages but retained with coefficients of generalisability.

While Golding was correct to point out that when rank order is maintained across situations this constitutes evidence of consistency and hence should be captured statistically, he has failed to do justice to the importance of differences in levels of responding across different situations. Clearly the situation does have an effect in the above example: in the encounter group individual differences in friendliness gave rise to a wide variation in behaviour whereas in the job interview everyone behaved more similarly. It is possible to imagine contexts where this discrepancy in response range is of more interest than the fact that rank order was maintained. For example, in educational research it would be useful to know of a teaching method which had the effect of reducing the discrepancy between the most and the least able students even if the brightest still performed best and the dullest worst.

A second point of criticism of person by situation interaction studies using analysis of variance designs concerns the difficulty of independently specifying the person and the situation factors, which is a requirement for analysis of variance (Alker, 1977). In an analysis of variance design, different situations have to be selected to form the various levels of the situation factor, e.g. in Moos's (1969) study, patients were observed in the different situations that are found in a psychiatric hospital. The dimension of variation by which situations may be distinguished is often specified in terms of the type of behaviour the situation permits. Thus, in a psychiatric hospital, or any institution for that matter, the study room is characterised by the quiet, solitary pursuits typical of the introvert, whereas the games room is characterised by the noisy, social activity typical of the extravert.

Support for Alker's point that person and situation factors will tend to be confounded is to be found in the growing body of studies in which taxonomies of situations based on behaviour are being successfully developed. For example, Frederikson (1972) proposed a taxonomy of situations based on behavioural consistency. He argued that cross-situational consistency of behaviour should not be taken as a sign of an underlying personality dimension, but as evidence that the *situations* are similar. His view was supported in a factor analysis of responses to an anxiety inventory, in which subjects rated the intensity of fourteen possible responses to each of eleven anxiety-provoking situations. Three situation factors emerged from the pattern of these responses: interpersonality stress situations, dangerous/inanimate situations, and facing-the-unknown situations.

A similar line of research by Price (1974) and Price and Bouffard (1974) has demonstrated that there is a consensus as to which behaviours are regarded as appropriate and in-appropriate for particular situations. Some situations were found to contain relatively few constraints and hence many different behaviours were regarded as permissible, e.g. in your own room or in the park; other situations contained many constraints, e.g. in church, or at a job interview, and only a limited range of behaviour was considered appropriate.

Argyle has argued that situations are discontinuous (Argyle, 1976, 1977). Each situation has its own set of rules deter-mining the behaviour, social roles, specialist equipment, language and even the personality characteristics that are considered appropriate for the situation. For example, a seminar is a situation where there are rules about the topic of conversation which will be conducted in the specialised language of the subject. The member of staff will probably be expected to fulfil the role of seminar leader and, although there is little specialised equipment beyond books, papers and note-taking materials, if a member of the group brought out some knitting, this would immediately be recognised as inappropriate. The seminar also sets limits on the range of personality displayed by its members, e.g. there are few opportunities for people to give and receive love and affec-tion. Since some of the rules distinguishing between situations pertain to behaviour, Argyle's classification of situations also confounds person and situation variables.

Behaviour is regarded as characteristic of persons and, since behaviour emerges from these studies as an important characteristic of situations, it is interesting to consider to what extent taxonomies of persons and situations are similar, or even equivalent.

Some evidence for the correspondence between persons and situations is given in a recent paper by Bem and Funder (1978), who have demonstrated the value of describing persons and situations with comparable terminology. They argue that a situation can be described in terms of the charac-teristics of a person best suited for it. It is then possible to compare a particular person with the ideal for the situation and to determine from the degree of match or mismatch how that particular person would respond to that situation. Bem and Funder give a hypothetical example of a young man considering applying to Stanford University. He might be told that successful Stanford students are intelligent, single-minded and ambitious. He would then compare his own personality with this image and predict how he would react to the Stanford environment which fostered these qualities. Bem and Funder developed a technique for describing both persons and situations with the same items. It is a form of Q sort (Stephenson, 1953), a method for describing personality in which a set of items is sorted into categories ranging from highly characteristic of the person in question, through irrelevant, to highly uncharacteristic of the person in question. When a Q sort is applied to a *situation*, it results in a template characterising that situation, and a comparison between a particular person and the situation is easily made by assessing the similarity between the template and the person's Q sort on the same items. Bem and Funder describe a number of experiments using this technique. However, the critical test of the approach, namely, determining whether prior knowledge of an individual's similarity to the template for a particular situation can reliably predict their subsequent behaviour in that situation, has yet to be conducted.

The problem of deconfounding person and situation variables ends up as a mixed blessing. As the Bem and Funder study shows, using the same dimensions for classifying persons and situations can yield fruitful material; on the other hand, Alker's point still remains — analysis of variance requires that persons and situations be independently specified. While Alker is probably right that in real life person variables do often distinguish between situations (see also Bowers, 1973; Mischel, 1973), it is clearly feasible in laboratory research to allocate people at random to independently specifiable situations; and there are real-life contexts, such as the experience of different teaching methods at school and university, where it also occurs.

Both of the above criticisms apply to person by situation interaction research, where analysis of variance designs have been used. It is important to remember that such experiments are only one of several forms of interactionist research

(Pervin and Lewis, 1978). Analysis of variance designs have been accused of being mechanistic (Overton and Reese, 1973). They merely come up with the proportions of variance accounted for by different factors rather than exploring processes by which one variable affects another. In order to study how interaction effects actually *operate*, Overton and Rees recommend an organismic approach to these questions, in which all the variables involved are seen as being interdependent: any change in one will affect all the others in the system.

By far the most telling criticisms of interactional research have come from probably the most experienced workers in this field: Cronbach and Snow (Cronbach and Snow, 1977; Snow, 1977, 1978). Their work has mainly been confined to the study of aptitude (person) by treatment (situation) interactions in educational research; nevertheless their criticisms at a conceptual level are equally applicable to any field.

Cronbach started out with high hopes that aptitude by treatment interaction research would prove useful for psychology in general and for its application in such fields as education (Cronbach, 1957). However, over the years these hopes have receded (Cronbach, 1975). The main problem is that although it is possible to draw some, albeit rather tentative, generalisations about straight aptitude by treatment interactions (e.g. the effects of directed versus independent study on bright and dull students), such interactions are always open to modification by another variable, e.g. sex of subject, which yields an aptitude by treatment by sex of subject interaction. Then this interaction is open to moderation by yet another variable, say time of day, which yields an aptitude by treatment by sex of subject by time of day interaction. And so on, *ad infinitum*. As Cronbach expressed it 'you enter a hall of mirrors' (Cronbach, 1975, p. 119).

Interactions in many areas of research, including personality, are notoriously hard to replicate, and this becomes understandable in view of all the different higher-order interactions which could be going on unobserved in different experiments. Many of the variables that enter into these complex, higher-order interactions are of a transitory nature and specific to a particular location or stage in a culture's development. By the time their effects have been unravelled, they will have been replaced and become part of history (Gergen, 1973, makes a similar point about social psychology). Cronbach concludes that psychology cannot be regarded as a cumulative science awaiting the organisation of the amassed facts into a grand, unifying theory. Instead, Cronbach recommends that we study local events and be satisfied with only being able to achieve short-term control. Each new generation must solve the problems posed by a fresh set of circumstances.

In the face of such pessimism, interactionism can scarcely be held up as the new paradigm for personality research. Yet Cronbach argued that all areas in psychology are gradually discovering that interactions are of greater significance than main effects. For personality there is clearly no turning back to the simplistic notions of a pure trait position or pure situationism since both have been shown to be inadequate. Given that we must accept that we are in an interactionist era, are there any redeeming features to redress the balance, at least in part, in favour of interactionism?

Interactionism and consistency

To answer this question it is necessary to remember how this chapter began: with a discussion of the different types of consistency on which the personality theorist's perspective is based. While the demonstration of type A consistency is not in dispute, the other three types were challenged by Mischel. Although his attack was only partially successful, it was certainly damaging. One of the redeeming features of interactionism is that it has provided a solution to the consistency issue by showing that all types of consistency can be demonstrated, but only in certain people in certain situations: consistency is the product of interaction, not main effects.

The first study to make this point was that of Bem and Allen (1974). While Bem has never been an advocate of the strong trait position, he was interested in the conditions under which consistency may be found. Bem and Allen hypothesised that individuals who regard themselves as consistent will actually behave more consistently than those who regard themselves as inconsistent. The personality variables they studied were friendliness and conscientiousness. Ratings on these traits were obtained from the subjects themselves, their mother, their father and a peer. In addition, behavioural indices of these two traits were also obtained, e.g. for friendliness, subjects' behaviour in small group discussion was observed and for conscientiousness a neatness score based on the subjects' personal appearance and the state of their living quarters was estimated. The subjects were also asked to assess how friendly and conscientious they thought themselves to be.

For the analysis, the subjects were divided into two groups on the basis of their self-ratings for consistency: a high variability (inconsistent) and a low variability (consistent) group. The consistency for each subject across the ratings and the behavioural indices of each trait was then assessed. For friendliness the hypothesis was confirmed: the low variability group were more consistent across the measures than the high. For conscientiousness the results were less straightforward. It turned out that the experimenters' choice of neatness as a behavioural index of conscientiousness was inappropriate. In the low variability group the neatness measure and other behavioural index of conscientiousness, returning course readings at school, bore no relation to one another. This zero correlation for the low variability group affected their total consistency measure, giving the impression that low variability subjects were inconsistent. This finding demonstrates Bem and Allen's central point: the experimenter's definition of a trait may differ from the subject's (in their study, the subjects did not believe that neatness and returning course reading were both aspects of conscientiousness) and this may make the subjects appear inconsistent when in fact they are consistent across the situations they themselves consider relevant to the trait in question.

Bem and Allen's study investigated type D consistency and showed that one way to demonstrate it is to study subjects who regard themselves as consistent on the trait under investigation and to establish that the subjects and the experimenter agree on the behaviours that define the trait. Several more recent studies have adopted Bem and Allen's approach and, by taking the moderating role of self-perceived consistency into account, types B, C and D consistency have been found.

Vestewig (1978) used this approach in a study of risk taking. Generally, risk taking has been regarded as primarily determined by situational variables: a person will assess the degree of risk in a particular situation rather than be consistently daredevil or cautious regardless of the odds. However, Vestewig hypothesised that certain people would be consistently risky or cautious and that these could be located through their self-perceptions. In this experiment he first asked all subjects to complete a questionnaire which included an item requiring them to rate themselves on their consistency in gambling-type tasks or games of chance. Then the subjects performed two gambling tasks where each task involved making a series of choices between cautious or risky responses. When the whole sample was considered, it was found that while subjects were consistent in their responses within each task, there was little consistency across tasks. A different picture emerged when the sample was divided into high and low self-perceived consistency: subjects who perceived themselves as behaving consistently were more likely to have adopted similar strategies on both tasks resulting in greater consistency across tasks than subjects who did not regard themselves as consistent. This finding was more marked for male than female subjects – a result which Vestewig tentatively explained as due to the males' slightly greater previous gambling experience. Whatever the reason for the sex difference, Vestewig has demonstrated that for certain people risk taking is not task-specific, as was previously believed.

Vestewig's study confirmed Bem and Allen's finding that consistency is more likely to be found in subjects who regard themselves as consistent. These two studies show that consistency does occur in some people. Does this imply that some people and some behaviours are chronically inconsistent? An area where inconsistency is typically regarded as the norm is the relationship between a person's verbally reported attitudes and their actual attitude-related behaviour (type D consistency) – a source of much discomfort for social psychologists (Eiser, 1979). A study by Gibbons suggests a way of reducing this type of inconsistency.

Gibbons (1978) was interested in the consistency between attitudes about sexual standards and behavioural reactions to pornography. It is a common finding that attitude scores do not correlate with behaviour and Gibbons hypothesised that self-focused attention might act as a moderator variable to affect the relationship between self-report and behavioural measures of attitudes. He found that the consistency between a pre-test attitude measure and reactions to pornographic material (rated excitement) was enhanced when the subject's attention was self-focused simply by placing a mirror in the booth where the pornographic material was inspected and rated. The effect of the mirror was remarkably strong: for the self-focused group (mirror present), there was a significant positive correlation between the previous attitude measure and the excitement ratings ($r = 0.60$); for the non-self-focused group (mirror absent), the correlation was negative and nonsignificant ($r = -0.21$).

Gibbons has thus shown that consistency can be enhanced by making subjects more self-aware. The role of self-awareness was studied in more detail by Turner (1978). His measure of self-awareness was a self-report measure of private and public self-consciousness: the extent to which people reflect on their behaviour in relation to themselves as compared with thinking about the effects of their behaviour on others. Turner studied the consistency between self-reported dominance and dominant behaviour in small-group problem-solving. He obtained two self-reports of dominance: one which asked subjects to express their typical level of dominance and another in which the subjects expressed the maximum possible level of dominance of which they regarded themselves capable. In addition, private and public self-consciousness scores were obtained for each subject. The results showed that the maximal self-reports were more consistent with actual behaviour than the typical, indicating that subjects are more accurate about what they are capable of than what they think they typically do. It was also found that consistency between self-reported dominant behaviour and actual dominant behaviour was higher for subjects with high private self-consciousness and low public self-consciousness than for subjects with low private self-consciousness and high public self-consciousness. Turner concluded that people who reflect about their behaviour in relation to themselves rather than thinking about the effects they have on others are more likely to have accurate self-knowledge than those who are concerned with how they appear to others. Accurate self-knowledge will lead to consistency between self-reports and actual behaviour.

Conclusions

The personality theorist's perspective, whether it be represented by single- or multi-trait theories, is committed to the view that personality is a major determinant of behaviour. Traits are inferred from observations of behavioural consistency. The concept of consistency is therefore central to the personality theorist's perspective.

This chapter began by proposing a typology of the different forms of behavioural consistency and then assessed the evidence for each of the four types. The evidence suggests that while type A consistency is reasonably well-established, types B, C and D are more problematic and certainly not as reliable as personality theorists have tended to assume. We are neither automatons driven solely by an internal personality programme nor entirely slaves of circumstance. The opposite extreme to a pure trait position is situationism, and that too has proved inadequate. Common sense, backed up by psychological research, tells us that the way we behave is a function of both who we are and the situation we find ourselves in.

The interactionist model now predominates over either a pure trait or pure situationist position. However, the interactionist model does not invalidate the personality theorist's perspective; on the contrary, it has given it a whole new lease of life. The personality theorist's perspective has survived the cricitisms raised by the consistency issue thanks to interactionist research. The perspective has not gone unchanged: instead of being based on fanciful assumptions of absolute consistency, it has had to adapt to the reality of relative consistency. This will mean far more research along interactionist lines in the future to determine how both person and situation variables interact to determine behaviour. Cronbach's pessimistic outlook suggests that this research will not produce straightforward, generalisable findings, but there is no going back. The way forward must be taken, however uninviting it may appear.

5 The Lay Perspective

Some of the most intuitively appealing insights into personality are to be found outside the realm of academic or professional psychology. Novelists and playwrights have for centuries been astute observers of human nature, and we judge their work by their ability to portray convincing characters. Most creative writers appear to believe in the importance of the person rather than the situation in the determination of behaviour; it is through the characters' reactions to external events, and their choices of environments, that we discover more about their personalities. It is interesting to speculate on the type of novel or play a thorough-going behaviourist would write. Presumably, the characters would remain undeveloped and all the effort would go into devising situations for them to respond to.

Few of us are novelists or playwrights, but we are all amateur psychologists. We think we know a great deal about the workings of our own minds and the minds of others, and probably much of this knowledge is correct in so far as it serves us well in ensuring we function effectively in our everyday lives. Most people do not need to take a psychology course to know that if information is not rehearsed while in short-term memory it is liable to be lost, or so it would seem from the number of us who mutter telephone numbers to ourselves in the brief interval between finding the number in the book and dialling it. Nor is it necessary to have studied Eysenck or Cattell to know that someone who has been described to you as 'sociable' is probably a good person to attach yourself to at a party, because they are likely to be talkative and friendly as well.

It is one particular aspect of our amateur psychologising, namely, our ability to develop theories about our own personalities and other people's, that constitutes the subject-matter of this chapter, which concerns the lay perspective on personality. Psychologists are just as interested in studying what people think about themselves and others as they are in studying how people actually behave. Particularly in social psychology, understanding behaviour often requires the study of subjects' own theories about it. The study of naive psychology or people's causal explanations of their own and others' behaviours is known as attribution theory, and is a rapidly expanding area of social psychology (see Mower White in this series). The lay perspective may be seen as a part of attribution theory, since the latter is concerned with the personality characteristics we attribute to ourselves and others to explain behaviour.

The lay perspective may be distinguished from the personality theorist's perspective since the latter attempts to describe what personality actually is rather than people's beliefs about it. However, the personality theorist cannot avoid also being a naive psychologist. The descriptive and intuitive beliefs which form the lay perspective have also served to shape the sorts of scientific questions posed about personality, and hence have partially determined the answers which have been found. More important, since personality can never be observed directly but can only be inferred, the lay perspective will inevitably have influenced the form these inferences have taken, and thus helped in the construction of the personality theorists' representations of personality.

The lay perspective is similar to the personality theorist's perspective in that both perspectives give rise to personality theories. After all, both are looking at the same phenomenon and trying to make sense of it. The elements of lay theories are the words (traits) provided by the language for describing personality, and the theoretical propositions of lay theories refer to the relations believed to hold between traits.

The Generality of Implicit Personality Theory

The specialised trait language, and the beliefs we hold about which traits are likely to co-occur in the same individual and which are not, are collectively referred to as implicit personality theory (Bruner and Tagiuri, 1954; Schneider, 1973). The adjective 'implicit' is used to indicate that a lay person's understanding of personality is a partly unconscious process in the sense that the person is not necessarily capable of fully articulating it. Imagine how difficult it would be to answer a question such as 'What are your beliefs about which personality traits co-occur?' On the other hand, if you were confronted with a particular individual and asked to make a personality judgment such as whether the person is kind or cruel, on the basis of other information about the individual's personality, you may well be able to do so.

The most important question to be asked about implicit personality theory is to what extent everyone shares a *similar* set of beliefs about personality. If it turns out that we all operate with highly idiosyncratic theories, then the study of implicit personality theory will be of far less interest to psychologists than if it turns out that implicit personality theories are reasonably uniform from person to person. This is an empirical question which has been studied in a number of ways.

Methods of studying implicit personality theory
In everyday life we make use of implicit personality theory in two ways. When we compose a spoken or written description of ourselves or others, a part of that description will probably consist of personality traits: we are able to convert our direct experience of a person into a more abstract form expressed in a series of traits. These descriptions are usually meaningful to others, as is demonstrated by the second use of implicit personality theory: inferring the presence of additional traits on the basis of a brief trait description. For example, an employer might sum up his impression of an employee as 'conscientious' and write this in a character reference when the employee applied for a new job. The potential new employer, on reading the reference, would form an impression of the applicant on the basis of this limited description and might well infer that the candidate was also 'reliable', 'orderly' and 'hardworking' rather than 'careless', 'slapdash' or 'lazy'. These two

manifestations of implicit personality theory in everyday life have formed the basis of two techniques used in laboratory investigations: personality description and trait inference (Rosenberg and Sedlak, 1972a).

In studies of naturalistic personality descriptions, subjects are free to say or write anything they like about a person of their choice. The investigator is particularly interested in the use of trait words and in whether certain groups of traits repeatedly co-occur in different subjects' descriptions. For example, in Rosenberg and Sedlak's study of college students' personality descriptions, 'intelligent', 'friendly', 'self-centred', 'ambitious' and 'lazy' were frequently-used traits, but they were not all used to describe the same person. If a person had been described as 'intelligent', then 'friendly' would be likely to also occur in the description, whereas 'self-centred' would not (Rosenberg and Sedlak, 1972b). The advantage of naturalistic personality descriptions is that they provide a close approximation to real life and the experimenter's influence is minimal because the choice of traits is left to the subject. For these reasons, they are particularly popular in the study of children's implicit personality theories; here the experimenter is interested in the extent of the child's trait vocabulary as well as in the patterns of trait co-occurrences. The major disadvantage of naturalistic descriptions is the problem posed by the scoring of the protocols. Individual researchers have tended to develop their own scoring schemes, and this often makes it difficult to compare the results of different studies.

The way subjects describe other people's personalities can also be studied, rather more artificially, by the experimenter supplying a range of personality traits from which the subject selects those that best fit the person being described. This is known as the *trait sorting* method, and its main advantage is that it presents no scoring problems. On the other hand, the results are circumscribed by the experimenter's choice of traits. A trait sorting task was used by Rosenberg, Nelson and Vivekananthan (1968). They asked subjects to think of up to ten people they knew who were as different from each other as possible, and then to distribute sixty-four personality traits (supplied by the experimenter) amongst these ten people. An alternative to trait sorting is *trait rating*; here each trait in a list provided by the experimenter is rated in terms of how well it characterises the person in question.

Naturalistic descriptions, trait sortings and trait ratings all provide the experimenter with information about how subjects use traits to describe other people. The second aspect of implicit personality theory, its use in inferring the presence of additional traits on the basis of limited information, is studied under even more artificial conditions. Typically, subjects are presented with brief trait descriptions of hypothetical individuals (these are sometimes as brief as one word) and asked to decide whether or not such a person would possess a series of other traits listed by the experimenter. For example, the given description might be 'A polite person' and the subject might be asked to judge whether a polite person is likely to be 'thoughtful', 'impulsive' and 'friendly'. Judgments are usually obtained in the form of ratings on scales such as the following:

How likely is it that a polite person would also be:

	Very unlikely			Neutral		Very likely	
Thoughtful?	1	2	3	4	5	6	7
Impulsive?	1	2	3	4	5	6	7
Friendly?	1	2	3	4	5	6	7

An example of an early study which used the trait inference technique is Hays' (1958) investigation into the co-occurrence likelihoods of the following traits: 'warm', 'cold', 'dominant', 'submissive', 'intelligent', 'stupid', 'generous', 'stingy'. Subjects were asked to estimate the likelihood that a person described as 'warm' would also be 'cold' and so on for all the possible pairs of traits in both orders (i.e. warm and dominant, dominant and warm), amounting to 112 estimates in all.

Investigations into implicit personality theory, whatever method they use, are rather like shining a torch on a very dark night. With at least 4,500 commonly used trait words in our vocabulary (Allport and Odbert, 1936), the number of judgments we are theoretically capable of making about patterns of trait co-occurrence is enormous. No wonder the bulk of these judgments is never made explicit. The aim of research is to illuminate a carefully selected portion of these judgments with the hope of discovering the principles by which these beliefs are organised.

The structural representation of implicit personality theory
In the studies of implicit personality theory using the methods described above, enough similarity between subjects' judgments was found to justify ignoring individual differences, allowing one instead to concentrate on representing the organisation of beliefs about trait relations. This organisation can be safely assumed to be typical of most people. From all the methods it is possible to derive scores indicating the believed co-occurrence likelihood of trait pairs. In naturalistic personality descriptions, this measure is based on the frequency with which trait pairs are found to co-occur across the protocols. In trait sortings it is derived from the similarity between subjects' trait distributions, and in trait influence studies a quantified assessment of the relationship between traits is already available in the trait rating.

Having obtained estimates of the co-occurrence likelihoods of all the possible trait pairs studied in a particular investigation, the researcher is faced with a similar problem to that confronted by the multi-trait personality theorists described in Chapter 3: how to discover the organisational principles underlying this mass of data. The problem requires some form of multivariate analysis, and the popular techniques are factor analysis, cluster analysis and multidimensional scaling. All these techniques are designed to represent the interrelations within a set of items (in this case personality traits) in such a way as to reveal the highly interrelated subgroups, which are then regarded as manifestations of the same underlying dimensions.

If subjects show a general agreement in their beliefs about trait co-occurrences, then representations of these beliefs, whatever the technique used, should be similar across different studies. This view is supported by Rosenberg and Sedlak's review of the structural representations of implicit personality theory, where they find considerable agreement across studies (Rosenberg and Sedlak, 1972a). The general finding is

that beliefs about trait co-occurrences have a common underlying dimensional structure and, although the precise number
of dimensions varies from study to study, it is usually between
three and five. It is a well-replicated finding that three of
these dimensions correspond closely to the dimensions of
word meaning discovered by Osgood (1962): evaluation,
activity and potency. Thus traits such as 'popular' and
'sociable' are contrasted with 'unhappy' and 'vain' on the
evaluative dimension (good–bad); 'industrious' and 'determined' contrast with 'wavering' and 'insignificant' on an
activity dimension (active–passive), and 'stern' and 'critical'
contrast with 'sentimental' and 'naive' on the potency dimension (hard–soft). This organisation is shown in Figure
5.1. These studies usually explore the structure of between

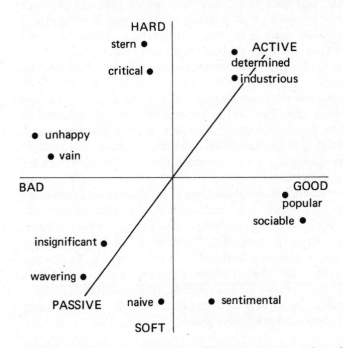

Figure 5.1 *The two-dimensional configuration of twelve traits
showing the position of the three axes good–bad, active–
passive and hard–soft (freely adapted from Rosenberg et al.,
1968)*

sixty and eighty traits, not merely twelve as shown in the figure for the sake of clarity.

Where more than three properties are found to underlie the data these additional factors may be variants on one of the Osgood factors, for example, the evaluative dimension often breaks down into separate dimensions for social good-bad and intellectual good-bad. Not surprisingly, there is least consensus among naturalistic personality description studies, where the unstructured nature of the task allows individual differences to be more prominent. Nevertheless, the Osgood factors do emerge (e.g. Rosenberg and Sedlak, 1972b), although the active-passive dimension tends to be relatively weak in these data (Rosenberg and Sedlak, 1972a). The three Osgood factors emerge most clearly in studies where the experimenter provides the traits and hence the task is more structured. In both trait sorting studies (e.g. Rosenberg *et al.*, 1968) and trait inference studies (e.g. Rosenberg and Olshan, 1970), all three factors have been reliably found.

The multidimensional representations of implicit personality theory provide us with a picture of how beliefs about trait co-occurrences are organised. The majority of the studies show that the words we use to describe personality may be grouped according to three to five dimensions. A person need not be described with traits drawn exclusively from one dimension but, however many dimensions are involved, it is extremely unlikely that traits from both ends of the same dimension would be used. A description containing a trait at the favourable end of the evaluative dimension, such as 'sociable', will probably also contain other favourable traits such as 'popular', 'humorous' and 'warm', but would not contain unfavourable traits such as 'rude' and 'cruel'. Although these representations have only been developed on samples of trait words, it is assumed that they have revealed the principles of organisation which run through the entire population of trait words.

Using Implicit Personality Theory to Form Impressions

In the previous section we have seen how everyone shares a

similar set of beliefs about personality, and how these beliefs are organised into an implicit personality theory. So far, the lay perspective has been presented only in its static form in that the structure of implicit personality theory has been described. We next consider the use people make of their implicit personality theories for forming impressions of other people.

Assessing impression formation from trait choices
The question that has puzzled psychologists, from Asch (1946) to the present day, is how we combine the pieces of information contained in a brief description of a person to produce an overall impression, and then use the resulting impression to make additional inferences about that person.

Consider the task Asch (1946) set his subjects. Two groups heard a brief description of an imaginary person who was either:

(A) intelligent, skilful, industrious, *warm*, determined, practical, cautious; or

(B) intelligent, skilful, industrious, *cold*, determined, practical, cautious.

The subjects were then required to write down their impressions, in the form of a short essay, of the person they had just heard described. In addition, they also completed a check-list task in which they had to select one trait from each of eighteen pairs of opposites (e.g. generous–ungenerous, strong–weak) which was the more compatible with the impression they had formed.

From their essays and their choices on the check-list, it was clear that groups A and B had formed strikingly different impressions even though there was only a difference of one word between the two descriptions. Group A, whose description contained 'warm', formed far more positive impressions than Group B whose description contained 'cold'. Asch (1946, p.263) gave examples of these contrasting pictures as revealed in the essays:

A (warm): A person who believes certain things to be right, wants others to see his point, would be sincere in an argument and would like to see his point won.

B (cold): A rather snobbish person who feels that his

success and intelligence set him apart from the run-of-the-mill individual. Calculating and unsympathetic.

The same picture emerged from the check-list choices. Group A selected the positive traits such as 'generous', 'good-natured' and 'strong' more frequently than did Group B.

Asch's task presented no difficulty for his subjects; but the problem for Asch, and subsequent psychologists, was to explain how they had arrived so easily at uniform impressions on the basis of discrete bits of information and why it was that a difference of just *one* of these bits of information had such an effect.

Asch proposed two contrasting models of impression formation: the 'elementaristic' model and a Gestalt view. In the elementaristic model, the uniform impression is seen as the result of the summation of all the separate bits of information. According to this model, impressions formed by groups A and B were the result of adding intelligent + skilful + industrious + warm or cold + determined + practical + cautious. Asch rejected the elementaristic model since it failed to explain the disproportionate effect of changing the single element 'warm' or 'cold'. The Gestalt model was more promising: the separate pieces of information were seen as being capable of influencing each other in an interactive way rather than an additive way. Thus the inclusion of 'warm' or 'cold' in the list influenced each of the other traits, which explains how they had a disproportionate effect. The interactive effects of one element upon another were seen as changing the nature of those elements, and hence resulting in an impression, or Gestalt, which was greater than the simple sum of the parts.

To test the Gestalt model, Asch (1946) carried out several experiments in which the content of the description was varied. He discovered that not all traits were capable of exerting as profound an influence on the final impression as 'warm' and 'cold' had done. For example, when identical descriptions to those in the 'warm' or 'cold' experiment were used with the replacement of 'warm' or 'cold' by 'polite' or 'blunt', there was no marked difference between the impressions formed by groups A and B. Asch concluded that some traits were more influential or 'central', while others were more 'peripheral'. Central traits changed the Gestalt more dramatically than peripheral ones by exerting a stronger influence on each of the other elements.

In a re-analysis of some of Asch's experiments, Wishner (1960) came up with a different explanation for the central versus peripheral trait effects. Wishner's first step was to discover people's beliefs about the co-occurrence likelihoods of the traits Asch used in his descriptions and in his check-lists. In effect, he charted the structure of the particular sub-section of implicit personality theory which Asch had studied. This was done by selecting fifty-three of Asch's traits and asking college students to rate their instructors on these traits. From these ratings, he was able to estimate the co-occurrence likelihood of each trait combination and express it in the form of a correlation. A high positive correlation indicates co-occurrence is likely; a high negative correlation indicates co-occurrence is very unlikely; correlations around zero indicate no consensus on co-occurrence likelihood was found. Some of these correlations between the traits in Asch's descriptions and those in the check-list are shown in Table 5.1.

Wishner argued that it should be possible to predict which traits would have a central effect in a description from prior knowledge of their correlations with the traits in the check-list. Where a check-list contains a large proportion of traits with strong correlations with only one of the traits in the description, then this trait will behave like a central trait. Take Asch's 'warm' or 'cold' experiment. The traits forming the rows of Table 5.1 are each one member of the pairs in Asch's check-list. They are shown in order of magnitude of their difference in choice by Asch's 'warm' and 'cold' groups, e.g. 'ungenerous' was chosen by 9 per cent of the 'warm' group and 92 per cent of the 'cold' group; 'sociable' was chosen by 91 per cent of the 'warm' group and 38 per cent of the 'cold' group. It will be seen that the correlations in the 'warm' column for the first nine traits include the largest in the whole table (algebraic sign does not affect the size of the correlation). In other words, 'warm' correlated more strongly with those traits in the check-list that showed the greatest difference between the 'warm' and 'cold' groups.

Since this was something of an *ad hoc* analysis, Wishner

Table 5.1 Estimates of the correlations among some of the traits used by Asch (1946) (from Wishner, 1960, p. 101)

Check-list traits	Warm	Unintelligent	Clumsy	Indus- trious	Determined	Practical	Cautious
				Description Traits			
Ungenerous	−33	04	−07	−12	−10	−09	−15
Irritable	−57	01	18	−18	−20	−24	07
Humorous	24	−16	−12	−04	38	01	−24
Sociable	70	00	−07	26	30	16	−11
Popular	50	−33	−26	24	35	35	01
Self-centred	−30	14	−03	−13	−01	−20	−08
Unhappy	−54	21	07	−36	−35	−22	08
Humane	34	−06	00	28	−12	27	29
Imaginative	48	−17	−17	24	43	18	−31
Restrained	−13	15	03	04	−14	08	35
Unattractive	−10	36	−04	−23	−08	−05	−15
Unreliable	−28	31	34	−41	−15	−44	−15
Strong	07	−28	−10	14	39	31	01
Dishonest	−43	28	06	−30	−14	−28	−08
Important	17	−50	−28	30	35	23	−18
Serious	02	−09	−34	27	18	25	24
Persistent	18	−30	−28	20	60	12	16

went on to test his hypothesis using a new list of traits in the description and a new check-list. The traits in the description, which were uncorrelated with one another, were: 'scrupulous', 'cautious', 'good-looking', *'humane'* or *'ruthless'*, 'flexible', 'serious' and 'fearless', with one group hearing 'humane' and the other hearing 'ruthless'. The check-list contained six traits highly correlated with 'humane' and 'ruthless' and six with low correlations with these traits. The check-list traits were uncorrelated with the other traits in the description. The correlations had been estimated from an earlier rating study. Wishner repeated the Asch experiment using these traits. He predicted, and found, that the difference between the 'humane' and 'ruthless' groups in their check-list choices was largest on those check-list traits with high correlations with 'humane' and 'ruthless'.

Wishner's experiments demonstrated that so-called central

effects depend on the relations between the traits in the description and the traits in the check-list. Where a large proportion of the check-list consists of traits with high correlations with one of the traits in the description, this trait will operate as a central trait. The more recent work on the structural representation of implicit personality theory reviewed in the previous section allows us to follow Wishner's line of reasoning a little further. We have seen how the beliefs about trait co-occurrence (expressed as correlations in Wishner's study) may be represented in terms of three to five dimensions including good–bad, hard–soft and active–passive. This means that traits, along with most other words, are characterised by these three properties to a greater or lesser extent, e.g. 'sociable' is primarily good and 'sentimental' is primarily soft. The multivariate studies of implicit personality theory indicate that the most likely candidates for central traits will be those most directly measuring one of the underlying dimensions, since it is these traits which will have strong correlations with a large number of other traits associated with the same dimension and weak correlations with traits associated with the other dimensions. Thus, by setting a trait representing one dimension in a context of traits representing other dimensions in the description, and by having a substantial number of check-list traits representing the central trait's dimension, central trait effects will be found. 'Warm' and 'cold' emerged as central traits in Asch's study since they are excellent examples of the good–bad dimension, and the words in the check-list with a large evaluative component were bound to correlate with it. Wishner's choice of 'humane' and 'ruthless' was apposite since they are excellent examples of the hard–soft dimension, and so it was easy to find traits for the check-list that were either strongly correlated or uncorrelated with the potency (hard–soft) dimension. Only the activity dimension remains to be explored and, using Wishner's methodology, it should be relatively straightforward to demonstrate that, say, 'active' and 'passive' have central effects.

While Wishner advanced our understanding of what is meant by a central trait, he did not attempt to develop Asch's Gestalt model of trait combination. His continued support for Asch's view that people form unified impressions out of a series of elements is rather surprising given that his experiments had shown how the effects of different descriptions were due to the relations between only one of the elements in the description and the check-list traits. Since in Wishner's experiments central effects were explained without proposing any form of combination between the elements in the description, a more parsimonious conclusion is that subjects were not attempting to combine the elements in the description at all but made their check-list choices on the basis of the trait in the description which was most relevant (correlated).

Quantitative models of trait integration

People's beliefs about trait co-occurrences are studied by providing them with a description of an imaginary person in terms of a set of traits (which we will refer to as *given* traits) and asking for judgments about the likelihood that other traits (which we will refer to as *probe* traits) would also characterise that imaginary person. For example, the imaginary person might be described by the given trait 'bold' and subjects might be asked to judge whether such a person would be likely to possess a series of probe traits such as 'fearless', 'timid', etc.

The first study to investigate quantitatively how traits in a given description are combined to produce a unified impression which is then used as the basis for subsequent inferences about probe traits was done by Bruner, Shapiro and Tagiuri (1958). They developed a technique which has been adopted in most subsequent studies in this area. It involved obtaining ratings on the probe traits in relation to the givens presented singly as well as in combination. It was then possible to see how responses on the same probe trait differed depending on the number and the nature of the given traits. Bruner *et al.* used four given traits in all: 'considerate', 'independent', 'intelligent' and 'inconsiderate'. These were presented singly, in twos and in threes (all four were not presented in combination because of the incompatibility of 'considerate' and 'inconsiderate').

There were fifty-nine probe traits. Each of the eleven

possible combinations of given traits was used; each combination was seen by a separate group of subjects. The subjects rated all fifty-nine probe traits for their co-occurrence likelihood with the given trait or traits. Thus, in a single-trait group, the subject might be asked, for example, to rate the likelihood that an 'intelligent person' (given trait) would also be 'aggressive' (probe trait). A subject in a three-trait group might be asked to rate the likelihood that a person who is 'considerate', 'independent' *and* 'intelligent' would also be 'aggressive'.

For the purpose of analysis, the ratings were simplified to a yes or no (+ or −) decision. The single given trait decisions were then compared with the multi-trait decisions on the same probes. For example, the single given trait 'intelligent' was regarded by most subjects as co-occurring positively with 'aggressive':

intelligent   ⟶   aggressive? = +

and the single given trait 'inconsiderate' was also regarded as co-occurring with 'aggressive':

inconsiderate   ⟶   aggressive? = +

When 'intelligent' and 'inconsiderate' were presented together as two given traits then an 'intelligent and inconsiderate' person was also seen as being 'aggressive':

intelligent + inconsiderate   ⟶   aggressive? = +

The addition of another given trait with the same relation to 'aggressive', e.g. 'independent', in the three given traits condition resulted in a positive decision.

Where the single inferences led to different decisions, then decisions in the two givens condition were roughly half positive and half negative. Where there were three given traits with two having single inferences to the probe of the same sign and one different, the combined judgments tended to be the same as the two decisions of like sign. These findings were all based on the inspections of proportions of subjects who responded in a particular way; no statistical checks were made.

More recent quantitative studies of impression formation have involved a higher level of mathematical sophistication. The most notable figures in this field are Anderson (1974, 1978) and Warr (1974). Their investigations are designed along the same lines as the Bruner *et al*. study; they compare ratings from single given traits to the probes with ratings from combinations of these given traits to the same probes.

Although both Asch and Wishner favoured a Gestalt model of trait combination, Anderson has followed the lead set by Bruner *et al*., and worked on elementaristic models. Anderson's models have been developed to account for how information is combined (integrated) in a variety of social decisions, including trait inferences. For example, in the attribution of blame, the amount of blame attributed to a person involved in an unpleasant event is given by the following equation (Anderson, 1976):

Blame = Intent + Consequence − Extenuation − Personal Goodness.

While in the above equation the model is an *additive* one, much of Anderson's work has been concerned with demonstrating where an *averaging* rather than an additive model provides a better account of how information is integrated (e.g., Anderson, 1962, 1965, 1974, 1978). The critical experiment devised by Anderson to distinguish between the averaging and additive models of impression formation involves four given traits, two of which produce extreme ratings on the probe trait when presented as a pair, and two which produce less extreme ratings on the same probe when presented as a pair. For example, the given traits 'sneaky and deceptive' might produce a more extreme rating on the probe 'dishonest' than the given traits 'cowardly and boastful'.

When all four traits are presented in combination, an additive model predicts a more extreme rating on the probe trait than the more extreme of the two paired conditions. Thus a 'sneaky, deceptive, cowardly and boastful' person would be rated as more dishonest than a 'sneaky and deceptive' person. An averaging model predicts that the four given traits condition will result in a less extreme rating than the more extreme of the two paired conditions. Thus a 'sneaky, deceptive, cowardly and boastful' person would not be rated as extremely on the probe 'dishonest' as a 'sneaky and deceptive' person would be, but would be rated as being more dishonest than a 'cowardly and boastful' person. This example is summarised in Table 5.2 with imaginary ratings to illustrate how the effects of the averaging model are quantifiable. Generally, Anderson has found support for an averaging model rather than an additive model in studies of impression formation.

Table 5.2 An illustration of averaging effects in trait combination

Given traits	Ratings on the probe trait 'dishonest' ranging from −5 (definitely not) to +5 (definitely)
Sneaky and deceptive	+4
Cowardly and boastful	+2
Sneaky, deceptive, cowardly and boastful	+3

Warr and his colleagues have also studied trait combination in impression formation. In particular, they have been concerned with the effect on the probe trait ratings of varying the relation between the givens and the probes, and they have found certain conditions in which the averaging model does not apply. Warr (1974) used a Bruner *et al.* design in which the given traits were presented either singly or in pairs, in relation to the same probes. He found that the effect of increasing the given information from one to two traits sometimes led subjects to make more extreme ratings on the probe traits than they had to either of the two givens presented singly, and sometimes resulted in less extreme ratings than the more extreme of the two givens presented singly. He called these, respectively, push-over and pull-back effects.

Push-overs and pull-backs were found to occur according to the magnitude of the discrepancy between the probe trait ratings for the givens presented singly. Where the discrepancy was large, i.e. one of the givens produced a very extreme rating on the probe trait and the other given produced a more neutral rating, then pull-backs would occur. For example, the given traits 'attractive' and 'orderly' might result in a pull-back when presented together in relation to the probe 'likeable': while 'attractive' would be rated as extremely likely to co-occur with 'likeable', 'orderly' would be much less likely to do so. Pull-backs support Anderson's averaging model: the addition of the second, less strongly related element results in a less extreme combined inference.

Push-overs occurred where there was only a small discrepancy between the probe trait ratings when the givens were presented singly. For example, the givens 'attractive' and 'humorous' would probably result in similar extreme ratings on the probe 'likeable' and, when presented together, the combined inference would be even more extreme. Push-over effects are not predicted by Anderson's averaging model.

Push-over and pull-back effects were found to occur both when the two givens were evaluatively similar (e.g. 'attractive and orderly', 'cruel and mean') and dissimilar (e.g. 'attractive and cruel', 'mean and orderly'). However, when the discrepancy between the two givens was large and they were evaluatively dissimilar, then a phenomenon called *discounting* occurred. Consider the given trait combination 'hostile and sociable' in relation to the probe trait 'rude'. When presented singly, the given trait 'hostile' would probably yield a far more extreme rating in relation to 'rude' than the given trait 'sociable'. Subjects would be more confident to say that 'hostile' and 'rude' co-occur than to say that 'sociable' and 'rude' do not co-occur. Given such a large discrepancy between the two single given inferences, instead of 'sociable' producing pull-back effects in the combined condition, it may actually be ignored. If this occurs, the rating for the probe trait 'rude' will be the same in the combined condition as it is when 'hostile' is presented as a single given. This example is summarised in quantitative terms in Table 5.3.

It seems that when trait combinations involve a large discrepancy, credulity is stretched to breaking point and the less likely trait is discounted. Discounting represents a second instance where the averaging model does not apply and it has been observed not only by Warr (1974) but also in other studies (e.g. Wyer, 1970).

The quantitative studies of impression formation, illustrated here by the work of Bruner *et al.*, Anderson and Warr, have all inferred how the elements of given information are combined by looking at the output derived from the combined versus single given information. The effects of varying the input (given traits) are observed on the output (probe trait ratings) and from the magnitude of the output, intervening combinatorial principles are inferred.

Table. 5.3 An illustration of discounting effects
in trait combination

Given trait or traits	Ratings on the probe trait 'rude' ranging from −5 (definitely not) to +5 (definitely)
Hostile	+5
Sociable	−2
Hostile and sociable	+5

Anderson describes his averaging and additive models of trait combination as 'cognitive algebra' (Anderson, 1974) but this is something of a misnomer since he is not in fact attempting to describe the cognitions involved in trait integration. He has developed mathematical models capable of predicting the size of probe trait ratings in relation to particular givens, but these models do not refer to the mental operations required to achieve the observed behaviours. While there is nothing wrong in principle in attempting to explain trait integration and inference by mathematical models alone, it is also interesting to investigate the requisite cognitive processes since there remains the possibility that these processes may deviate markedly from those implied by the idealised mathematical models.

Cognitive models of trait integration and inference
Implicit personality theory forms a part of our general knowledge, and is therefore comparable to our knowledge about other aspects of the world we live in. Most of this knowledge consists of useful ways of categorising objects. Knowledge about ways of distinguishing between, say, edible and inedible objects in the external world is essential for survival. Similarly, knowledge about traits and trait relations provides ways of distinguishing between different people and predicting how they will behave.

Language may be seen as providing a commonly-shared set

of useful categories for dividing up the world from a particular culture's viewpoint. Language reflects our general knowledge; e.g. we have categories such as 'fruit' and 'toy' to distinguish between these two broad classes of objects, and words such as 'apple' and 'ball' to refer to particular members of the broad categories. Knowing that an object is an 'apple' results in one set of behaviours whereas knowing that an object is a 'ball' results in another. The meaning of words represents our general knowledge of the objects to which the words refer: an apple is a fruit and is hard, so is good to eat but is not for bouncing; a ball is a toy (albeit of similar shape to an apple) and is made of plastic or rubber and hence bad to eat but good for bouncing.

Cognitive psychologists have studied the way words and meanings are represented and processed in semantic memory and several theories have been developed (see Greg, this series for a full discussion). Theories differ with respect to the way meaning is represented; for example is the meaning of 'apple' represented by the memories of all the apples we have previously encountered, or is it best represented in terms of a list of the characteristics we have found generally true of apples?

There are also different ways of conceptualising how we use the knowledge encoded in words and their meanings. When a person is asked to verify whether a particular instance belongs to a particular category, e.g. 'Is an apple a fruit?', there are two major classes of theory which have been developed to account for how we answer such questions: set-theoretic and network accounts. Set-theoretic accounts (e.g. Smith, Shoben and Rips, 1974) propose that we retrieve all the characteristics of fruit and apple and compare them. If a sufficient number are mutual, then we affirm that an apple is a fruit. Network accounts (e.g. Collins and Loftus, 1975) propose that words are stored as nodes connected by a network of paths which represent the relations between the words. Thus, if there is a path directly connecting fruit and apple, then we will confidently affirm that an apple is a fruit.

Cognitive models of the representation and processing of the categorising concepts embodied in language have traditionally been limited to words referring to concrete objects such as animals, fruit, vegetables, furniture, etc. and it is only recently that they have begun to be applied to the language of personality description (Cantor and Mischel, 1979a; Ebbesen and Allen, 1979; Harris and Hampson, 1980). In the extension of the models, the principles and issues are similar: an account of the representation of the meaning of trait words, and of the processing of the believed relations between traits is needed. First is the question of representation: is the meaning of a trait word represented by a collection of people we know who possess that trait, or is it represented in terms of the characteristics we associate with the trait? For example, the meaning of 'argumentative' might be represented by the memories of all the argumentative people we have encountered, or it might be represented by the characteristics of argumentative people, such as talkativeness, insensitivity and aggression. Second is the question of how this knowledge is processed: what happens if we are asked, instead of 'Is an apple a fruit', a question like 'Is an extraverted person argumentative?' Is the way people answer such a question best explained by set-theoretic or network accounts?

In the investigation of the semantic representation of concrete object categories, both set-theoretic and network accounts have proved useful and it has been demonstrated that the two approaches are fundamentally similar (Hollan, 1975). Both accounts have also been applied successfully to the language of personality description: Ebbesen and Allen (1979) found support for a set-theoretic account of the representation of trait meanings, whereas Harris and Hampson (1980) were able to give an account of trait integration using a network model. The studies of the cognitive processes involved in trait integration are of particular interest here because they illustrate how failing to take these processes into account can lead to false assumptions being made. Not surprisingly, the models of trait integration proposed by Anderson and by Warr have made the assumption that all the elements in a given trait description are taken into account before a judgment concerning the probe trait is made. However, it is precisely this assumption which has been challenged by Harris and Hampson (1980).

The first of their studies tested various models of the

cognitive processes involved in trait integration. The basic model was derived from the network account of semantic memory (Collins and Loftus, 1975). It was proposed that traits form nodes in a mental network connected by paths whose length is an inverse function of the correlation (positive or negative) between the traits: correlations near zero correspond to long paths, whilst large (positive or negative) correlations correspond to short paths. The sign of the correlation between two traits is assumed to be an inherent property of the path connecting them. For example, 'warm' and 'sociable', which are highly positively correlated, would be connected by a shorter path than 'warm' and 'tidy' which are less strongly correlated. 'Warm' and 'rude' would also be connected by a short path since they are highly negatively correlated.

This model differs from the network model of Collins and Loftus in that it proposes that all negative relations are directly stored. While models of semantic memory generally allow for the direct storage of some negative relations (Anderson and Reder, 1974), for reasons of cognitive economy not all possible negative relations are assumed to be represented. Given that implicit personality theory represents a fairly discrete area of knowledge, it does not seem unreasonable to assume an exhaustive representation of the negative as well as the positive correlations between traits.

When a person is asked to decide whether someone of a given trait description would be likely to also possess the probe trait, activation spreads out in every direction from the given trait node until the probe trait node is reached. The subject's decision is based on the speed with which the path is completed and the sign of the path. It is postulated that the longer the path (i.e. the weaker the correlation between the traits) the less confident the decision.

Such a model of the cognitive processes involved in making a trait inference readily lends itself to investigation using either a rating or a reaction time measure. In the rating task, subjects' confidence that a person of the given trait description would also possess the probe trait can be indicated on a scale running from definitely does not possess the probe (no), through don't know, to definitely does possess the probe (yes). In the reaction time task, subjects can be asked to respond 'yes' or 'no' and the interval between the presentation of the probe trait and their response can be timed in milliseconds. The model makes two predictions about reaction times: first, that decision times will follow the same pattern as probe trait ratings, the more confident the rating the faster the reaction; and second, the direction of the response (yes or no) will make no difference to its speed.

Both these predictions were supported in an experiment in which only single givens were used. Probe traits rated with high confidence as co-occurring with the given traits yielded faster reaction times than probe traits with less strong relations with the givens. Whether the probes were rated positively or negatively had no effect on either confidence ratings or reaction times. The first experiment therefore supported the basic model of the cognitive processes involved in making an inference from a single given trait to different probe traits.

The next question to be asked was how the model should be extended to explain inferences made from *two* given traits. The basic model suggests that when a subject is presented with two given traits and asked to make a decision about a probe trait, the two paths connecting each of the givens to the probe will be activated. At this point it is possible to construct a number of alternative models to describe the inference process. We tested three such models. The first is based on the seemingly unlikely view that the two given traits are not integrated. It assumes that the two paths are activated simultaneously and the subject makes an inference on the basis of the first path completed between the two givens and the probe; the second path to be completed is ignored because the inference has already been made before this path is completed. The other two models are alternative ways of representing the integrative processes assumed by Anderson and by Warr. In the second, simultaneous activation is again assumed but the decision about the probe is assumed to be held back until both paths have been completed and thus the final decision utilises both pieces of given information. In the third model, instead of assuming simultaneous activation, serial processing is assumed: the path between one of the givens and the probe is activated, and then the path between the other given and the probe is activated. The final decision is held up until first one and then the other path is completed.

Using the Bruner *et al.* design, comparing responses to single versus combined given traits on the same probes, the three models lead to different predictions about subjects' reaction times. The first (non-integrative) model predicts that subjects will be as fast in the combined condition as the faster of their two single given condition responses. In the combined condition, the shorter path will be completed first and form the basis of the response while the longer path will be ignored. The second (integrative) model predicts that subjects will be as slow in the combined condition as they were in the slower of the two single given conditions because they will not respond until both paths, activated simultaneously, have been completed. The third model (also integrative) predicts the longest reaction time of the three in the combined condition, since each path between given and probe is activated sequentially and the subject decides after both have been completed in turn. The third model predicts that reaction times in the combined condition will be at least as slow as the sum of the two single conditions.

The experiment to test between these three models involved two groups of subjects, one who performed the rating task and one who performed the reaction time task. The procedure for both groups was virtually identical. The given traits were 'warm', 'practical' and 'warm and practical'. Half the twelve probe traits were strongly related to 'warm' and half were strongly related to 'practical'. The task was to judge whether a person of the given trait description would possess the probe traits. Each subject repeated the task three times, making judgments with respect to each of the three given trait descriptions. It was therefore possible to compare each subject's judgments on the same probes across the two single and the combined given conditions. The results of the rating and reaction time tasks were strikingly similar and are shown graphically in Figure 5.2a and b.

Figure 5.2a shows the rating data. The mean rating for the six probes related to 'warm' and the six probes related to 'prac-

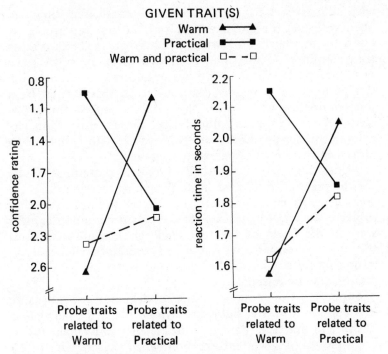

Figure 5.2a *Mean confidence ratings for probe traits related to 'warm' and probe traits related to 'practical' in each of the given trait conditions (adapted from Harris and Hampson, 1980)*

Figure 5.2b *Mean reaction times for probe traits related to 'warm' and probe traits related to 'practical' in each of the given trait conditions (adapted from Harris and Hampson, 1980)*

tical' are shown for each of the three given trait conditions. In the 'warm' condition, probes related to 'warm' were rated with more confidence than probes related to 'practical'. In the 'practical' condition, the reverse pattern emerged: probes related to 'practical' were rated with confidence whereas probes related to 'warm' were not. In the combined condition, where subjects had to judge about a 'warm and practical' person, their ratings indicate that they were basing their judgments on the more strongly related of the two given traits. For the probes related to 'warm' they were as confident when the given traits were 'warm and practical' as they had been with just the given trait 'warm'; and for the probes related to 'practical' they were as confident in the two given trait condition as they had been with only the single given trait 'practical'. Thus, in the 'warm and practical' condition the presence of 'practical' did not detract significantly from the confidence with which the subjects judged the probe traits related to 'warm', nor did the presence of 'warm' detract significantly from the confidence with which they judged the probe traits related to 'practical'.

Figure 5.2b shows a virtually identical pattern of results for the reaction time data (note that short reaction times are equivalent to confident ratings). These findings show that subjects were just as fast in the combined condition as they were in the faster of the two single given conditions. Thus the first, non-integrative model of trait inference receives strong support whereas the two models assuming trait integration may be rejected.

Support for the non-integrative model is surprising because it is counter-intuitive. Subjects have been asked to imagine a 'warm and practical' person so surely they must make use of both pieces of given information when making the probe trait decision? However, the reaction time data clearly show that the probe trait decisions were based on one given trait only. It could be argued that the two given traits used in this experiment were not typical because they themselves were unrelated. 'Warm' people are not regarded with confidence as also being 'practical'. Perhaps the non-integrative model only holds where the correlation between the givens is close to zero or negative and one of the given traits is discounted, as has been observed in previous studies. While it is possible that 'warm' and 'practical' are unrepresentative of more usual trait combinations, it is difficult to see how invoking the concept of discounting helps to explain the results obtained in the above experiment. If a given trait is to be discounted, it must, presumably, be inspected first in order that a decision can be made to discount it. According to the reaction time data, no such inspection of the less strongly related trait could have taken place.

To check the generality of the findings with other kinds

of given trait combinations, we have carried out similar experiments using the *related* given traits 'clever and successful' and 'humorous and likeable'. In both cases it was observed that subjects were basing their probe trait decisions in the combined given condition on the more strongly related of the two givens, as indicated by their single given decisions on the same probes. From these findings it looks as though the non-integrative model holds generally in trait inference. So far only the two given trait condition has been investigated but the model is easily extended to three or more given traits: it always predicts that the most confident single given decision will determine the multiple given response. Some indirect evidence in support of the model is to be found in Wishner (1960). In his re-analysis of Asch's experiments he was able to show that differences in check-list choices were obtained by changing only one of the traits in a seven given trait description. The so-called central trait in the given trait description was the one which, unlike the others, correlated strongly with a substantial number of the check-list traits.

In conclusion, this section has demonstrated how it is possible to apply the theory and methods of cognitive psychology to investigate the processes underlying impression formation. Such studies are a welcome addition to the studies of impression formation made by Wishner (1960), Warr (1974) or Anderson (1965) which rely on the numerical output of the impression formation process alone. Quantitative models of trait integration are forced to make assumptions about the underlying cognitive processes, such as 'every item of given information is inspected', which the direct investigation of cognitive processes may show to be invalid.

A limitation of much of the work described so far in this chapter has been the artificiality of the stimulus materials used. Typically the given information with which the subject is expected to form an impression consists of one or more trait words presented in the absence of any of the other information that is normally present in everyday life (such as physical appearance, social roles, knowledge of typical behaviours, and so on). The failure of research to study how such forms of non-linguistic information are integrated in impression formation leaves the generality of the findings using traits alone in question. Investigations to test both output and processing models would benefit by broadening the range of stimulus materials and one convenient way of providing non-linguistic information would be to use videotapes of the targets in which the combination of given information could be varied. The next section discusses investigations of how children acquire implicit personality theories. Here there has been more of an effort to use realistic forms of given information since the subjects have frequently been too young to be presented with linguistic materials.

The Acquisition of Implicit Personality Theory

The existence in adults of a widely shared set of beliefs about trait co-occurrences which is used to describe others and to make trait inferences begs the question of how this knowledge is acquired in the first place. Presumably children have to acquire the language of personality description and knowledge about trait relations just as they have to acquire language and knowledge in other domains.

We have seen that implicit personality theories are used by adults for the purposes of personality description and inference and it will be assumed that they serve the same functions for children. In order both to describe personality and to make personality inferences, the child must have some understanding of the concept of personality. In particular, before either personality description or inference can take place, it is necessary for the child to have the ability to infer underlying personality characteristics on the basis of observations of overt behaviours. Only then is it possible to accumulate a set of beliefs about the co-occurrence of personality traits, and hence to be able to infer the presence of additional traits on the basis of limited information. The ability to infer a trait from behaviour is essential for the construction of an implicit personality theory. The first question is, therefore, when does this ability first appear?

Once the basic ability has been established it is then possible for the child to acquire a more and more extensive implicit personality theory. The content and organisation of the child's implicit personality theory is the second area for investigation. Here research has focused on the child's trait vocabulary and beliefs about relations between traits.

Studies of the acquisition of implicit personality theory may be divided into two groups according to the age of the subjects: children under 7 years of age and children of 7 years and older. The studies of children under 7 are mainly concerned with whether or not young children have the ability to make personality inferences. In older children, in addition to studying any changes in this ability, the emphasis is also on the content and organisation of implicit personality theories. Having considered this research, it will then be appropriate to discuss the theories which have been proposed to explain the findings on the acquisition of implicit personality theories and to consider to what extent the acquisition of this form of social cognition should be regarded as distinct from general intellectual development.

Implicit personality theories in children under seven years
Although children under 7 years are not in possession of a wide trait vocabulary, they are nevertheless fairly sophisticated social perceivers. They can distinguish between people according to their race from 3 years onwards (Brand, Ruiz and Padilla, 1974); they are aware of sex roles from as early as 4 years and are able to describe their mother and father in different terms (Dubin and Dubin, 1965). In the main, the under 7s describe people by referring to external, physical attributes using only a few, global trait terms such as 'good' and 'nasty'.

The young child's ability to distinguish between people according to race, sex role and on broad terms such as the 'good' versus 'bad' dichotomy appears to support the view that young children are only capable of using broad, and hence uninformative, concepts. However, it is possible that this view of the young child embodies an underestimate of the abilities involved.

Snodgrass (1976) observed that some kindergarten children were able to make spontaneous trait inferences about characters described in brief vignettes. The descriptions were composed of several concrete examples of behaviour that could be described by a single trait term; e.g., 'aggressiveness' would have been presented by several instances of the character getting involved in fights. The children were then asked to tell 'what else' they could about the character. Although the incidence of spontaneous trait inference was found to increase with age, such inferences did occur even at the kindergarten level. It is unfortunate that Snodgrass did not report the trait terms used by the young children, since it would have been interesting to compare their choice of words with the older children's trait language. The ability demonstrated in Snodgrass's study, and indeed whenever a young child uses a concept to distinguish between people, is that of being able to perceive the co-occurrence of a variety of surface characteristics and to attribute their presence to an underlying cause. In the case of the vignettes, the child had to appreciate that the several instances of behaviour all had essential features in common that could be attributed to a single, internal characteristic. When a child distinguishes a 'good' person from a 'nasty' one, this requires moving from observable behaviour to an abstract concept. Although the variety and subtlety of the young child's concepts are limited, the essential processing ability of inferring an abstract concept from co-occurring surface attributes would appear to be present from this early age.

A study supporting this view has recently been carried out by Craig and Boyle (1979). They showed 5-, 6- and 7-year-olds videotapes of pairs of people interacting. The two people on a tape each behaved in distinctively different ways; for example, one would be friendly while the other was shy, or one would be polite while the other was aggressive. After watching the tape the child was asked what each of the actors was like. After the child had given a spontaneous description, he or she was then asked specifically about the actors' personalities (for example, 'Is he shy? Is he polite?'). One of these traits would be compatible with the actor's behaviour and the other not. The spontaneous descriptions were broken down into units and coded, one of the categories being for trait terms.

It was found that the older children used more trait terms and fewer references to physical appearance in their spontaneous descriptions than the younger ones. The older children were also more accurate in their answering of the specific questions. However, the most interesting feature of the results was the ability shown by the 5-year-olds. In their responses to the specific questions, twelve out of the sixteen children scored significantly better than chance level. This indicates that even children of this young age are able to recognise when the correct trait is being used to describe behaviour. Craig and Boyle suggest that young children may have difficulty retrieving trait terms from memory, and hence use them less readily in spontaneous descriptions. Nevertheless, their ability to recognise the correct application of traits shows that the capacity to think in trait terms is present.

Contrary to this view of the young child's precociousness, investigators have stressed the importance of external, physical characteristics in young children's descriptions of other people (e.g., Livesley and Bromley, 1973; Watts, 1944). They interpret this as indicating that the child is unable to go beyond physical appearance to the underlying psychological characteristics. However, is this a misinterpretation? When a child says 'I don't like John, he's fat', could this not be the child's way of expressing the negative aspects of John's personality? Lacking the verbal sophistication to say 'I don't like John because he is greedy, unself-disciplined and spoilt' the child simply describes him as fat.

Implicit personality theories in children over seven years
Most of the research on the acquisition of implicit personality theories has been conducted on children of 7 years and older. These studies have investigated age changes in both the ability to make personality inferences, and the content and organisation of implicit personality theories.

Studies of the ability to make personality inferences indicate that as the child gets older he or she is likely to make more personality inferences and to acquire the ability to integrate conflicting information to form a unified impression. For example, Gollin (1958) presented children with conflicting information about a target in the form of a film showing a little boy in a number of situations behaving socially desirably in some and undesirably in others. The child's task was to write a free description of the boy. Gollin scored the response both for trait inferences and for attempts at integrating the conflicting information. The number of inferences and attempts at integration showed a marked increase with age. Livesley and Bromley (1973) also observed that the ability to integrate conflicting information develops with age. Conflicting statements are modified with qualifying and relational terms in older children.

Studies of the age changes in the content of implicit personality theories indicate that around the age of seven there seems to be a marked increase in content as indicated by the number of trait terms used spontaneously by the child. Livesley and Bromley (1973) obtained free descriptions from children aged 7 to 15 years of a variety of adult and child targets. Content analyses of these descriptions showed that the greatest change in the number of trait terms used occurred between 7 and 8 years. Their result confirmed previous findings (e.g., Scarlett, Press and Crockett, 1971; Watts, 1944).

There is some disagreement as to whether a child's trait vocabulary continues to develop steadily or whether the bulk of it is acquired at around 7 to 8 years. Yarrow and Campbell (1963) failed to observe marked age changes in the content of free descriptions obtained from children ranging in age between 8 and 13 years. Livesley and Bromley (1973) suggest that this may have been due to the scoring system used by Yarrow and Campbell which stressed the 'meaning' of statements as opposed to their 'abstractness'. As children grow older they may use progressively more abstract terminology to attribute the same personality characteristics to the target, e.g., 'He's always getting into fights' may later turn into 'He's violent'.

The disagreement between Livesley and Bromley and Yarrow and Campbell illustrates a difficulty with all free description studies. Usually one of the dependent variables is the frequency of trait terms in the description. Different investigators have employed different definitions of what counts as a trait term. Thus, in the previous example, 'He's always getting into fights' might not qualify as a trait term since it refers to concrete behaviour. The qualifier 'always' implies consistency, the hallmark of a personality trait, so on the basis of 'always' the statement might be regarded as having trait-like meaning. If the speculations in the previous section about physical characteristics having trait-like significance are also taken into account, then the difficulties of developing a scoring system to identify trait terms accurately across all age-groups become considerable.

An investigation into the age changes in the content of implicit personality theories was conducted by Peevers and Secord (1973). The interpretation of their findings was enhanced by including an adult group against which the progress of the younger age-groups could be measured. They scored naturalistic personality descriptions in terms of four major categories: descriptiveness, personal involvement, evaluative consistency and depth.

Descriptiveness referred to the degree to which a piece of information differentiated the target from other people; for example, 'John lives in a house' was coded as undifferentiating and hence of low descriptive value, whereas 'John is talkative' was coded as a dispositional statement and hence of more descriptive value. They hypothesised that young children would use less differentiating descriptions than older children.

The personal involvement category provided a measure of egocentricity which was defined as the degree to which a person described the target in relation to him or herself. The most egocentric statements are those where the target's behaviour is described in terms of its consequences for the subject; for example, 'He gave me a cookie'. At the opposite extreme, statements such as 'He is tall' contain no personal involvement and hence are not egocentric. It was hypothesised that younger children, being generally more egocentric, would make more personally involving statements than older subjects.

The evaluative consistency category was a measure similar to those used by Gollin and by Livesley and Bromley. To be evaluatively consistent, the description of a liked person had to contain only positive statements, whereas the description of a disliked person had to contain only negative statements. Peevers and Secord had an interesting hypothesis about evaluative consistency: they predicted that the youngest age-group (kindergarten) would be characterised by inconsistency because they would not be aware of such inconsistency. In contrast, the oldest age-group (college age) would also be characterised by inconsistency, but they would be deliberately inconsistent because they would be aware of the complexities of personality. The intervening age-groups would be expected to show more consistency.

The final category, depth, referred to the degree to which a description attempted to give a causal explanation; for example, 'John is talkative' is not as deep as 'John is talkative when with other people because he is trying to hide an underlying shyness'. Again, a simple age-related increase in depth was expected.

The subjects (kindergarten children, 8- and 12-year-olds, high-school juniors and college seniors) described three friends they liked, and one disliked acquaintance. Their spoken responses were tape-recorded and later transcribed. The findings were mainly in line with predictions. For the liked targets, there was an increase in the number of distinguishing terms and a decrease in the number of egocentric terms with age. The predicted evaluative inconsistency at college level did not occur, although it was present in the kindergarten subjects. Causal explanatory items coded as deep occurred infrequently and then only in subjects 12 years of age and older.

An unexpected finding was that disliked targets were described in a different style to liked targets. The older subjects reverted to more juvenile responses when describing the person they disliked by using more egocentric statements at a lower descriptive level. However, they used more of the mature category of dispositional descriptive statements for the disliked targets. One finding that Peevers and Secord noted with interest was the relatively large proportion of undifferentiating statements subjects of all ages included in their descriptions. Remarks about personal possessions, social roles and position in the family are relatively uninformative in the sense of distinguishing one individual from another, and yet were clearly regarded as important information by the subjects.

Honess (1980) pursued the question of developmental changes in the use of egocentric terms. He proposed that 'egocentric' was a misleading category including some terms which were collaborative as opposed to egocentric. For example, Peevers and Secord (1973) categorised personal involvement statements into egocentric and mutual categories. They found a decrease in the use of egocentric terms with age (e.g., 'He gave me a cookie'), and no differences between the post-kindergarten age-groups in the use of mutual (i.e., collaborative) terms (e.g., 'We go bike-riding together'). In his own study, Honess found a marked increase in collaborative terms such as 'We buy the same clothes', particularly for girls, at the start of adolescence compared with younger and older age-groups. He interpreted this as evidence of the pre-adolescent using friendship and the joint activities it brings as a way of learning to see oneself through another's eyes and thus to reduce egocentricity.

This study demonstrates another aspect of the problem with the scoring of personality descriptions which we encountered earlier in the discussion of the meaning of physical terms: the same statement is evidence of different kinds of thinking at different ages. 'John is fat' may be a trait term for a 5-year-old and a physical description for a 12-year-old; 'We buy clothes together' may be egocentric for a 5-year-old and collaborative for a 12-year-old.

Studies of age changes in the organisation of implicit personality theories have used a variety of different techniques for representing the relations between traits. As we have seen, one way of representing the content of adult implicit personality theories is via multidimensional representations of children's beliefs about trait relations at various ages with those of adults. Olshan (1970) carried out just such a study. She found that the same number of dimensions (four) was adequate for representing the data from 8-, 11- and 14-year-olds, but that the psychological identity of some of these dimensions changed with age. For example, the youngest age-group used the 'adult–child' dimension whereas for the two older age-groups this was replaced by the 'male–female' dimension. However, at all age-levels there was a strong evaluative component: each group perceived people in terms of both a social good–bad dimension and an intellectual good–bad dimension. The same evaluative dimensions are found in adult representations.

Another way of representing trait relations is to explore the hierarchical aspect of trait organisation. This approach was adopted by Honess (1979). He studied written personality descriptions obtained from four age-groups (8, 10, 13 and 16 years). He also administered to each subject a special form of repertory grid called an implication grid (Bannister and Mair, 1968). The child was presented with pairs of constructs and asked to estimate how likely it would be that a person characterised by one construct (e.g., 'friendly') would also be characterised by the other (e.g., 'honest'). The constructs were derived from the same child's written personality description, and covered physical appearance, abilities and personality traits. The implications grid provided a way of assessing the children's beliefs about co-occurrence of the features they believed to be important in describing others, and essentially the same procedure could be used for all age-groups.

Honess hypothesised that an increase in organisation with age would manifest itself in the implication grids in two ways. First, the number of implications (i.e., construct pairs estimated as likely to co-occur) would decrease with age because fewer implications indicate more differentiation of the construct system. A simple system where every construct implies every other is simple in the sense that it is wholly undifferentiated. Second, the degree of hierarchical organisation of the constructs was predicted to increase with age. This would be indicated by an increase in the number of implications for relatively abstract constructs. Thus in a mature system the construct 'warm' would be likely to co-occur with more constructs than 'wears glasses' because the former is more abstract than the latter. The results supported both hypotheses: there were age-related decreases in the number of implications and an age-related increase in the degree of hierarchical organisation.

Social cognition and intellectual development
The research into children's implicit personality theories is generally regarded as indicating that as children get older their personality descriptions become richer both in the number of trait terms used and the complexity with which

they are organised (Livesley and Bromley, 1973). As the number of trait terms increases they also change from being more global (e.g., 'naughty') and often physical (e.g., 'fat') to referring to more subtle dispositions capable of making finer discriminations between people (e.g., 'friendly', 'cowardly').

These findings have been interpreted as indicating that implicit personality theories develop in accordance with Werner's theory of cognitive development (Werner, 1957). The young child's concepts are global and unrelated; developmental change leads to greater differentiation of the concepts and more complex relationships are formed between them (Gollin, 1958; Honess, 1979; Watts, 1944). However, we have already challenged this interpretation of the young child's trait vocabulary. Although, for an adult, the young child's terms are global and physical, the child may be using them to make subtle distinctions between individuals on a dispositional basis. The findings may also be understood in terms of Piaget's theory of cognitive development (see Flavell, 1963). In particular, the supposed decrease in the use of egocentric terms (Livesley and Bromley, 1973; Peevers and Secord, 1973) is consistent with Piagetian theory.

In applying theories of cognitive development to social cognition, the assumption is made that development occurs via a series of stages such that the end product bears little relation to the original. Such an assumption cannot be made for the acquisition of implicit personality theory. We have seen that the basic ability of inferring traits from behaviour is present from an early age and there is no evidence to suggest that this essential ability is replaced by others as the child grows older, or that it differs in any profound way from the adult process of trait inference.

Another difficulty imposed by working within a theoretical framework borrowed from cognitive development is that it becomes impossible to separate the changes that *do* occur in social cognition from the changes associated with intellectual development in general. For example, does the observed increase in trait vocabulary at around 7 years reflect a general memory improvement or does it indicate a metamorphosis in the child's implicit personality theory? In Honess's study, the more intelligent children in each age-group exhibited more hierarchical organisation and fewer implications than the less intelligent children, which suggests that he was studying a manifestation of intellectual development rather than a specific aspect of social cognition (Honess, 1979).

Theoretical confusion will be reduced if it is accepted that social cognition presumably shares many of the cognitive processes that contribute to intelligence and hence, in these respects, it is not useful to distinguish between development in social cognition and general intellectual development. Nevertheless, there may also be certain processes which are either unique to social cognition or are used predominantly in this domain and hence are of particular interest. The ability to infer underlying dispositions from overt behaviour may be just such an ability. Subsequent research on the acquisition of implicit personality theory should make this distinction, and studies should be designed so that processes specific to implicit personality theory may be identified and their development investigated.

Conclusions

The psychological investigation of the lay perspective on personality has revealed that, from an early age, people have extensive and complex theories about personality which they use for descriptive and inference purposes. Implicit personality theories, along with other kinds of beliefs about others such as stereotypes, allow us to categorise people and their behaviour. The advantages of the categorising ability inherent in implicit personality theories are the same for the lay person as the advantages derived from the formal personality theories of the personality theorist's perspective: both the implicit and the explicit theories permit the discrimination between individuals and the prediction of subsequent behaviour. The aim of the present chapter has been to show that we have now reached a considerable degree of understanding of the lay perspective with respect to the contents of implicit personality theories, the manner in which they are used and the way in which they are acquired. The next chapter is concerned with the relation between the lay perspective and reality: to what extent are implicit beliefs about personality accurate reflections of reality?

6   The Lay Perspective and Reality

Imagine a study where the members of a discussion group which had been meeting regularly for a year were asked, when they met for the last time, to rate each other on twenty bipolar personality scales, such as good-natured–irritable, talkative–silent, careless–tidy, calm–anxious, imaginative–simple. Each group member's profile of scale scores is then calculated by averaging the scores awarded by all the other group members on each scale. It would then be possible to intercorrelate and factor analyse the rating scales to discover the underlying structure of the trait ratings. Would such a study tell us about the structure of the ratees' personalities; or would it tell us about the structure of the raters' implicit personality theories? In other words, do personality ratings tell us about the personality of the ratee, or the way the rater perceives personality?

In the previous chapter we have seen how the psychological study of the lay perspective involves observing people's use of trait terms when describing others, or when making inferences about how they will behave. Consider, for example, Wishner's (1960) study, where the correlations between traits were estimated by obtaining students' ratings of their instructors on these traits. Here trait ratings were being used to yield information about implicit personality theory. By contrast, in Chapter 3, we saw how trait ratings are regarded, in terms of the personality theorist's perspective, as one of the three sources of personality data; ratings are used as a way of measuring the ratees' personalities. Thus two groups of psychologists are conducting similar investigations but treating the data as though they measured two different things. This contradiction has arisen in part because those social psychologists who study the lay perspective and those who are personality theorists have tended to work in isolation, ignoring alternative interpretations of their data.

Psychologists studying the lay perspective are interested in the beliefs people hold about personality, and regard these as *beliefs*, not necessarily as accurate observations. Personality theorists are interested in the personalities of their subjects, and regard human raters as measuring devices capable of plugging into reality and observing it reliably. They tend not to consider whether rating data is irreparably contaminated by raters' beliefs about personality. A reconciliation between the lay perspective and the personality theorist's perspective ought to be possible, since both are concerned with the same subject-matter: human personality. Psychologists interested in the lay perspective need to acknowledge that implicit personality theories could scarcely be fabricated out of thin air, but must have *some* basis in reality. Personality theorists need to remind themselves that personality can never be observed directly, only inferred, and that the inference process is susceptible to distortion. It then becomes clear that personality cannot be said to reside exclusively within an individual, nor to be a figment of a perceiver's imagination, but is the product of an interaction between reality and our perception of it.

The work to be discussed in the first part of this chapter consists of those studies which have tried to bridge the gap between the lay perspective and the personality theorist's perspective. However, the majority of studies have not been conducted with the reconciliation of the two perspectives in mind. Rather, a combative stand has been adopted, in which the personality theorist's perspective is the focus of attention, and is either the subject of vigorous attack or vigorous defence.

The Three Interpretations of Personality Ratings

Measures of personality
The controversy between the two perspectives began with a series of experiments carried out by Tupes and Christal

(1961), Norman (1963) and Passini and Norman (1966). The purpose of these studies was to investigate personality using a version of personality ratings called the *peer nomination technique*. Thus, ostensibly, these studies were carried out under the aegis of the personality theorist's perspective. The same procedures were used in all three studies. The subjects (service men in the Tupes and Christal studies, college students in the others) were split up into small groups of six to sixteen people, and each subject was asked to assign the other members of the group to either pole of a series of twenty bipolar personality scales. These scales were selected from those used by Cattell (1947) to arrive at a comprehensive yet economical coverage of the personality sphere (see Chapter 3). They are listed in Table 6.1. The subjects' scores on each scale were calculated on the basis of the group data by subtracting the number of nominations to pole B from the number of nominations to pole A. This figure was then corrected for the size of the group and a constant was added to avoid negative numbers. The rating scales were then intercorrelated using subjects' scores from all the small groups in the sample and the resulting correlation matrix was factor analysed.

Not only was the procedure virtually identical across all these studies, but the results were too. Repeatedly, the same five factors emerged in the analyses in the different studies with loadings from the same scales (see Table 6.1). These factors were: extraversion, agreeableness, conscientiousness, emotional stability and culture. The only point on which these studies differed was the length of acquaintance of the participants. In the Tupes and Christal studies and Norman (1963), the samples varied in length of acquaintance from three days to three years. In Passini and Norman's study, the length of acquaintance was fifteen minutes during which no conversation was permissible between the group members so ratings were made on the basis of appearance alone.

Measures of implicit beliefs
Until Passini and Norman's study it had been assumed that the peer nomination technique provided information about

Table 6.1 The five factors representing the twenty peer
nomination scales (from Norman, 1963)

Factor name	Scale labels
Extraversion	talkative–silent
	frank, open–secretive
	adventurous–cautious
	sociable–reclusive
Agreeableness	good-natured–irritable
	not jealous–jealous
	mild, gentle–headstrong
	cooperative–negativistic
Conscientiousness	fussy, tidy–careless
	responsible–undependable
	scrupulous–unscrupulous
	persevering–quitting, fickle
Emotional stability	poised–nervous, tense
	calm–anxious
	composed–excitable
	non–hypochondriacal–hypochondriacal
Culture	artistically sensitive–artistically insensitive
	intellectual–unreflective, narrow
	polished, refined–crude, boorish
	imaginative–simple, direct

the structure of personality residing within the nominee.
Norman (1963) had discussed possible explanations for why
his five-factor structure differed from the larger number
favoured by Cattell (1947), and concluded that the additional
factors found by Cattell were derived from unreliable scales
and accounted for too small a percentage of the variance to
be worth considering. Norman (1963) was arguing about the
best way to represent the structure of personality, but the
results of Passini and Norman's study raised doubts about
whether Norman had in fact been measuring the personality
of the nominees.

The findings that an identical factor structure could be
derived from peer nominations made by *strangers* demonstrated that this structure could equally be regarded as a
representation of people's *beliefs* about the relations between personality traits as of their actual co-occurrence
within a set of observed individuals. Finding virtually identical factors in samples varying in acquaintance from fifteen
minutes to three years was interpreted by Passini and Norman
as evidence that people's nominations are based on their

beliefs about trait co-occurrences, i.e. their implicit personality theories, rather than their observation of trait co-occurrences in the nominees. On the basis of these studies it has been argued that personality factor structures based on observer ratings are more parsimoniously interpreted as reflections of the raters' implicit personality theories rather than the ratees' personalities (Mischel, 1968).

The claims made for these studies (both by their authors and others) concerning their threat to the validity of personality ratings are excessive with respect to what has actually been demonstrated. There is a methodological feature of the procedure used in all the studies which detracts from the significance of the findings. The subjects were required to assign their peers to one or other pole of the bipolar trait scales. The task therefore asked for a very crude personality judgment. A person was deemed either 'talkative' or 'silent', 'goodnatured' or 'irritable', 'sensitive' or 'insensitive', and so on, but could never be placed somewhere between the two as would be the case on a rating scale. In addition to what was already a highly restrictive task, subjects were told they had to allocate at least one third of the group to pole A of the scale and at least one third to pole B. Inevitably, subjects must have had to make some compromises and gone against their first appraisal when placing some nominees at poles in order to meet the quota. From the comments made in the reports of these investigations it is clear that subjects found the nomination task both difficult and unrealistic, e.g. 'The subjects in this study complained more than usual that they felt uncomfortable about filling out the rating forms' (Norman, 1963, p.581). In Passini and Norman's study, where subjects had to judge total strangers, the implausibility of the task was openly acknowledged in the instructions where the subjects were told that their data were to be used as 'a base line for comparing results obtained from other samples of subjects who were better acquainted with one another' (Passini and Norman, 1966, p.45).

In view of the highly constrained and unrealistic nature of the task, it is surprising that the peer nomination data were ever compared with the personality rating data obtained by personality theorists such as Eysenck and Cattell. Cattell

(1957) has listed the principles of a reliable rating study, which include such safeguards as insisting that the raters observe their ratees in a wide variety of situations for at least three months and preferably for a year, and that the rating scales be couched in non-ambiguous terms with clear indications of the behaviours to which they refer. The procedures used in these studies fall short of Cattell's recommendations and, while Tupes and Christal (1961) and Norman (1963) claimed to be investigating personality, the procedures used indicate that they forced their raters to fall back on their implicit personality theories rather than base their judgments on observations, and hence the similarity between these studies and those of Passini and Norman.

It is interesting that these studies reliably uncovered five dimensions instead of the three more commonly found in studies of structural representations of implicit personality theory (Rosenberg and Sedlak, 1972a). The three Osgood factors are discernible, however, with extraversion and agreeableness probably forming two aspects of evaluation, emotional stability and conscientiousness similar to activity, and culture similar to potency.

Since these studies are more correctly viewed as investigations of implicit personality theory they have no significance for the validity of personality ratings. However, even if Passini and Norman had been correct in regarding their study as an investigation into implicit personality theory, and the previous studies as attempts at investigations of personality proper, the argument that the studies all produced the same results because raters impose their implicit personality theories onto their observations, does not hold. Studies of implicit personality theory describe people's beliefs about the co-occurrence likelihood of traits. Rating studies of personality aim to study the actual co-occurrence likelihood of traits. Given that ratings could be distorted by implicit beliefs we have two possibilities as to what personality ratings are measuring:

(A) The actual co-occurrence likelihood of traits (personality);
(B) Beliefs about the co-occurrence likelihood of traits (implicit personality theory).

If it was demonstrated that A and B are the same, it could not then be argued, as Passini and Norman tried to do, that personality ratings do not plug into reality but distort observations to correspond with internal beliefs. To argue in this way ignores another equally valid interpretation of the results, that personality ratings measure both A and B and the results are similar because implicit personality theory is an accurate representation of actual trait co-occurrence. The only way to test between these two interpretations of a similarity between A and B is to obtain a measure of trait co-occurrence free from the dangers of contamination by implicit personality theory.

Measures of semantic similarity
Before reviewing the studies which claim to have done just this, there is another possibility as to the meaning of trait ratings which must be considered. It has been suggested (D'Andrade, 1965; Mulaik, 1964) that personality ratings measure neither actual nor believed co-occurrence likelihood of traits, but instead are a measure of the overlap in meaning or semantic similarity between the trait terms. D'Andrade obtained ratings of the similarity in meaning between each of the twenty scales shown in Table 6.1 by selecting one of the poles for each of the scales and presenting all possible pairs of these traits to a group of students who were asked to rate the pairs for similarity in meaning. The group data were then averaged so that a mean similarity rating between each and every other trait was obtained. Using this matrix of similarity ratings, D'Andrade then obtained correlations between each of the traits by treating the columns as tests and the rows as subjects. This procedure sounds strange but is legitimate. To illustrate, Table 6.2 is an imaginary section of D'Andrade's similarity matrix. To the extent that the column traits are similar in meaning (correlated) the subjects (i.e. the row traits) will have approximately the same similarity ratings with the traits. Thus 'secretive' is equally similar to 'silent' and 'cautious' as are 'reclusive' and 'undependable'. The same is true where the column traits are dissimilar (uncorrelated): there are consistent differences in the similarity ratings from all the 'subjects' between 'cautious' and 'careless'.

Table 6.2 Hypothetical section of a similarity matrix
of the kind used by D'Andrade (1965)

	silent	cautious	careless
secretive	6	6	4
reclusive	5	5	4
undependable	4	4	6

Having estimated the correlations between the traits,
D'Andrade was then able to factor analyse them. The results
of the analysis were virtually identical to those obtained by
Tupes and Christal, Norman, and Passini and Norman. The
same five factors emerged and the pattern of scale loadings
was identical except for five misplacements. D'Andrade had
shown that the pattern of trait relations, so reliably obtained
when using these twenty bipolar scales to rate other people,
may also be obtained when no other people are involved
and subjects are simply required to rate the similarity in
meaning between trait terms. His findings suggest that the
five-factor structure of these scales is due to the overlap in
meaning between them and not to either beliefs or observations of their actual co-occurrence.

As a result of D'Andrade's study, we now have three
possible interpretations of trait ratings:
(A) The actual co-occurrence likelihood of traits (person-
     ality);
(B) Beliefs about the co-occurrence likelihood of traits
     (implicit personality theory);
(C) Overlap in meaning between traits (semantic similarity).

D'Andrade does not insist that his findings undermine the
validity of interpretation (A). He recognises the possibility
that (C) could be an accurate representation of (A):

> it is possible that the so-called psychological traits dealt
> with in this paper exist both as components in the terms
> used to describe the external world and in the external
> world as well. Such an isomorphism, if it exists, might be
> the result of the external world affecting first the dis-
> criminations made by speakers of a language, who then
> eventually develop a sememic structure within the language

to encode these discriminations. (D'Andrade, 1965, pp. 227-8).

Mulaik (1964) obtained ratings of twenty real people, twenty stereotypes and twenty personality traits on seventy-six bipolar rating scales similar to those used by Osgood (1962), e.g. strong–weak, active–passive, etc. The ratings of real people were regarded as measuring actual characteristics, the ratings of stereotypes were regarded as measuring implicit beliefs and the ratings of traits were regarded as a measure of conceptual similarity. Similar factor structures were found in all three sets of rating data but Mulaik resisted coming to any dogmatic conclusions on the basis of this evidence. He argued that the most parsimonious explanation is that people possess a pre-existing set of beliefs about the conceptual similarity between traits and that these beliefs distort our view of both real people and stereotypes. However, he also stated that if it could be shown that 'raters of the meaning of trait words make such ratings according to their knowledge of how traits go together in persons and not according to their knowledge of meanings as such' (Mulaik, 1964, p.510), then he would be prepared to accept the explanation that the similarity between all three sets of data is due to accurate observation resulting in accurate beliefs encoded into the meaning of trait words.

The studies described so far have suggested three possible interpretations of what personality ratings are measuring, but they have been unable to demonstrate the superiority of any one interpretation because they have lacked a measure of trait co-occurrence that could be regarded as an objective measure of what happens in the external world unbiased by the human observer. Nevertheless, these studies succeeded in raising doubts about the status of personality ratings which it was important to resolve. For the lay perspective, it is important to decide whether people's beliefs about trait co-occurrence (their implicit personality theories) are isomorphic with reality or are distortions of the external world. If it were established that human observers are biased in their perception of personality in others because of their pre-existing and inaccurate beliefs about trait co-occurrence, then

Table 6.3 Investigations into the epistemological status of implicit personality theory

Studies using immediate behaviour ratings	Measures of personality and implicit beliefs	Statistical method of comparison	Results and conclusions
D'Andrade (1974) (reanalysis of Borgatta, Cottrell and Mann, 1958, and Mann, 1959)	Bales's social-interaction categories: 1 Immediate behaviour ratings 2 Ratings from memory 3 Conceptual similarity ratings	Correlations between the inter-category correlation matrices obtained in each measure	1 had a low correlation with 2 and 3 which were highly correlated. Pre-existing beliefs about item similarity distort ratings from memory.
Shweder (1975, part 1) (reanalysis of Newcomb, 1929)	Behavioural items: 1 Immediate behaviour ratings 2 Ratings from memory 3 Conceptual similarity ratings	Correlations between the inter-item correlation matrices obtained in each measure	1 had low correlations with 2 and 3 which were highly correlated. Pre-existing beliefs about item similarity distort ratings from memory.
Studies using self-report questionnaires			
Lay and Jackson (1969)	Personality Research Form items: 1 Actual responses 2 Co-occurrence likelihood estimates	Multidimensional scaling of co-occurrence likelihoods, factor analysis of actual responses	Dimensions similar across 1 and 2 People's beliefs are accurate representations of reality
Stricker, Jacobs and Kogan (1974)	MMPI Pd scale items: 1 Actual responses 2 Conceptual similarity sortings of items	Factor analysis of the actual responses, each subject's response pattern compared with the factor structure	Subjects' response patterns similar to the factor structure. People's beliefs are accurate representations of reality

Studies using self-report questionnaires	Measures of personality and implicit beliefs	Statistical method of comparison	Results and conclusions
Mirels (1976)	Personality Research Form items: 1 Actual responses 2 Co-endorsement likelihood estimates	Item by item comparison between 1 and 2, no dimensional analysis	21 out of 26 item pairs had significantly different co-endorsement estimates as compared with actual patterns of co-endorsement. People's beliefs are inaccurate
Jackson, Chan & Stricker (1979)	Personality Research Form items: 1 Actual responses 2 Mirels's data on co-endorsement likelihood estimates	Co-endorsement likelihoods for item pairs were correlated with measures of actual item co-occurrence	1 and 2 highly similar, Mirels's results attributed to his method of analysis of 1 which used a conditional probability index. People's beliefs are accurate representations of reality
Shweder (1975, part 2)	Questionnaires by Bales (1970); Sears, Maccoby and Levin (1957): items from the MMPI: 1 Actual responses 2 Ratings of conceptual similarity Measures of personality	Comparison of multi-dimensional scaling solutions of the Bales items, factor analyses of the Sears, Maccoby and Levin items and correlations for the MMPI items between 1 and 2	1 and 2 highly similar in all three studies. People's beliefs distort their judgments of actual behaviour

the validity of the personality theorist's perspective would be in serious doubt. As we saw in Chapter 4, rating data is a source of evidence for type C consistency (different behaviour, same situation) and therefore the status of rating data is critical for the validity of the personality concept, and indeed for the entire personality theorist's perspective. If trait co-occurrence (type C consistency) does not actually happen in the external world and instead is constructed by people's cognitive processes, then there would be no sense in constructing personality theories to account for a phenomenon mistakenly attributed to the external world when in fact it only exists inside people's heads. The next section reviews studies specifically addressed to these issues.

Investigations into the Epistemological Status of Implicit Personality Theory

The distinguishing feature of studies claiming to test the epistemological status of implicit personality theory is that they all intend to compare people's beliefs about the relations between traits with actual trait relations. Individual studies differ in the procedures used but, despite the variety of ingenious methodologies, it is highly doubtful whether any have in fact succeeded in fulfilling this intention. A selection of these studies, chosen because they represent the different methodologies and are frequently cited, are briefly summarised in Table 6.3 and are discussed in more detail below.

Studies using immediate behaviour ratings
The first two studies listed in Table 6.3 took as their 'objective' measure of trait co-occurrences immediate (i.e. on the spot) ratings of behaviour and compared these ratings with ratings based on memory and ratings of the conceptual similarity of the rating scales. D'Andrade (1974) presented data from two studies he had found in the literature in which ratings of behaviour recorded on the spot were compared with ratings of the same behaviour made from memory (Borgatta, Cottrell and Mann, 1958; Mann, 1959). In both studies the behaviour under investigation was small-group interaction,

and the forty categories used to rate it included six Bales interaction-process analysis categories (Bales, 1970). D'Andrade limited his attention to these six categories. Both studies provided immediate ratings of the group members' interaction on the Bales categories (see Table 6.4 (i)).

Table 6.4 The three sets of interactional-analysis categories (from D'Andrade, 1974)

(i) Immediate rating categories	(ii) Memory rating categories	(iii) Semantic similarity categories
1 Shows solidarity, raises others' status, jokes, gives help, reward	1 Shows solidarity and friendliness	1 Shows solidarity
2 Shows tension release, shows satisfaction, laughs	2 Is responsive to laughter	2 Jokes, laughs
3 Gives suggestions, direction, implying autonomy for other	3 Makes the most suggestions	3 Suggests, gives direction
4 Disagrees, shows passive rejection, formality, withholds help	4 Disagrees most	4 Disagrees
5 Shows tension increase, asks for help, withdraws 'out of field'	5 Tends to be nervous	5 Shows tension, nervous
6 Shows antagonism deflates others' status	6 Tends to be antagonistic	6 Shows antagonism

They also provided ratings made by the group members of each other after meeting nine times on a similar, but not identical, set of categories (see Table 6.4 (ii)). To these two sets of ratings, D'Andrade added a third which consisted of ratings of the semantic similarity between another set of similar, but not identical, categories (see Table 6.4 (iii)). Thus he was able to compare immediate ratings with ratings from memory and semantic similarity ratings on what he regarded as equivalent categories. This was done by correlating each category with every other within each set of data and then comparing the three correlation matrices (see Figure 6.1).

In both studies, it was found that the immediate ratings matrix (i) did not correspond to either the memory ratings

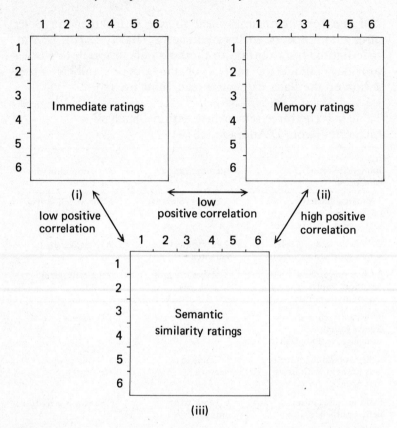

Figure 6.1 *Diagrammatic representation of D'Andrade's (1974) results*

matrix (ii) or the semantic similarity matrix (iii). The greatest correspondence was obtained between the semantic similarity matrix (iii) and the memory ratings matrix (ii). The degree of correspondence was measured by calculating the correlations between matrices. D'Andrade concluded from these findings that ratings of behaviour made from memory are subject to systematic distortion which is produced by the rater confusing the similarity in meaning between the terms with the memory of whether the two categories did or did not actually co-occur in the same people. Ratings from memory are used both in studies claiming to be measuring implicit personality theory and in studies claiming to measure personality, but in either case D'Andrade's findings imply that they will be distorted by the effects of semantic similarity which does not correspond to reality. The 'human behaviourscope', as he puts it, is not a reliable measuring instrument.

D'Andrade's study has been criticised by Block, Weiss and Thorne (1979), in particular for the fact that he failed to do what he had claimed, that is to compare ratings obtained in three different ways on the same categories. In Table 6.4 the categories used in each of the three rating tasks are shown and it can be seen that not only are all three sets of categories full of ambiguous wordings allowing for all kinds of idiosyncratic interpretations (e.g. (ii) 2: 'Is responsive to laughter'), but there is also considerable variation in wording across the three versions of the same category (e.g. category 1). This is not a pedantic point because, as constructors of questionnaires and rating scales know to their cost, the slightest change in wording of an item can have substantial effects on how that item is interpreted by respondents. A study such as D'Andrade's has to pay meticulous attention to the use of identical categories before it may be argued that the correlational structure of one set of responses differs from another for reasons other than category wording.

A study by Shweder (1975, part 1) was similar in many respects to that of D'Andrade. Shweder too made use of a previous study (Newcomb, 1929) in which immediate ratings and memory ratings were compared. The subjects in this study were boys on summer camp. The rating categories consisted of thirty items measuring various aspects of extraversion, e.g. 'Takes the initiative in organising games', 'Gets up before the rising hour', 'Gets into trouble of a mischievous or adventurous nature.' Each boy was rated twice on these items, first by his counsellor as soon as possible after the occurrence of the behaviour (immediate ratings), and second at the end of the camp, by six observers and the counsellors (memory ratings). In addition, Shweder also obtained semantic similarity ratings of these items from a student group. In an analysis similar to that used by D'Andrade, Shweder compared all three sets of ratings. His results were in agreement with those obtained by D'Andrade. The memory ratings were highly similar to the semantic similarity ratings whereas the immediate ratings had relatively low correlations with both — see Figure 6.2. Shweder argued that the semantic similarity ratings were the product of a pre-existing conceptual scheme which caused the distortion of the memory ratings.

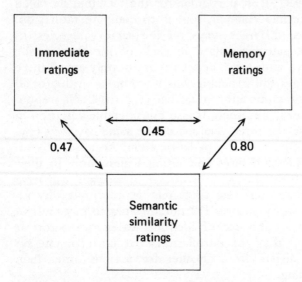

Figure 6.2 *Correlations between the three matrices of ratings (from Shweder, 1975; correlations are the means of the correlations for two groups reported separately by Shweder)*

The first point to make in commenting on Shweder's re-analysis of Newcomb's data is that the rating categories, although identical across the three sets of data, were in many cases as unsatisfactory as D'Andrade's, because they too did not refer unambiguously to specific behaviours. While 'Gets up before the rising hour' is a good item in that it is clearly def ned, many were more vague, such as 'Engages in group mis demeanour' or 'Actively moves about most of the day'; these items must be open to idiosyncratic interpretations depending upon raters' personal definitions of 'misdemeanour', 'actively' and 'most'. In addition it is difficult to see how the counsellors making the immediate ratings could have carried out the instructions to rate the item as soon as possible after it had occurred, since their ratings required a general impression of a day's activity. These categories, then, cannot be claimed to be measuring clearly defined behaviours as they occur, which is the essential requirement for ratings of actual behaviour. Therefore Shweder's (and D'Andrade's) immediate ratings cannot be taken as acceptable objective measures of reality, but are more appropriately viewed as a measure of reality filtered through the raters' perceptual and cognitive processes.

The disparity between the memory ratings and the immediate ratings suggests that the cognitive filter has a much larger effect the further it is distanced in time from the initial observations. Shweder regards this disparity as evidence of the inaccuracies of implicit personality theory, because he regards the immediate ratings as an accurate measure of reality. However, since his view of the immediate ratings' status is dubious, an equally plausible interpretation of the disparity is that with an interval between observation and rating the rater is more susceptible to the distorting effects of the cognitive filter. This interpretation is supported by the correlations Shweder reports between the three ratings matrices (see Figure 6.2). If the immediate ratings are subject to essentially the same distorting influences as are reflected in the memory ratings and the semantic similarity ratings, although to a lesser extent, the correlations between the immediate matrix and the other two matrices should be numerically similar and positive. This is indeed the case: the correlations are not only similar and positive but of such a magnitude that a strong correspondence between all three matrices is indicated (0.45 and 0.47).

In sum, Shweder's study is limited by his failure to obtain a genuine measure of actual behaviour against which to compare the other ratings. It is therefore impossible to reach any firm conclusions from his results about the accuracy of either semantic similarity or ratings from memory. The disparity between the memory ratings and the immediate ratings, although not particularly large, does suggest that the cognitive filter of the human observer has a more biasing effect with separation in time between the events themselves and ratings of them.

Studies using self-report questionnaires
The next group of studies shown in Table 6.3 used a different measure of actual trait co-occurrence against which to assess people's beliefs. The measures of personality in the external world were self-report questionnaires, and these measures were compared either with semantic similarity ratings or co-occurrence estimates of the questionnaire items, the aim being to see how far people's beliefs about the overlap in meaning between the items (semantic similarity) and the beliefs people hold about which items co-occur (co-endorsement estimates) correspond to the actual patterns of co-occurrence as revealed by the respondents' questionnaire responses.

Lay and Jackson (1969) found a strong correspondence between co-endorsement estimates and actual co-endorsement of the questionnaire items. Stricker *et al.* (1974) found a strong correspondence between semantic similarity estimates and the actual co-endorsement of the items. In both these studies, the correspondence was interpreted as evidence in support of the validity of people's beliefs: responses to questionnaires were regarded as accurate measures of actual behaviour and, since people's beliefs corresponded to this measure, then the beliefs were regarded as accurate too. Mirels's (1976) study failed to find any correspondence between co-endorsement estimates and actual co-endorsement, but Jackson *et al.* (1979) have demonstrated that this failure was due to the type of statistical analysis Mirels used and when the data were analysed along the lines favoured by Jackson *et al.* the strong correspondence was found.

In complete contrast, Shweder (1975, part 2) interprets his finding of correspondence between semantic similarity estimates and actual co-endorsement to mean that when people respond to a questionnaire they base their responses on their beliefs about the semantic similarity between the items rather than on their knowledge of their own behaviour. He regards this as the more parsimonious explanation which would only be refuted were it to be demonstrated that semantic similarity and co-endorsement corresponded to actual behaviour.

Shweder is correct to regard self-report questionnaire data

as liable to contamination by implicit beliefs, and Lay and Jackson are wrong to regard them as accurate representations of reality. Asking someone to fill in a questionnaire provides the investigator with a specific behaviour sample (the respondents' self-perceptions) and these cannot be assumed to be unbiased and isomorphic to actual behavioural occurrence. Again, these studies have failed to find a satisfactory measure of actual behaviour. However, it is not, as Shweder argues, more parsimonious to regard questionnaire responses as illusions because they correspond to semantic similarity ratings. Such a view begs the question of where these illusory beliefs came from. It is more parsimonious to regard the correspondence between the way people fill out questionnaires, co-endorsement estimates and semantic similarity between the items as due to all three being descriptions of the same data: actual behaviour patterns. Such an interpretation is more parsimonious than Shweder's because it avoids having to develop a theory for the origins of the so-called 'illusory' beliefs people hold about semantic similarity and co-endorsement. However, a choice between the two interpretations cannot be made until a satisfactory measure of actual behaviour uncontaminated by pre-existing beliefs is obtained.

None of the studies summarised in Table 6.3 have succeeded in comparing people's beliefs about personality with the true co-occurrence likelihoods of personality traits, because the measures were all liable to contamination by observers' pre-existing beliefs. Whether these beliefs should properly be regarded as contaminating cannot be established until they have been compared with the reality they claim to represent; until then we cannot assume either that they are accurate or inaccurate. The studies in Table 6.3 have not advanced our understanding in this debate. The failure of investigators to arrive at a convincing measure of the external reality we call personality must raise doubts about the wisdom of such an enterprise. Will it ever be possible to construct rating scales non-ambiguously describing behaviour which raters can use to observe and record reality accurately? If human observations are ruled out because of their susceptibility to bias, then perhaps there are mechanical recording devices which could be used instead. Instruments to measure noise versus no noise, although acceptably objective, do seem to fail to capture the complexities of human personality.

The manipulation of reality

Given the extreme difficulties posed by attempting the objective measurement of personality, another way of approaching the problem of assessing the biasing effects of people's beliefs is for the investigator to step in and manipulate reality. By controlling the reality confronting the human observer, the investigator can see when and how the human observer deviates from that reality. Such an investigation cannot help answer the question of whether observers' beliefs about personality are accurate or inaccurate, but it can tell us more about the effects these beliefs have on observations.

A study by Berman and Kenny (1976) of observer bias illustrates this approach. In the first part of their study they discovered people's beliefs about the co-occurrence of a variety of trait pairs and located pairs believed to be correlated positively, negatively or not at all. They then presented subjects with descriptive statements about fictitious targets of the form: 'John was rated high on the trait sociable' and 'John was rated high on the trait friendly'. In these descriptions the co-occurrence of the trait pairs within each target was varied such that it sometimes corresponded to the believed positive, negative or zero correlation and sometimes did not. Thus while John might be described as highly friendly and sociable (corresponding to the believed correlation), Dave might be described as high on friendly but low on sociable (which goes against beliefs). After two viewings of a series of sixteen statements in which eight targets' ratings on two traits were presented, the subjects performed an immediate recall task in which they tried to remember how each target was described on the two traits (high or low). This procedure was repeated nine times with different targets' names and traits. Finally, at the end of the nine blocks, the subjects performed a delayed recall task in which they tried to remember how all the eighteen targets had been described.

The result of Berman and Kenny's study showed that subjects' recall of manipulated trait correlations was strongly influenced by the pre-existing beliefs about the actual corre-lations between traits. Thus both John and Dave would be recalled as rated high on both sociable and friendly because that corresponded to pre-existing beliefs, even though only John and not Dave had been presented in that way.

Berman and Kenny interpret their findings as powerful evidence against the validity of human observations; how-ever, their interpretation has been strongly criticised by Block (1977b), who regards the study as irrelevant for the personality rating issue. In a typical personality investigation where human observers are used, the data base consists of observations of targets' behaviour, not a series of statements about their personality trait ratings. The task in Berman and Kenny's experiment required subjects to remember the asso-ciation between the target's name and a trait rating. The statements were presented twice to the subjects before the immediate recall test, but presumably immediate recall could have been improved to 100 per cent accuracy given enough presentations. The delayed recall test was even more difficult: subjects had to recall each targets' rating on eighteen traits. Memory for ratings on traits in the earlier presentations would have been subject to retroactive interference: thus the task difficulty was confounded with delay of recall. Block regards the study as an experiment on paired associate learning and is therefore not surprised by the influence of pre-existing beliefs about trait correlation: it is well established that prior associative links influence recall in the early stages of this type of learning.

Block has criticised Berman and Kenny's study for being essentially an experiment about memory rather than an ex-periment about the accuracy of the human observer. This criticism is correct. Berman and Kenny were not testing the validity of personality traits as accurate categories for human behaviour, but rather they were studying the effects these categories have on memory. Their study demonstrates how these categories bias recall of inconsistent information in the direction of making it more consistent, e.g. Dave is actually described as high on 'friendly' but low on 'sociable' which is inconsistent with pre-existing personality categories and hence at recall this inconsistency is ironed out and Dave is remembered as being both highly friendly and sociable.

Although Berman and Kenny's study does not bear directly on the epistemological status of implicit personality theory, it does lend support to a possible interpretation which accounts for all the findings presented in Table 6.3. Let us assume that people's pre-existing beliefs about which personality traits and personality-related behaviours are likely to co-occur are accurate to the extent that they are correct on most occasions. The lay perspective is similar to the personality theorist's perspective in that it does not guarantee 100 per cent accuracy in its predictions but rather it is able to come up with a reasonable estimate of what may co-occur. In a given instance it may be wrong, but this rough and ready guide about personality is better than no guide at all.

This may seem rather a major assumption to make. It will be recalled (see Chapter 4) that Mischel coined the phrase 'personality coefficient' to ridicule the correlation of around 0.30 which is a typical finding in studies correlating personality test scores with a sample of behaviour. Mischel argued that this low correlation was indicative of the fact that behaviour is inconsistent and therefore the concept of personality is invalid. If Mischel's summary of the evidence on consistency is correct, then both the lay perspective and the personality theorist's perspective are operating with an invalid concept of personality: to describe a person in terms of a personality trait is entirely unhelpful since it does not form the basis for reliable predictions or inferences.

However, we have already seen how Mischel's extreme position has been modified in the light of interactionist research; and a recent paper by Epstein (1979) presents some strong evidence for the view that, for most people much of the time, behavioural consistency is the rule and not the exception. Epstein was able to demonstrate consistency where others have failed by correlating personality measures with measures of behaviour based on averages over several samples of that behaviour. Epstein argued that previous studies such as those reviewed by Mischel have obtained low correlations between test scores and actual behaviour because only one behavioural event in one situation was sampled, and such one-off samples are subject to error associated with the characteristics of the situation in which the behaviour was sampled. Only by averaging over situations and occasions is this error reduced and the 'personality coefficient' boosted to respectable proportions (Epstein reported correlations as high as 0.90).

Epstein's demonstration of behavioural consistency supports the validity of the personality concept and suggests that it is entirely reasonable to assume that the lay perspective is accurate for characterising most people much of the time. Where it lets us down in particular is when we make personality judgments after the passage of time. In this case implicit personality theory acts like other categorising systems to organise and simplify the stored information in such a way that certain details, in particular those discordant with the categories, are lost at recall.

Given the view that implicit personality theories tend to work and therefore must, to some extent, be accurate, certain predictions may be made. First, the structure of personality described by personality theorists and the structure of implicit personality theories will share some common features. The personality theorists' investigations into personality will thus risk being contaminated by implicit beliefs — hence some similarity would be expected. But more importantly, both perspectives are concerned with the same subject-matter and if both provide fairly accurate pictures of personality then there should be some overlap between these pictures. This is indeed the case. We have already seen how personality theorists are in considerable agreement about the major dimensions of personality with extraversion and neuroticism being found in all the major investigations. Studies of implicit personality theory typically come up with extraversion and emotional stability (neuroticism) plus one to three other dimensions (see Table 6.1). Implicit personality theory is therefore neither as simple as Eysenck's tripartite structure (extraversion, neuroticism and psychoticism) nor as complex as Cattell's structure (involving at least twenty different factors).

However, there is evidence that the various representations of personality structure proposed by different personality theorists have a number of factors in common which bear a close resemblance to those found in studies of implicit personality theory. Vagg and Hammond (1976) carried out a partial replication of H.J. Eysenck and S.B.G. Eysenck (1969) in which the Eysenck, Cattell and Guilford personality inventories were factor analysed. Four factors were found to be measured by all three inventories and were invariant across the sexes. The first two factors were identified as Neuroticism and Sociability, which confirmed the Eysencks' findings. However, Vagg and Hammond located two additional factors which had gone unrecognised by Eysenck and Eysenck; these were labelled as Sensitivity *v.* Practicality and Group-centred Morality *v.* Self-centred Independence.

The factors discovered in peer nomination studies (see Table 6.1) are similar to the factors found by Vagg and Hammond. The factors of Neuroticism and Sociability are directly comparable to the lay perspective's Extraversion and Emotional Stability. Vagg and Hammond's factor of Sensitivity appears, on inspection of the high loading items, to be comparable to the lay perspective's factor of Culture. 'Would not enjoy writing on drama, concerts' and 'Prefers engineering to philosophy' had high negative loadings on the Sensitivity factor and scales such as 'Artistically sensitive-artistically insensitive' and 'Imaginative-simple, direct' loaded on the Culture factor. The fourth factor located by Vagg and Hammond, Morality, is comparable to the lay perspective's Conscientiousness factor. High loading items on Morality include 'Most people shirk their duties' and 'Anyone will lie to keep out of trouble' which are comparable to high loading scales on Conscientiousness such as Persevering — quitting, fickle and Scrupulous-Unscrupulous. Thus the results of Vagg and Hammond and similar studies (e.g. Sells, Demaree and Will, 1970, 1971) suggest that the personality theorist's perspective and the lay perspective are converging on a similar representation of personality.

A second prediction about implicit personality theory which may be derived from the view that it provides a reasonably accurate picture of reality is that studies of the effects of observer bias should demonstrate that essentially the same structure is obtained in both on-the-spot ratings and in ratings made after a delay. The effects of delay on personality ratings should be comparable to the effects of delay in story recall where the same basic story structure is retained and it is the details which get lost with time (Bower, 1976). Support for this prediction is to be found in studies comparing immediate and delayed recall ratings (D'Andrade, 1974; Shweder, 1975) in which the correlations between the rating structures obtained on the spot and after a delay were moderate and positive.

The view that implicit personality theory does provide a reasonably accurate, if somewhat idealised, picture of reality accounts for the findings summarised in Table 6.3 in the following way. The interpretation of the studies using immediate behaviour ratings has already been presented, briefly it is as follows: while observers are liable to bias from implicit personality theory even in their immediate ratings, these effects will be more marked when there is a delay between observation and rating, hence the moderate correlations between immediate and delayed ratings and the high correlations between semantic similarity ratings and delayed ratings. Semantic similarity ratings may be regarded as measuring implicit personality theory, since people's beliefs about personality are encoded in the language of personality description. The studies using self-report questionnaire data showed a strong similarity between respondents' actual co-endorsement of items and people's beliefs about which items would be likely to be co-endorsed. This similarity may be understood if self-report data are regarded as the product of implicit personality theory: they require rating one's own behaviour after an interval between the actual behaviour and the rating and they may require an assessment of a disposition on the basis of a review of several behaviours on different occasions, both of which are likely to be influenced by implicit personality theory. The inconsistencies in one's own behaviour are just as likely to be subject to biased recall as are the inconsistencies in other people's behaviour.

Traits as Categories

In the previous section it has been asserted that the best explanation for the results of studies of the epistemological status of implicit personality theory, of the similarity between the lay perspective and the personality theorist's perspective, and of the biasing effects on memory, is to regard implicit personality theory as providing a set of categories for the understanding of personality which results in a reasonably accurate representation of reality. Throughout the previous discussion the issue of what is meant by reality has not been discussed. The philosophical stance adopted here is that there is a real world in which we operate, but our access to it is inevitably limited by the restrictions imposed by the human information processing system. Our view of the real world is therefore the product of the structures that exist in it and the way this information is filtered to us via perception and cognition.

In this section the view of traits as categories will be developed by relating the study of personality to theories and techniques typically found in cognitive psychology.

Personality traits are categorising concepts and therefore do not refer to directly observable events. Traits categorise particular behaviours performed in particular situations. They perform a necessary summarising function and provide a convenient shorthand for communicating about social behaviour. For example, instead of saying 'Carol is the sort of person who will greet a newcomer at work and show her round' we say Carol is friendly and helpful. Traits categorise both behaviours and the situations in which they occur. The situational element should not be underestimated; it is only possible to be friendly and helpful when there is a person in need of friendship and help, and these needs are often partially created by situational factors.

The significance of situational factors as components of traits is supported by studies of situational taxonomies (see Chapter 4) in which situations have been shown to be classifiable in terms of the behaviours that occur in them.

The constructivist position

The meaning of traits may be assumed to be encoded in terms of the behavioural and situational features to which they refer. Thus it is assumed that the meaning of traits is encoded in features which represent the cluster of attributes in the real world to which the trait is applied as a label. It is not being suggested that the traits themselves exist in the real world as observable events but rather that the cluster of behavioural and situational features to which they refer are observable events in the real world.

How does this view of traits cater for beliefs about trait relations and the epistemological status of these beliefs? Any two traits are likely to be believed to co-occur (and hence be semantically similar) to the extent that the behavioural and situational attributes to which they refer overlap. Each trait categorises a unique set of behavioural and situational real-world attributes, and hence its meaning is represented by a unique set of behavioural and situational features in semantic memory. However, given our rich language of trait description, there are many similarities between traits. Thus traits such as 'friendly', 'talkative', 'helpful' and 'sociable' are believed to have a high co-occurrence likelihood and are rated as semantically similar because these traits have a number of attributes in common. For example, they all require some form of social situation in which to occur since being friendly, talkative, helpful and sociable all require other people. These traits also all require communicative behaviour of a positive nature. These overlapping attributes increase the co-occurrence likelihood of these behaviours. It is likely that a person who is being friendly will also be helpful, and both these categories may themselves be categorised by the more abstract trait category of 'sociable'.

The sort of trait co-occurrence being described here is equivalent to one of the forms of behavioural consistency described in Chapter 4, namely type C consistency: different behaviours, same situation. The situation is essentially the same because it contains a person or people and the opportunity to approach them in a positive way. There are a number of forms this behavioural approach may take. Lay implicit personality theories and psychologists' personality theories assume that the same person will be characterised by the group of traits applicable to these behaviours in this situation. While this may not always be the case it forms a sound working hypothesis. Given that a person has arrived in a situation where there is an opportunity to perform one of the sociable behaviours, they are likely to perform several. Indeed, insofar as the traits are hierarchically structured, it will be impossible to perform only one, e.g. in order to be 'friendly' it is usually necessary to be 'kind' and 'helpful' and by being all those three the person is also being 'sociable'. Thus we have type C consistency.

Type C consistency refers to real-world consistency in the sense described above and forms the basis of the personality concept and its appraisal, both from the personality theorist's perspective and the lay perspective. All the other types of consistency are exaggerations of the real state of affairs. Thus, having observed people exhibit sociable traits in one situation, we erroneously assume they will exhibit them in another situation, either similar to the first or different, (types A and B consistency). We may even go so far as to predict a person's different behaviour in different situations (type D consistency) on the basis of overlapping attributes. For example, if a person was observed being talkative at a party, it may then be inferred that the person is a good public speaker since both activities require verbal fluency in the face of an audience. We know from the review of the relevant research in Chapter 4 that while type A consistency can be observed, types B and D are less reliable; and here we have further evidence for a well-documented phenomenon known as the *fundamental attribution error* (Ross, 1977). We tend to attribute characteristics to persons rather than situations, and hence to underestimate the importance of situations. When we assume types B and D consistency we are underestimating the importance of the situation variables and their control over behaviour, and exaggerating the importance of person variables. The personality concept has therefore been unwisely over-extended as a result of a characteristic error of human thinking. Nevertheless, its original foundation in type C consistency may be regarded as referring to a consistency which does have a basis in real life. Where personality trait ratings are concerned with type C consistency and are made with proper attention to reliability, they may be regarded as accurate representations of reality, because they are observations of genuine clusters of behavioural and situational attributes. The trait language is also an accurate representation of this reality. What we must remember is that traits are categorising concepts referring to both behavioural and situational attributes. Hence traits should not be treated as though they referred exclusively to people; they also refer to situations. Viewed in this way, 'personality' becomes a characteristic composed of both persons and situations, a construction based on the human information processor's observations of reality.

Having arrived at a new definition of personality which emphasises its constructive nature and gives it a rather insubstantial form hovering somewhere between the mind of the human observer and external reality, how is this phenomenon to be studied? The problem is not as difficult to resolve as it may first appear because it turns out to be a familiar one for cognitive psychologists. Personality is not the only aspect of the world to be apprehended via categorising concepts which to a certain extent construct the phenomenon being observed. The same is true even of the most straightforward objects such as tables and chairs. Psychologists have been aware for some time (Bruner, 1957) that the perception and understanding of the external world involves a categorisation process which serves to reduce and simplify a surfeit of stimulation. One of the earliest applications of this view of our understanding of personality is to be found in Kelly's theory of personal constructs (G.A. Kelly, 1955).

Kelly regarded models such as 'man the rat' (behaviourism) and 'man the computer' (information processing) as failing to pay attention to the fact that man actively seeks to understand and predict his environment. He is therefore more properly regarded as 'man the scientist'. The aspect of Kelly's theory of particular relevance here is the assumption that while the external world maintains an independent existence, human beings are only able to apprehend it indirectly via their perceptual and cognitive processes. As a result we build up a representation of that reality inside our heads, a representation which is composed of constructs; and these are used to make predictions about reality and hence to permit us to operate in it. Kelly proposed that constructs are bipolar: they contrast similar aspects of reality with dissimilar. We use constructs to categorise every aspect of reality, including other people and ourselves. For Kelly, an implicit personality theory can be described in terms of constructs. For example, I might have a construct 'kind–cruel' and, given a list of twelve friends and relations, I could arrange them in rank order from kind to cruel. This construct enables me to choose whom to go to for help and whom to avoid. Of course, I may have to modify my construct in the light of experience if, say, I encountered a friend who had to be cruel to be kind. I might then decide that 'kind–cruel' was too simplistic, failed to capture the full complexity of reality and hence did not give accurate prediction. Kelly's theory allows for such a process of continued modification of constructs, and the construct system as a whole is seen as interrelated and open to change. Although Kelly is ardently idiographic — we are each seen as having a unique set of constructs — he acknowledges that successful communication and social life rests on the correspondence between the way we each construe the world. In the personality domain, the findings from studies of implicit personality theory support the view that we share similar constructs for understanding and predicting each other's behaviour.

Kelly did not attempt to specify how constructs might be represented and stored in semantic memory, nor the mechanisms by which they might be called up and used to process incoming information. He was working before the rise of cognitive psychology and so it is not surprising that he did not think in these terms. Currently, the cognitive approach to the constructivist view of personality is much in vogue (Cantor and Mischel, 1979a). Recent developments in cognitive psychology have been applied successfully to personality with the result that we now have a better understanding of the categorising process effected by our beliefs about personality. In particular, this work has been able to shed light on when and how our beliefs about personality result in a biased perception of reality.

Cognitive studies of personality categories
In the main, the cognitive studies of personality categories have examined the effects of these categories on memory for personality information. The discussion of the studies in

Table 6.3 concluded that comparisons of immediate personality ratings and ratings from memory showed that memory has a distorting effect. Our beliefs about type C consistency are not always accurate for a particular individual's behaviour. There are several recent studies which suggest how these distortions might arise.

The work of Cantor and Mischel (1977, 1979a, 1979b) has borrowed extensively from Rosch's theory of object categorisation (Rosch, 1975, 1978; Rosch and Mervis, 1975; Rosch, Mervis, Gray, Johnson and Boyes-Braem, 1976).

In particular, Cantor and Mischel have made use of Rosch's concept of *prototypicality*. In object perception, prototypes form standards against which input is compared and around which it is organised. The prototype is the best exemplar of a particular category and incoming information is compared with this standard to determine how prototypical of the category the new instance is. For example, in a furniture store a shopper has to be able to distinguish between different categories of furniture in order to find out what he or she is looking for. This sounds easy and we do it all the time. Nevertheless you would probably agree that some items of furniture are better exemplars (or more prototypical) of their categories than others. Thus while a desk, at a pinch, belongs to the category 'table', an oblong pine kitchen table is unmistakably everything we mean by a table. The kitchen table is more prototypical of the table category than is a desk.

Variations in prototypicality come about because membership of object categories is not an all-or-none affair; instead, it depends on an object possessing a greater number of the distinguishing features of one category than those of another. For example (still in the furniture store) consider where the best place would be to locate sofa beds (i.e., sofas that can be converted into beds). They have many of the attributes of both the sofa category and the bed category, and therefore are extremely difficult to categorise. Similar problems occur in categorisation tasks involving natural object categories: we tend to think whales are fish and bats are birds.

Cantor and Mischel have proposed that categories for classifying people may be likened to categories for classifying objects. Person categories will be characterised by more or less prototypical members. The person categories they favour are widely held, stereotypical personality types such as the extravert, the door-to-door salesman or the rapist (Cantor and Mischel, 1979a). When presented with a new person, they argue that we compare this person's features with those associated with the prototypical member of the personality type to decide whether the new person belongs to the category. Once having categorised a person as a more or less prototypical member of a category, this will have implications for future information processing connected with this person. Specifically, Cantor and Mischel (1977) hypothesised that, if we have categorised a person as a prototypical member of a particular category, we will be biased to attribute (rightly or wrongly) all sorts of characteristics typical of that category to that person, beyond those characteristics we have been told about or observed. They tested this hypothesis in a recognition memory experiment in which subjects were presented with trait descriptions of fictitious targets and were later required to rate a list of traits in terms of how confident they were that the traits had appeared in the descriptions. There were four targets: an extravert described with several extraverted traits, an extravert control described with traits unrelated to extraversion, an introvert described with several introverted traits and an introvert control described with traits unrelated to introversion. The list of recognition traits for the extravert and extravert control targets contained some traits which had appeared in the original descriptions and some novel traits which varied in their degree of relatedness to extraversion. The recognition lists for the introvert and introvert control targets were similarly constructed with the novel traits varying in their degree of relatedness to introversion. Relatedness had been assessed previously in a trait rating task with different subjects. In addition to performing the recognition tasks, subjects also rated each target for how extraverted or introverted they seemed.

The ratings confirmed that subjects recognised two of the targets as being a prototypical extravert and a prototypical introvert and the other two as unrelated to extraversion and introversion. The results of the recognition task demonstrated that the prototypes extravert and introvert did have a biasing effect on memory. Although subjects recognised accurately which traits had appeared in the original descriptions, they also gave more confident recognition ratings to the novel traits highly related to the prototypes than to the less related or unrelated traits. These latter effects only occurred for the prototype targets and were not observed in the control targets. Their findings suggest how distortions observed in ratings from memory in the studies of D'Andrade (1974) and Shweder (1975) came about. Once the ratees had been categorised as prototypical of a certain personality type, the raters would tend to recall erroneously that the ratee possessed characteristics typical of that type, even if these characteristics had not in fact been observed.

Cantor and Mischel (1979b) confirmed and extended these prototypicality effects by varying the degree of prototypicality of the targets. They used a pure target described with all extravert or all introvert characteristics, a mixed target who appeared as partly introverted and partly extraverted, and an inconsistent target who had contradictory introvert and extravert characteristics. Subjects performed two recall tasks, immediate and delayed, in which they had to write down as much of the description as they could remember. They also wrote a short personality impression of each target. It was found that subjects recalled more information about the pure targets than the mixed or inconsistent targets. They also wrote more about the pure targets in their impressions. Cantor and Mischel concluded that the degree of prototypicality of a target with respect to a particular personality type category 'may indeed influence the ease with which information about that character can be encoded, retrieved and elaborated' (Cantor and Mischel, 1979b, p. 204).

A study by Lingle, Geva, Ostrom, Leippe and Baumgardner (1979) has demonstrated that the encoding, retrieval and elaboration of information about a person may be influenced by factors other than the prototypicality of that person with respect to a personality type. They argued that an impression of a person can be organised around a theme which influences subsequent information processing about the person. They borrowed from another area in cognitive psychology (the study of text processing and recall) where it has been shown that subjects remember texts more easily when they are supplied with an appropriate thematic title (Bransford and Johnson, 1972). The theme suggested by the title determines which facts will be recalled and the nature of further inferences made about the event described in the text. Lingle *et al.* hypothesised that themes would be correspondingly influential in the memory of personality impressions which are comparable in many ways to textual information.

In their experiments Lingle *et al.* manipulated the organising theme associated with the descriptions of the targets by having subjects make decisions about the targets' suitability for a particular occupation. After reading an eight-trait description of a target they rated the target's suitability for an occupation. Using this technique it was possible to vary the theme applied to the same target, e.g., one target was described with four traits suitable for a pilot and four traits suitable for a comedian. One group of subjects rated the target for suitability as a pilot and the other group for suitability as a comedian. Having read the descriptions and made the occupational ratings, subjects then recalled as many of the traits in the original description as they could and also wrote down additional traits they thought would be characteristic of such a person. It was found that subjects' recall for traits relevant to the occupational decision was better than their recall for occupational-irrelevant traits under both conditions of immediate and delayed recall. Subjects also produced more additional traits relevant to the occupational judgment than irrelevant.

In the experiments by Cantor and Mischel and Lingle *et al.*, the organisation of the personality description in memory was influenced at the time of presentation by manipulating the prototypicality of the target or the organising theme. In everyday experience with personality impressions we often encounter significant information about a person some time after we have formed our initial impression and, occasionally, this new information has a marked effect on our impression of that person. For example, two people may have been going out for several weeks before they get around to discussing, say, capital punishment, and if one person's views are in opposition to the other's, this may result in a reappraisal of their impressions of each other. This naturalistic observation suggests that the organisation of impressions in memory is not fixed but can be changed by the addition of new organising material at a later date. The possibility that past material can be reconstructed in this way was investigated by Snyder and Uranowitz (1978) in their study of sexual stereotypes. All subjects read the life history of a woman and were instructed to form an impression of her. The subjects were then divided into two groups: one group was told that the woman was a lesbian, the other that she was a heterosexual; half the subjects in each group were given this labelling information immediately after reading the life history and the other half one week later. All subjects returned one week later after reading the life history to answer a series of multiple-choice items on factual information in the life history. Some of these items referred to areas believed to be relevant to sexual preference such as whether the woman had been out with men when she was a teenager. Subjects' responses on these multiple-choice items revealed a significant effect of the sexual label regardless of when they received the labelling information. Thus subjects receiving the lesbian label made more errors reflecting stereotypic beliefs about lesbian life histories and subjects receiving the heterosexual label made more errors reflecting stereotypic beliefs about heterosexual life histories. Thus Snyder and Uranowitz had demonstrated that organising information can cause us to reconstruct an impression formed at an earlier date.

These examples of cognitive investigations into personality categories have demonstrated how the study of personality can benefit from borrowing cognitive methods and theories. One possible criticism of these studies is that, like so much of the cognitive research on which they are based, the link between their findings and what actually happens in everyday life is often tenuous. Such a criticism is, however, not strictly true in this case. Compare these cognitive studies with the earlier investigations of trait inference where subjects are required to infer the presence of additional traits on the basis of a brief given trait description. How often in real life do we ask ourselves questions such as 'Is a warm person likely to be happy?' We use our implicit personality theories more frequently to describe a person to someone else, or to make predictions which require recalling our impressions of a person and using them to make judgments. Therefore experiments concerned with how impressions are organised in memory and recalled are highly relevant to everyday life.

Conclusions

This chapter has been concerned with the accuracy of implicit personality theories. When people attribute personality traits to others are they describing what is actually there or are they imposing their own conceptual scheme on to the world? In the first section we saw how people's descriptions of others in the form of personality ratings have been variously interpreted by different investigators as measures of personality as it exists in the real world, measures of people's erroneous beliefs about personality, and measures of people's understanding of the meaning of the personality concepts they were rating. In the second section a number of studies attempting to determine what personality ratings do measure were described, and it was concluded that none of these studies succeeded in answering the question. Since the human observer does not have direct access to reality, any measures of personality are liable to contamination by the observation process. It was concluded that personality traits are most parsimoniously regarded as categorising concepts which refer to clusters of co-occurring behavioural and situational attributes which may be said to exist in the real world.

The third section described some studies exploring the implications of the view of traits as categories. These studies are comparable to those described towards the end of the previous chapter on the cognitive processes involved in impression formation. Both sets of studies have investigated the cognitive representation of people's beliefs about personality and the way personality-related information is processed.

A question running through the presentation of the lay

perspective over the last two chapters has been the extent to which the lay perspective is reconcilable with that of the personality theorist. The aim of the discussion has been to demonstrate how the investigation of the lay perspective has forced us to reappraise what we mean by the concept of personality. By concluding that personality is a valid concept if it is accepted that traits are categories encoding consistencies which do occur in the real world, it is possible to integrate the two perspectives. Thus our understanding of personality has advanced significantly by taking the lay perspective into account. Personality is best viewed as a construction of the observer and the observed.

The view of traits as categories is in accord with the personality theorist's perspective. Trait theories categorise the variety of personality data in terms of a small number of underlying dimensions. The logic is therefore similar to that of the lay perspective except that the personality theorist's perspective arrives at trait categories in an explicit manner with the aid of statistical tools such as factor analysis.

The next chapter will present the third perspective on personality, the self-perspective, and show how it too can contribute to the constructivist position.

7 The Self Perspective

In previous chapters we have seen how personality may be viewed as a construction derived from actual behaviour via an observer's perception of that behaviour and of the situation in which the behaviour takes place. This chapter is concerned with the special case where the observer and the observed coincide; that is, it is concerned with the perception of our own personalities.

To begin with, you will find below a series of ten statements describing a familiar personality constellation. Beside each one is a rating scale. You may find it interesting to read each statement and decide how accurately it describes you, marking the rating scale accordingly (1 = very inaccurate, 5 = very accurate). I suggest you do this before reading any further.

1 You have a great need for other people to like and admire you.   1 2 3 4 5
2 You have a tendency to be critical of yourself.
                                                                        1 2 3 4 5
3 You have a great deal of unused capacity which you have not turned to your advantage.   1 2 3 4 5
4 While you have some personality weaknesses, you are generally able to compensate for them.   1 2 3 4 5
5 Your sexual adjustment has presented some problems for you.   1 2 3 4 5
6 Disciplined and self-controlled outside, you tend to be worrisome and insecure inside.   1 2 3 4 5
7 At times you have serious doubts as to whether you have

made the right decision or done the right thing.

1 2 3 4 5

8 You prefer a certain amount of change and variety and become dissatisfied when hemmed in by restrictions and limitations.   1 2 3 4 5

9 You have found it unwise to be too frank in revealing yourself to others.   1 2 3 4 5

10 At times you are extraverted, affable, sociable, while at other times you are introverted, wary and reserved.

1 2 3 4 5

What did you decide? Probably you found some statements considerably more accurate for you than others. Calculate the mean accuracy score for all ten statements.

The statements do not, in fact, describe a familiar personality constellation in the strict sense since they are not the result of psychological investigation. These statements are a selection from those culled by Forer (1949) from a newsstand astrology book. He used them in the original study of what has now become known as 'gullibility'. He found that when people had been led to believe that these and similar statements formed their own personality profiles derived from a personality test, they regarded these statements as accurate descriptions of themselves. Typically, the statements were rated at around 3.5 on a 5-point scale. Since all Forer's subjects were given the same series of statements, the fact that they believed them to be accurate descriptions of their own personalities led Forer to the conclusion that people are gullible with respect to their self-perceptions. The implication is that people do not know themselves and are prepared to believe virtually anything they are told about themselves.

Of course, you knew from the outset that the statements were not a personalised description of yourself based on some form of assessment and this may well have lowered your ratings. Nevertheless, perhaps you considered that some of the statements were fairly accurate in describing you.

Do We Know Ourselves?

There have been several attempts at explaining why people find Forer's statements so acceptable: demand effects, social desirability, desire to be like others, and the perceived universal applicability of such statements. However, virtually all investigators have concluded that the high level of accuracy attributed to the statements reveals the inherent 'gullibility' of their subjects. It seems that when it comes to being told what we are really like we will swallow anything. Such a conclusion is frequently accompanied by a cautionary note on the use of clients' opinions in the validation of the clinician's assessment or interpretation of their problems. The gullibility studies are taken to imply that clients are likely to find acceptable anything with a ring of plausibility. It appears we do not know ourselves. This ignorance leads us to follow astrological forecasts, have our handwriting interpreted and our palms read and even, if we can afford it, to undergo psychoanalysis. All these procedures tell us something about who we are as well as what may happen to us. Apparently we need to be told who we are.

How does this disparaging view of self-knowledge square with the assumptions of the personality theorist's perspective? Traditional trait theorists such as Eysenck or Cattell believe that we are knowledgeable about ourselves. They assume that people can fill out a questionnaire without running into large gaps in their self-knowledge. People are even assumed to be so intimately self-knowing that they may try to paint an inaccurately desirable picture of themselves – hence the necessity for lie scales and social desirability checks. There seem to be two contradictory positions about the status of self-knowledge: the gullibility studies suggest that we are naive, whereas trait theorists have assumed a considerable degree of sophistication. However, a critical reappraisal of the gullibility studies suggests that the trait theorists' more complimentary view of self-knowledge is nearer to the truth.

The gullibility studies

None of the proposed explanations for the acceptability of Forer's statements have received adequate empirical support. Several studies have shown that demand effects do not explain the acceptance of fake personality descriptions. Ulrich, Stachnik and Stainton (1963) and Orpen and Jamotte (1975) found that varying the prestige of the experimenter had no effect on accuracy ratings. Even altering the demand characteristics of the test situation does not alter acceptability. Sundberg (1955) returned profiles composed of both genuine and astrological statements and asked his subjects to select which were *bona fide* and which were fake. They were unable to distinguish between the two types of statement beyond chance level.

Do subjects accept astrological-type statements because they express socially desirable qualities? This seems unlikely from mere inspection of some of the statements, e.g. difficulties with sexual adjustment are not usually seen as socially desirable! Hampson, Gilmour and Harris (1978) tested the social desirability hypothesis by obtaining accuracy and social desirability ratings of astrological statements and genuine statements derived from subjects' test scores on a personality inventory. They found that while astrological statements received the highest accuracy ratings they were regarded as the least socially desirable. These findings added to the conflicting results produced in previous research. Several studies have investigated what has become known as the 'Pollyanna' personality description (Thorne, 1961), so called because it contains entirely favourable statements. In some cases favourable descriptions are rated as being more valid than unfavourable descriptions (Weisberg, 1970; Collins, Dmitruk and Ranney, 1977) whereas no difference in acceptability between favourable and unfavourable descriptions has also been obtained (Dmitruk, Collins and Clinger, 1973). Several studies suggest that the effects of social desirability may be modified by the personality characteristics of the subjects concerned, e.g. Collins and Dmitruk (1979) found that unfavourable statements were rejected by repressors but accepted by sensitisers. Mosher (1965) found that high scorers on the Marlowe Crowne Social Desirability Scale (approval seekers) were more likely to accept favourable descriptions of themselves and less likely to accept unfavourable descriptions than low scorers.

If demand effects and social desirability cannot provide an adequate explanation of the acceptance of fake personality descriptions, perhaps people deserve being described as gullible after all. However, the accusation of gullibility contains two implicit assumptions: first, if we are gullible then it follows that we are unable to distinguish between true and false personality statements about ourselves: second, to accuse people of gullibility when they rate astrological statements as acceptable also implies that the astrological statement is itself inaccurate.

In experiments in which subjects rated the accuracy of personality profiles composed of genuine and fake personality test results in addition to astrological statements (Hampson, Gilmour and Harris, 1978), it was found that they were able to distinguish between the true and false statements about themselves and hence were not gullible. They gave significantly higher accuracy ratings to the genuine than the fake statements but, surprisingly, the astrological statements were perceived as being the most accurate. Since the subjects were not being gullible why did they find the astrological statements superior to the genuine ones?

Examination of the astrological statements indicates that they often refer to qualities shared by most people. When subjects were asked to rate genuine and astrological personality statements both in terms of accuracy for self and applicability to others, they regarded the astrological statements as more accurate and more applicable to others than the genuine statements. Hampson *et al.* thus concluded that people do not warrant being described as gullible. They are able to distinguish between true and false personality information and the repeated finding that astrological statements are regarded as more accurate than genuine information cannot be put down to the appeal of generality as such. It appears to reflect the fact that people are aware of the personality characteristics they share with each other and regard such information, when applied to themselves, as more reliable than information describing the ways in which they differ from other people. This interpretation suggests that the aspects of personality that interest psychologists are not the same as those that interest people in general. While psychologists are interested in what makes people different from one another, people in general are concerned about those aspects of their personality which they have in common with others.

The fact that people can fill out personality inventories and are able to distinguish between true and false descriptions of themselves does not tell us how they arrived at this self-knowledge. In the first part of this chapter we shall look at some theories concerning the status and origins of self-knowledge: what it means to know ourselves, what self-knowledge consists of and how it is obtained; then we shall go on to look at the significance of self-knowledge for subsequent behaviour. While it may seem from the reappraisal of the gullibility studies that self-knowledge is reliable, there is evidence from other sources that this is not always the case. Inevitably, therefore, much of the discussion will be concerned with the accuracy of self-perception.

Sources of Information About the Self

We possess the ability to stand back and observe ourselves even though we may not always be truthful about what we see. This reflexive quality of human nature has long been a source of fascination for both philosophers and psychologists. For some, it is this capacity to be aware of ourselves and regard ourselves as objects to ourselves that distinguishes man from the other animals.

Our self-observations can take several forms: we may attempt to perceive ourselves as we think others see us; we may attempt to observe our private thoughts and feelings and thus find out things about ourselves that would not be available to others unless we chose to tell them; and we may simply observe our own behaviour in the same way that we observe another person's behaviour and make inferences about the sort of person we are from these self-observations. The first form of self-observation, perceiving ourselves as we think others see us, assumes that other people constitute a major source of information about the self. In order to obtain self-knowledge, we find out how we appear to others. Such is the view of a school of thought known as symbolic interactionism.

Other people
Symbolic interactionism is primarily associated with the

names of Charles H. Cooley and George H. Mead. The 'symbolic' part of the term refers to the assumption that the environment should be regarded as consisting of objects whose significance lies in their social meaning. We are surrounded by a world of symbols, not a world of objects. 'Interactionism' refers to the fact that, via symbols, we are able to communicate with one another and to do this requires the ability to regard the world from another's perspective. The unit of analysis for symbolic interactionism is not an isolated individual but the interaction between two people: the self and the other. One of the results of interacting with another and taking the other's perspective is that the self is confronted with itself. It is in this way, argue the symbolic interactionists, that we are made aware of ourselves.

It was Cooley (1902) who aptly described the self-awareness derived from taking the other's perspective as the 'looking-glass' self. However, Mead is probably the best-known member of this tradition. Unlike most academics today who, unfortunately for their students, believe in the maxim 'publish or perish', Mead succeeded in becoming a highly acclaimed academic without writing a single book. He did, however, write several papers and it is through these and the books published after his death based on students' notes and previously unpublished manuscripts that it is possible for us today to learn about his conceptualisation of the self. Although he was a philosopher, he taught a course on social psychology and it was through giving these lectures that he developed his ideas on the self.

Mead believed that the essential quality of the self is that it is reflexive: the self can be an object to itself (Mead, 1934). We experience ourselves in the same way that we experience other people and objects in our environment. However, Mead argued, this experience can only come about through interacting with other people via the medium of language. It is by this process that we acquire a picture of ourselves referred to by Mead as the 'generalised other' which is the 'me' that 'I' am aware of. The generalised other is composed of other people's attitudes towards us. It is the product of socialisation: without interacting with others we would have no looking-glass in which to see ourselves. The self is therefore both social and socialised. By being made aware of ourselves through the attitudes of others we are aware of the effect our behaviour has on other people.

The self is composed of two parts, or phases, as Mead called them: the 'me' (the generalised other) and the 'I', and the 'I' reacts to the 'me'. The 'I' is the part of the self that decides how the 'me' will behave next. Once we begin to carry out the actions decided by the 'I', they immediately become part of our history, part of the 'me', so the 'I' can never be captured, it has always become part of the 'me' by the time we are aware of it.

The major contribution of Mead's theory of the self is his insistence on its social origins. Interaction with other people is essential for the development of the self. 'Selves can only exist in definite relationships with other selves' (Mead, 1934, p.164). This means that if a baby was abandoned on a desert island and miraculously survived to adulthood in the absence of human beings this person would have no self and would not be aware of itself. The sense of self, which feels so fundamental, is regarded by Mead not as an inherent property of human nature, but as the product of experience. Of course, we cannot test Mead's theory by depositing a baby on a desert island, but we may be able to draw some conclusions from those rare cases of children who appear to have been reared in the total absence of human beings. This strange occurrence has occasionally been documented.

One of the most detailed reports comes from India and concerns two girls who were believed to have been reared by wolves (Maclean, 1979). They were aged 3 and 6 years when they were first discovered. They were described as behaving in every way like their foster-parents the wolves. They ran on all fours, ate raw meat and howled. During the day they slept curled up together in a dark corner and at nightfall they would become restless and alert. They were fearful of human beings and ignored other children.

The Indian minister who found them tried to teach them language. Unfortunately, the younger girl died not long after they had been found and taken into his care, but the older girl did acquire a few words and learned to walk upright. Perhaps, as she began to interact with her new caretakers and learned to perceive her surroundings as possessing symbolic meaning, she began for the first time to experience the dawning of a sense of human selfhood. Tragically, she too fell ill and died before it would have been possible to discover whether this was indeed what had begun to happen.

Mead's insistence that the self depends on social inter-action suggests another intriguing possibility. In the past ten years advances have been made in teaching sign languages to chimpanzees. The Gardners, for example, brought up a chimp called Washoe as if she was a human infant and taught her the rudiments of a sign language (Gardner and Gardner, 1969). She became proficient at signing her material needs and preferences for toys and play companions. In making these signs she referred to herself, e.g. 'Washoe eat'. The claim made by the Gardners and other researchers, that they have succeeded in teaching their chimpanzees a language equivalent to a human language, has been challenged (e.g. Fodor, Bever and Garrett, 1974; Seidenberg and Petitto, 1979); nevertheless, this work does raise the possibility that in teaching language to a chimpanzee we may also be giving it a sense of self.

Symbolic interactionism regards the self as the product of language which, as a proposition about the nature of the self, is impossible to refute since we cannot interrogate an organism which does not have a language to find out whether it has a self. It also assumes that the self is an all-or-none concept: an organism is either linguistically sophisticated and self-aware or it is not self-aware. This restricted view does not permit the possibility that an organism could be self-aware in so far as it is capable of distinguishing between its physical self and its environment even though it may not be fully self-aware in the sense that it is capable of thinking about itself. Evidence for partial self-awareness is available for chimpanzees and pre-verbal human infants. This evidence is derived from studies in which the subject is shown its reflection in a mirror (it is confronted with its looking-glass self in the literal sense). There are two sorts of responses to mirror reflections: one is to treat the reflection as though it were another organism which is usually evidenced by the subject attempting some form of social behaviour with the reflection; the other is for the subject to recognise the correspondence between the reflection and the self. This recognition is evidenced by self-directed behaviour such as, in the case of the chimpanzee, grooming parts of the body which would otherwise be invisible.

In a study using two chimpanzees Gallup (1970) demonstrated that after prolonged exposure to mirrors (approximately 80 hours) the chimps would stop responding socially to the image and behave as though they recognised the correspondence between the reflection and themselves. To confirm this, Gallup anaesthetised the two animals and, while they were unconscious, he painted their eyebrow ridges and the tops of their ears with red dye. On regaining consciousness, the animals were observed for the frequency with which they spontaneously touched these parts of their bodies when no mirror was present. This base rate was then compared with the amount of touching that occurred in the presence of the mirror and it was found that there was a dramatic increase in touching of the dyed areas when the animals viewed themselves in the mirror. This finding confirmed that the chimpanzees were capable of self-recognition since they did not attempt to reach out and touch the strange red patches on the chimpanzee in the mirror but instead they touched the appropriate parts of their own bodies.

A similar investigation conducted on human infants is reported by Lewis and Brooks (1975). Instead of dye, the mothers dabbed rouge on their baby's face when pretending to wipe it. The rouge was applied to the nose and then the baby was placed in front of a mirror and observed to see if it would touch its nose. The babies ranged in age from 9 to 24 months and only the older babies (15–18 months and 21–24 months) showed evidence of self-recognition. Both these studies go against the symbolic interactionist position by demonstrating that organisms without language are capable of a partial form of self-awareness. However, it should be noted that Gallup was unable to observe any evidence of self-recognition in a lower species of primates (stump-tailed macaques and rhesus monkeys). Consequently, if it is conclusively established that chimpanzees are capable of acquiring language, then the symbolic interactionist position may be seen as being supported since it could be argued that physical self-recognition only occurs in animals capable of the more complete self-awareness involving language.

Symbolic interactionism proposes that other people are a major source of information about the self and this proposition is open to empirical investigation. If it is the case that our self-perceptions are based on the way we perceive others to perceive us, then a number of predictions may be made. First, there should be a high correlation between people's self-perceptions and their perceptions of the way other people see them. Second, there should be a high correlation between people's self-perceptions and others' actual perceptions of them. Third, there should be a high correlation between people's perceptions of how other people perceive them and how other people actually perceive them. Studies investigating these three predictions have been reviewed by Shrauger and Schoeneman (1979) who concluded that only the first prediction had received substantial empirical support: people's self-perceptions do correlate with their perceptions of how other people see them. There was no substantial support for a correspondence between people's self-perceptions and the way others actually see them, or for a correspondence between people's perceptions of the way others see them and the way others actually see them. Shrauger and Schoeneman point out that even if all three predictions had been supported, it still would not constitute conclusive support for the symbolic interactionist position since the direction of causal relations would remain unknown. Is it the way others see us and the way we think that others see us that causes us to hold certain self-perceptions? Or, conversely, does holding certain self-perceptions cause the way we are perceived by others and our perceptions of the way we are perceived by others?

The only way to determine the direction of causality is to study changes in self-perception, perception of other's perceptions and others' actual perceptions over time taking repeated measures of each of these viewpoints; unfortunately, this type of study has not been carried out. An approximation to it is to study the effects on self-perceptions of feedback about the self from others. Studies in the laboratory have

been able to manipulate the content of feedback and observe
its effects on self-perceptions. The general finding is that self-
perceptions are changed by feedback but, as Shrauger and
Schoeneman caution, the significance of these findings is in
doubt because the demand effects in self-perception are such
that subjects may feel obliged to report changes in self-
perceptions which may not have actually occurred.

The symbolic interactionist position claims that other
people are a major source of our self-knowledge and studies
have shown that it is only our perceptions of other people's
perceptions of us that tally with our self-perceptions. There is
a disparity between these perceptions and others' actual perceptions of ourselves. It seems that we as self-perceivers,
seeking information about ourselves from other people, have
a tendency to distort the facts. This distortion could be due
to the privileged access to past and present experience which
is granted to the self-perceiver. This additional information
may affect the self-perceiver's perceptions of the self and also
of others' perceptions of the self resulting in the disparity
between the self-perspective and the perspective of others.
Other people are not in possession of all the information
when they observe another and this inaccessible information
could form a large component of self-knowledge.

Privileged information

When we think about ourselves one of the questions we
frequently end up asking is 'Why did we do so and so?' Why
did we chose that job? Why did we quarrel with that friend?
Why did we like that book and not the other? These are also
the sorts of questions other people ask us in daily conversation. We may sometimes have difficulty in answering them,
but usually we are able to explain our preferences and behaviours in a way that is satisfactory to ourselves and others,
e.g. we chose the job because it paid well, we stopped seeing
the friend because of a political disagreement, we preferred
one book to another because it was better written. It is
generally assumed that we arrive at these explanations by
going over in our minds the factors which affected our
decision and the way we thought about them.

The assumption that we have access to the cognitive

processes which determine our thoughts and actions has recently been challenged by Nisbett and Wilson (1977). They have gathered together an impressive array of evidence from cognitive and social psychology which suggests that we do not have access to our higher cognitive processes. According to Nisbett and Wilson, we explain our behaviour by reporting our beliefs or theories about it rather than by analysing what actually occurs. Their evidence against introspective awareness is drawn from a range of previous literature as well as some experiments of their own. Much of the evidence comes from experimental social psychology, where the findings suggest that people are often unaware of the cognitive processes the experimenter has demonstrated to be responsible for a behaviour change. For example, in reattribution studies, attempts are made to change behaviour by causing subjects to change their attributions with respect to that behaviour (Storms and Nisbett, 1970; Valins and Ray, 1967; Zimbardo, Cohen, Weisenberg, Dworkin and Firestone, 1969). However, while the experimenters assume that the behaviour change is accompanied by a conscious appraisal of the reattribution process, post-experimental questioning of the subjects typically reveals that they are unaware of the stimuli controlling their behaviour and regard the experimenters' explanations as interesting theories but inaccurate for them.

This type of study is well illustrated by Storms and Nisbett's (1970) reattribution study with insomniacs. The distinguishing features of insomnia are physical symptoms such as rapid heart rate, breathing difficulties, feeling too warm, and mental alertness and activity. Storms and Nisbett hypothesised that if they could persuade their insomniac patients to reattribute these symptoms to some cause other than to the stresses and strains in their daily lives which they believed produced the insomnia, then they would be able to ignore the symptoms and get to sleep. In other words, by changing the subjects' cognitions about their symptoms, a behavioural change would follow.

To test this hypothesis, Storms and Nisbett studied three groups of insomniacs using estimated time to get to sleep as the dependent variable. Subjects in all three groups first reported the time it took them to get to sleep on two consecutive nights in the absence of experimental manipulations. Then, for the next two nights the three groups received different treatments. The arousal group was given a placebo pill to take just before going to bed and was told that the pill would produce rapid heart rate, breathing difficulties, body heat and mental alertness — all the symptoms of insomnia. The relaxation group were told that the pill would have the effect of reducing all these symptoms; and a control group was given the pill but not informed about its possible effects.

Storms and Nisbett predicted that the arousal group would get to sleep faster with the pill than without it, whereas the relaxation group would take longer to get to sleep when given the pill. Their argument was that the arousal group would re-attribute their symptoms to the pill's effects rather than to the difficulties they had experienced during the day. The relaxation group, on the other hand, would believe that their insomnia must be particularly bad if they were still ex-periencing all the symptoms in full even though they had taken a pill designed to reduce them. The results were in line with this argument: the arousal group got to sleep 28 per cent quicker on the pill nights whereas the relaxation group took 42 per cent longer. The control subjects reported no differences.

When the experimenters asked the experimental subjects why they had slept better or worse on the two pill nights, they did not explain the change in the same terms as the experimenters. The arousal subjects attributed their improve-ment to positive events in their daily lives such as having taken an exam that had been worrying them or having made up with their girl friend. The relaxation subjects would attri-bute their increased insomnia to equivalent negative events in their lives. When the connection between the pill and the changes in sleep patterns was pointed out, subjects were in-sistent that they had not associated the pills with their in-somnia and doubted if any of the other subjects would have explained the effects along the lines proposed by the experimenters.

The studies of helping behaviour provide another illustration of this phenomenon. It is a reliable finding (Latané and Darley, 1970) that a person is much more likely to go to the aid of someone in distress if the person is the only bystander; the more people present who could help, the less likely it is that any one of those people actually will help. However, when subjects were asked whether they thought their helping was influenced by the number of other bystanders, they strongly denied any such influence. Of course, they may be aware of the effect of other people and find it socially undesirable to admit to it.

On the basis of these and other studies, Nisbett and Wilson argued that we probably never have direct access to our cognitive processes. Having discredited the powers of introspection, they still had to give an account of why it is that people are capable of producing explanations for their behaviour and descriptions of their thought processes, even though these explanations and descriptions are often, though not always, inaccurate. Nisbett and Wilson suggest that the origin of such explanations and descriptions lies in *a priori* causal theories. These are theories about stimulus–response relations which are widely shared within a culture and may be derived from explicit rules, e.g. 'I was driving slowly because it was a built-up area'; or beliefs about our own and other people's behaviour, e.g. 'I am feeling happy today because the sun is shining'.

In some instances there may be no *a priori* theory in existence to provide an account of a particular situation. In this case, a person will cast around for the most plausible explanation and this search process will be open to the biases of human thinking uncovered by Tversky and Kahneman (1973, 1974; Kahneman and Tversky, 1973). For example, the representative heuristic results in people assuming the similarity between a stimulus and a response implies the two are causally related. *A priori* causal theories will not necessarily be wrong, but when they are right it cannot be concluded that introspection has been accurate but rather that by lucky accident the *a priori* theory coincided with the actual state of affairs.

Nisbett and Wilson's argument is disturbing: it suggests that we have areas of apparent self-knowledge about which we feel entirely confident and others find reasonable, but which are not the product of self-examination and are frequently grossly inaccurate. Such an anti-introspectionist view is extreme. Not only does it challenge the validity of the use of introspection in cognitive studies such as reports on problem-solving processes (e.g. Newell and Simon, 1972) or mental rotation (e.g. Shepard, 1975), but also it challenges the current trends in social psychology where more attention is being paid to people's own explanations of their behaviour (Harré and Secord, 1972) and current theorising in the area of therapeutic behaviour change where changes in abnormal behaviour are seen as the product of a change in the patient's cognitions (e.g. Bandura, 1977).

In presenting such an extreme view, Nisbett and Wilson have provoked strong reactions (e.g. Smith and Miller, 1978; Rich, 1979; White, 1980). Their most cogent critics have been Smith and Miller who, in addition to making methodological comments on Nisbett and Wilson's own studies, have put forward three major criticisms of their position. The first criticism is that Nisbett and Wilson have presented a position which is not open to refutation: it has been argued that people's self-reports on their mental processes are not usually correct but that even when they are, this is due to the lucky coincidence of the *a priori* theory with the actual state of affairs and is not due to accurate introspection. Stated in this way, the theory is unverifiable and Smith and Miller argue that the issue should be presented in a different and verifiable manner. Instead of claiming that people's introspections are never correct, the issue should be under what conditions, if any, are people's introspections valid.

The second major criticism made by Smith and Miller is that Nisbett and Wilson have not paid attention to the distinction between what subjects may regard as the cause of their behaviour, given their ignorance of experimental manipulations, and what the experimenter, who is fully cognisant of all the variables, regards as causing the subject's behaviour. This is particularly important where a between-subjects design has been used, as in the Storms and Nisbett study of insomniacs. Individual subjects did not know about the differential effects on the arousal, relaxation and control groups as did the experimenters and, in the absence of this knowledge and in the light of their own personal history of insomnia, it was not inaccurate of the subjects to relate the cause of the change in their sleep patterns to events in their daily lives rather than to taking the pills.

The third major criticism was directed towards Nisbett and Wilson's inadequate distinction between mental processes and mental content. They argued that while we have access to mental content, we do not have access to mental processes. However, it is hard to maintain such a distinction. Take, for example, Shepard's work on mental rotation where subjects are asked to imagine rotating a shape presented visually through, say 180 degrees (Shepard, 1975). Subjects can be stopped in mid rotation and asked to describe the appearance of the shape at that point. Will their introspections be concerned with content or process?

Despite the doubts about the viability of their extreme position, Nisbett and Wilson have demonstrated that subjects in certain social and cognitive experiments were unaware of the stimuli determining their behaviour and were unaware of their unawareness, although this ignorance seems less remarkable in the light of Smith and Miller's comments. However, Nisbett and Wilson do not deny that we do have access to mental contents such as memories of our past experiences and there must be situations in which our rich self-knowledge results in a better understanding of ourselves than is possible for an outside observer; for example, the idiosyncratic emotional reactions to places or people of special significance which are inexplicable to the observer, ignorant of this private information.

Nisbett and Wilson are not the only psychologists to have adopted an extreme position about the limitations of self-perception. While they claim we do not have access to our mental processes, Bem (1972) has claimed that, regardless of whether we have access to this information, we do not use it as a basis for our self-knowledge. Instead, we make use of the same information which is available to an observer in understanding ourselves.

Self-observations of behaviour

Bem's theory of self-perception is strongly influenced by Skinnerian behaviourism from which it derives an underlying assumption which at first seems to stand the world on its head. Skinner argued that we do not know about our internal states until we have learned to discriminate between them and label them. Statements such as 'I have a headache' or 'I feel depressed' appear, on the face of it, to refer to internal stimuli available exclusively to the speaker: the speaker knows that he or she feels depressed or in pain and makes a statement to that effect. But how do we know that what we are feeling, which is a private event, corresponds to what other people call depression or a headache? Skinner argued that statements referring to private events are learned in the same way that names for objects in the environment are learned: by pointing and naming. The child falls over and bumps his head and the mother comforts him saying 'There, there, you've got a headache now from bumping your head.' The radical assumption in such an analysis is that the problem for psychologists to explain is not why we are unaware of some internal states, but how it is that we are ever aware of any internal states at all.

Bem has developed Skinner's discussion of the acquisition of language for describing internal states to the whole area of self-perception. He argues that we do not rely on the private information available only to ourselves but we use the same external information available to everyone when we make inferences about ourselves. For example, to decide whether we are enjoying a comedy show on television, we observe how much we are laughing and how little our attention is wandering away from the programme. Similarly, if a market researcher stops us in the street and asks us which we prefer: tea bags or loose tea, we remember we always buy tea bags and conclude we must prefer them. In both these instances, an observer would have been able to assess our internal state as accurately as we could since the inferences were based on overt behaviours. Bem does not deny that the self-perceiver has access to private information, nor that this information plays a role in self-perception, but he does argue that it is used far less than we have assumed.

The first experiments to test self-perception theory involved the self-perception of humour (Bem, 1965). Bem hoped to show how a person's attitude towards cartoons could be changed by manipulating external cues. In the first part of the experiment, the subjects answered questions about themselves into a tape recorder. They were instructed to answer truthfully if an amber light was illuminated on the recorder and to lie if the green light went on. Thus the subjects learned to believe themselves in the presence of the amber light and to disbelieve themselves in the presence of the green light. To control for the possible effect of light colour, half the subjects received the reverse training. In the second part of the experiment, the subjects were shown a series of cartoons which they had previously rated as being 'neutral' (neither funny nor unfunny) and were told to say into the tape recorder either 'This cartoon is very funny' or 'This cartoon is very unfunny' depending on the experimenter's instructions. While they were speaking, either the amber or the green light would be on. Finally, the subjects rated the humorousness of the cartoons again. The results showed that the external cues, the coloured lights, had affected the subjects' subsequent ratings. They changed their attitudes significantly more for the cartoons where they had made the statement in the presence of the 'truth' light than in the presence of the 'lie' light. Bem concluded that the subjects had learned to believe what they said in the presence of the truth light and to disbelieve what they said in the presence of the lie light. When asked afterwards, subjects reported being unaware of the effects of the lights.

When it first appeared, self-perception theory was regarded as an alternative to cognitive dissonance theory and there were several studies attempting to compare the explanatory powers of these two accounts (e.g. Bem, 1967). (For a full discussion, see Mower White, in this series.) The aspect of self-perception which concerns us here is the account of the self-perception of personality dispositions. According to Bem's theory, we decide what sort of person we are in the same way as an observer decides, that is by observing our behaviour and making inferences from it. For example, ask yourself 'Am I a generous person?' If you have any hesitations in saying 'yes' or 'no' then you may find yourself remembering how you have behaved in previous situations where you could have exhibited generosity: did you buy a round of drinks at the pub the other day, or give some money to the person collecting for a charity? On the basis of your past behaviour, you assess whether or not you deserve the label of 'generous'.

It is a common reaction to feel uneasy about Bem's theory. After all, it is undeniable that from the standpoint of the self, we have a different perspective on ourselves from that of the observer; we are in possession of information of which the observer is ignorant. Since this is the case, how can Bem assert that we come to know ourselves in the same way that another person knows us: through behavioural observation? Bem's position becomes somewhat more acceptable if it is stressed that it was always intended as an explanation for self-perception under conditions of uncertainty; it is a theory about how we come to know ourselves when the 'internal cues are weak, ambiguous or uninterpretable' (Bem, 1972, p. 2). In other words, when the information about ourselves to which we have privileged access fails us, it is then that we, like other people, can only understand ourselves by examining how we behave. There is a sense in which Bem's position is similar to that of the symbolic interactionists, who argue that our self-concept is the result of our perceptions of how other people see us. When we refer to our behaviour to decide what we are like, we make the same inferences on the basis of that behaviour as another person would (e.g. people who give to charity are generous) and hence arrive at an opinion of ourselves that would, presumably, match the opinion of us that we would expect another to hold. The findings reviewed by Shrauger and Schoeneman (1979) on the correspondence between self-perceptions and our perceptions of how others see us lends indirect support to Bem's theory.

Having considered the three sources of information about the self that have received considerable theoretical and empirical attention, it is reasonable to conclude that self-perceptions make use of them all. In part, we perceive ourselves as we think others see us, even though this view may not always correspond to how others actually see us; we augment this knowledge with the private information about ourselves to which only we have access, although there are times when this information is either unavailable or misleading; when these two sources are inadequate, we turn to self-observations of our behaviour to arrive at self-understanding. The most noteworthy point to emerge from this discussion is the disparity between self-perceptions and others' actual perceptions of us. Perhaps in this disparity there lies an explanation for our fascination with obtaining other people's perceptions of ourselves, be they our friends, psychologists, psychoanalysts or astrologers. Since we can never truly be an object to ourselves and see ourselves as others see us, our perceptions of ourselves and others are inescapably seen through our own eyes. Occasionally our attention is drawn to the disparity between our self-perceptions and another's perceptions of us, giving us a tantalising glimpse of how we appear from another perspective. No wonder we are fascinated and desire the impossible: to step outside ourselves and take a longer look.

The Consequences of Self-Perception

While the debate continues as to the sources of information on which self-perception is based, much of the past and present research effort on the self perspective has been directed towards the consequences of self-perceptions for the self-perceiver's behaviour. Social psychologists have studied the consequences of self-perception from two contrasting viewpoints. Motivational approaches regard self-perception as responsible for self-serving biases which cause us to seek ways of raising our self-esteem and avoiding negative self-appraisal. In contrast, the cognitive approach regards self-perception as just one aspect of the total human information processing system, and any biases or distortions are not explained in motivational terms such as self-serving, but instead are viewed as the inevitable result of the structure and functioning of the human information processing system. Both motivational and cognitive approaches aim to describe the consequences of self-perception typical for most people. However, the role of self-perception in the production of individual differences in behaviour has also been studied and will be discussed.

Motivational consequences

A currently influential motivational theory of the consequences of self-perception is the theory of objective self-
awareness proposed originally by Duval and Wicklund (1972)
and subsequently modified by Wicklund (1975, 1978). The
key propositions may be summarised as follows. Attention at
any one moment is assumed to be either directed wholly
towards the self or wholly towards external events. When
attention is self-directed, discrepancies between the ideal
and actual self are bound to emerge. These discrepancies will
give rise to feelings of negative affect which will motivate the
person to overcome the discrepancy in one of two ways:
either by behaving in such a way as to narrow the gap between the actual and ideal self, or by disregarding the discrepancy through avoidance of the state of objective self-
awareness.

As originally stated, Duval and Wicklund's theory proposes
that there is always a negative discrepancy between our
aspirations and our actual performance: on close self-examination we will always regard ourselves as failures. Even those
rare moments of positive evaluation where, for once, our
actual achievements have outstripped our ideals and aspirations will only give us brief satisfaction. Almost at once we
will adjust our aspiration level to exceed our recent success,
thus returning us to the normal state of negative evaluation
(Wicklund, 1975).

The same essentially negative view of the consequences of
self-perception is to be found in attribution theory, where a
phenomenon variously termed ego-defensive, ego-protective
or ego-biased attribution has been extensively investigated
since first being noted by the early theorists (Heider, 1958;
Jones and Davis, 1965; Kelley, 1967). The research has been
primarily concerned with situations involving positive and
negative outcomes such as achievement tasks and teaching.
The typical finding is that subjects are more likely to attribute successful performance to characteristics within themselves, e.g. persistence, intelligence, etc., while failure is
attributed to external factors beyond their control such as
luck or some feature of the situation. A well-known experiment in this area is a study of arithmetic teaching by Johnson,

Feigenbaum and Weiby (1964) in which they asked subjects to teach two pupils how to multiply by ten. They were given work sheets indicating that pupil A had done well on the task but that pupil B had done badly, (in fact there were no real pupils in the experiment). Next, the subjects were asked to teach the same two pupils to multiply by twenty and again pupil A appeared to have done well but the feedback for pupil B indicated either a good or poor performance. On subsequent questioning, the subjects who had been led to believe that pupil B had improved tended to attribute this improvement to their good teaching whereas the subjects who had been led to believe that pupil B had continued to perform poorly attributed this to B's inadequacies. In motivational terms, these and other findings indicate that we have a tendency to distort our world view in order to maintain or enhance our self-esteem. Both objective self-awareness and ego-defensive attribution assume that self-perception has motivational consequences which result in behaviour designed to preserve self-esteem. The implication is that such self-serving behaviour will prevent a person from obtaining veridical feedback, one consequence of which may be the perpetuation of a distorted or biased self-perception.

Cognitive consequences
The information-processing approach to self-perception provides an alternative explanation of the so-called distortions and biases of self-perception (Miller and Ross, 1975). It views them as inevitable products of the human information processing system. Instead of regarding us as constantly striving to bolster up a crumbling positive self-image, this approach reinterprets biases as the legitimate product of a system built to process information in a particular way which, while occasionally producing errors, is generally reasonably effective. The cognitive view of self-perception has been developed within an attributional framework. When we inquire into the causes of our own behaviour we carry out the three attributional tasks (Ross, 1977): we decide between situational and dispositional factors in the causes of our behaviour; we may infer the presence of additional dispositions, and we may make predictions about our future

behaviour. In contrast to the motivational approach which has also made use of an attributional framework, the cognitive approach has developed rational models of self-attributions, be they veridical or biased.

As with the motivational consequences, it is the cognitive consequences of self-perception that result in biases or distortions that are of particular interest here. The cognitive biases that have been observed in self-attributions are the fundamental attribution error, the false consensus bias and role bias. The most common of these is the fundamental attribution error which is the tendency to underestimate the role of situational factors and overestimate the role of dispositional factors in the causation of behaviour (Heider, 1958). An important variant on this bias is the actor–observer distinction. Jones and Nisbett (1971) argued that actors and observers differ with respect to their susceptibility to the fundamental attribution error. When we are asked the reasons for our own behaviour (i.e. when we are the actors) we tend to stress situational factors as causal, whereas when we are asked to explain another person's behaviour (i.e. when we are observers) we tend to stress dispositional factors in our explanations. Jones and Nisbett proposed that the discrepancy may be due to the different perspectives taken by actors and observers: for the actor, features in the situation are more salient, whereas for the observer, the actor is more salient. An experiment by Nisbett, Caputo, Legant and Maracek (1973) illustrates the operation of the actor–observer distinction: they found that male students explained their best friends' choice of girl friend in terms of the dispositional qualities of the best friends, whereas they described their own choice of girl friend in terms of her dispositional qualities. Thus in their own relationships, where they are actors, they explain their behaviour in situational terms (the girl friend's qualities), but for their best friends' relationships, where they are observers, they explain their best friends' behaviour in dispositional terms.

Ross (1977) argues that the actor–observer discrepancy may be explained in terms of another attribution error: the false consensus bias. We tend to see our own behaviours and attitudes as relatively common, normal and appropriate and to see alternative behaviours and attitudes as relatively uncommon, deviant and inappropriate. The false consensus bias is an important consequence of self-perception because it suggests that the way we see ourselves affects our views of others. Evidence for the false consensus bias was reported by Ross, Greene and House (1977). In one of their experiments they presented students with questionnaires containing four brief stories culminating in a behavioural choice. The subjects were asked to indicate how they would respond and also to estimate what proportion of their peers would respond in the same way as they had. For example, one story asked you to imagine that on leaving the local supermarket you are stopped by a man who asks you for your opinion of the shop. You reply favourably and the man then reveals that he has videotaped your response and asks permission to use it in a TV commercial. Your task is to choose whether or not to give permission and to estimate the proportion of your peers who would reply in the same way as you had. After making the behavioural choices, subjects were then asked to rate themselves on a series of personality traits, and to rate a typical peer who would have chosen the same option as they had and a typical peer who would have chosen the other option. The results showed that the subjects estimated that a higher percentage of their peers would choose in the same way as they had, and the traits ratings showed that subjects made more confident ratings about the typical person who would have chosen differently from them than for the typical person who would have chosen the same. Ross, Greene and House (1977) have demonstrated a bias towards perceiving a false consensus: subjects regarded their choices as relatively common and normal and hence not particularly informative of personality characteristics. In contrast, a person who chose differently from the subject was perceived as behaving in a relatively deviant and uncommon way which permits more confident personality inferences to be made.

The false consensus bias may be used to explain the actor-observer distinction in the following way. We regard our own behaviour as relatively normal and common and hence not particularly informative of personality dispositions — therefore we tend to explain our own behaviour in situational terms. However, when we observe someone behaving differently from the way we would have behaved in a particular situation we attribute the behaviour to personality traits rather than situational factors. Since this is bound to happen on some occasions we will inevitably see our peers as possessing more numerous and more extreme personality characteristics than ourselves.

The final bias to be discussed is the effect of social roles. Information about ourselves is obtained mainly in social interactions and these are frequently governed by the constraints of the roles adopted by the participants. Our perceptions of ourselves and others become biased when we ignore the fact that, in part, behaviour is a product of the social role, and wrongly attribute it in entirety to internal dispositions. Ross, Amabile and Steinmetz (1977) demonstrated role bias by assigning subjects at random to the role of questioner or contestant in a quiz game. The questioner was instructed to think up a difficult question from his own general knowledge to ask the contestant and to give the correct answer if the contestant was wrong or could not answer. The social roles therefore endowed the questioner with all the advantages and the contestant with all the disadvantages. The participants were subsequently asked to rate themselves on the level of their general knowledge. The questioners rated their general knowledge as higher than that of the contestants and this discrepancy was also displayed in the contestants' ratings and in the ratings of uninvolved observers. Ross, Amabile and Steinmetz argue that their experiment is a particularly strong measure of role bias since the advantages and disadvantages of the two roles were so blatant, and assignment had clearly been arbitrary. Nevertheless, contestants were led to perceive themselves as more ignorant than the questioners even though, if the roles had been reversed, the erstwhile contestants could have had the erstwhile questioners feeling equally ignorant.

The consequence of role bias for self-perception is that we may attribute characteristics to ourselves which are inevitable products of our roles and therefore uninformative of personal dispositions. Nevertheless, our sense of self is inextricably bound up with our social roles; for many of us our social role is a significant part of our identity, e.g. 'I am a teacher', 'I am a mother', 'I am a student.' In real life we are likely to choose roles for ourselves which require the kinds of behaviours for which we are dispositionally suited. So, as with many of the information processing biases, there is an element of rationality. It is reasonable to expect that you will be characterised by a number of traits that your self-appointed role exhibits. Where the bias creeps in is when the role is arbitrarily conferred or where it prescribes certain behaviours that do not necessarily correspond with the role-player's personality.

The motivational and cognitive consequences of self-perception which have received the most attention have been those which result in biases or distortions. There is a tendency for the studies to give the impression that, having demonstrated the operation of a bias and having given it a name such as 'self-serving' or 'false consensus', these biases have also been explained. Ross (1977) even argues that one bias, the false consensus bias, can explain another: the fundamental attribution error. However, by merely documenting these consequences of self-perception, investigators have not explained them and certainly explaining one bias in terms of another does not advance our understanding of how they come about. A recent line of research which may prove more fruitful in this respect is exemplified by the work of Markus.

Markus (1977) borrowed the terminology and techniques of cognitive psychology to aid in the understanding of self-perception in much the same way that Cantor and Mischel (1979a) have done in their investigations of the perception of others. She proposes that information about the self is organised into cognitive structures referred to as self-schemata. A self-schema is a generalisation which developed as a result of past experience and is used in subsequent processing of self-relevant information. For example, a person's knowledge about how generous or mean he or she has been in a variety of situations in the past will become summarised in a generosity schema in which the person's self-perception is one of either generosity or meanness or, if generosity has never been of relevance to the person, no schema will be present and the person can be described as aschematic in this respect. For those with schemata, their presence will have consequences for the way subsequent information related to generosity is processed.

Markus tested the hypothesis that self-schemata have consequences for the processing of self-relevant information by comparing female students with and without self-schemata with respect to dependence–independence. The presence or absence of this self-schema was estimated from three converging sources: self-ratings on this dimension, ratings of the importance of this dimension for the subjects, and checking 'dependent' or 'independent' on an adjective check-list. On the basis of these data, Markus was able to identify subjects with dependent self-schemata, independent self-schemata and those who were aschematic. In a range of experiments she then demonstrated how these groups processed information related to dependence–independence in different ways. For example, in a reaction time experiment, dependent subjects were faster to decide whether dependent traits were self-relevant than independent traits; for independent subjects the reverse pattern of reaction times was obtained and for aschematics there was no difference in reaction times for the two types of traits.

Markus's work represents an interesting development for two reasons. First, she has shown how a certain amount of substance can be given to rather vague notions of self-concept or self-perception by postulating the existence of cognitive structures which serve as information-processing categories and whose effects on subsequent information-processing can be predicted. Second, by specifying more precisely the mechanisms underlying self-perception, she has provided an explanation of individual differences in the processing of self-relevant information by showing how self-schemata may differ or even be absent. It is to individual differences that we now turn.

Individual differences in self-concept
So far this chapter has been concerned with the nature of self-knowledge, how it is obtained, and some of the consequences of self-knowledge for behaviour. These are questions

which apply to people in general and do not form the basis for making distinctions between them. However, self-perception has been used specifically as a means of differentiating between individuals. The aspect of the self-concept that has been used to this end is self-esteem and one approach to investigating the consequences of self-perception is to study how people's level of esteem affects their behaviour.

When we engage in self-examination we frequently find ourselves comparing the sort of person we think we probably are with the sort of person we would ideally like to be. If there is a reasonably close match between our actual self and our ideal, we will be content. However, if there is a discrepancy we will feel discontented and tense; if the mismatch is large, serious depression or anxiety may develop. Such is the view of one of the most influential writers on the self: Carl Rogers.

As a result of a lifetime's experience as a psychotherapist, Rogers developed a personality theory in which the self plays a central role and individual differences are described in terms of the self. The chief constructs in the theory are the organism and the self (Rogers, 1959). The organism refers to the person as a subjective perceiver of reality; it is the locus of personal experience which Rogers terms the phenomenal field. For Rogers, personal experience has an authenticity unequalled by any other information source, be it the views of significant others or the findings of scientific investigations. If something feels good to the organism, then it is good. As he says of himself: 'Experience is, for me, the highest authority' (Rogers, 1961, p.23).

The self is an important element of a person's subjective experience or phenomenal field: it refers to that aspect of a person's phenomenal field which consists of that person's subjective experience of him or herself. In experiencing oneself, evaluations by others will be added to that experience and the resulting self concept may become distanced from the organism because, while the organism may find a particular experience good, the self may reject it. In this event, an incongruence between the organism and the self will develop which will be threatening and anxiety-provoking for the person. In addition to a person's self concept, there is also an ideal self which represents how the person would really like to be. Incongruence between the self and the ideal self is also threatening and anxiety-provoking. In his non-directive approach to psychotherapy, Rogers's aim is to provide a supportive environment in which the client will feel able to explore the experience of the organism and achieve a harmony between it, the self and the ideal self (Rogers, 1961). This harmony provides the opportunity for personal growth.

While much of the evidence for Rogers's views is clinical in nature rather than experimental, he has never been disparaging about the value of scientific inquiry; as he says, 'The facts are friendly' (Rogers, 1961, p.25). In evaluating Rogerian non-directive therapy, techniques of studying the therapeutic process have been developed which are widely used today. Of more relevance here is the investigation of the self-concept and its state of congruence or incongruence with the organism and the ideal self. For this purpose, Rogers used Q technique (Stephenson, 1953). The subject is given a set of cards on each of which is written a descriptive statement that can be applied to the self, e.g. 'I express my emotions freely', 'I often feel humiliated'. The nature of the statements can be varied to suit the aims of the investigation. The task is to sort the cards into piles ranging from a pile for those statements 'least like me' to those 'most like me'. Subjects can be asked to sort the cards according to how they perceive themselves (the self) or how they wish themselves to be (the ideal self). The two sortings can then be correlated to obtain a measure of congruence, which is sometimes referred to as self-esteem. Using this technique, changes in self-esteem have been observed during the course of therapy (Butler and Haigh, 1954; Rudikoff, 1954).

The congruence between the self and the ideal self provides a measure which may be used to differentiate between individuals and predict differences in behaviour. Variants of the actual self versus ideal self definition of self-esteem have been used by a number of personality theorists and clinicians (e.g. Kelly, 1955; Sullivan, 1953).

An alternative approach to the assessment of self-esteem for the purpose of predicting individual differences in behaviour is to use a questionnaire intended to measure it directly. A popular one of this kind, as indicated by the number of references cited in Buros (1975), is the Tennessee Self Concept Scale. It consists of a hundred items covering different aspects of the self such as physical self, moral-ethical self, personal self, family self and social self. The test yields a total score which is regarded as a measure of self-esteem and also an estimate of the consistency between the different aspects of the self. The Tennessee Self Concept Scale has been used with some success in a variety of contexts. For example, delinquents are typically found to have low self-esteem, although it may be somewhat naive to accept these data at face value.

The measurement of individual differences in self-perception begins to merge imperceptibly with the measurement of personality as advocated from the personality theorist's perspective. Whenever a person fills out a self-report personality questionnaire such as the EPI or the I–E scale, that person is providing the investigator with an assessment of his or her self concept with respect to the dimensions in question. Self-report data are self-perceptions and hence can be regarded as assessments of the self concept. As such, they are vulnerable to all the inaccuracies and distortions discussed in this chapter. However, to acknowledge that questionnaire data are self-perceptions is not to dismiss them as invalid for, as we saw in Chapter 6, a truly objective measure of personality is probably unobtainable, and personality should be regarded as a construction involving a number of different perspectives, including the self perspective. Since self-perceptions can have consequences for behaviour they are legitimate objects for study and are properly regarded as an aspect of personality.

In conclusion, it is interesting to note that the fascination with the self and hence with individual differences is a phenomenon peculiar to Western cultures. Evidence from other cultures suggests that the self concept receives far less emphasis. Data of an anthropological nature collected by Luria during the 1930s but not reported until recently suggest that illiterate Russian peasants living in remote villages did not possess self concepts of a psychological nature

(Luria, 1976). In reply to a question such as 'Are you satisfied with yourself or would you like to be different?' the peasants would respond in terms of their material achievements and material aspirations by saying, for example, 'It would be good if I had a little more land and could sow more wheat.' For these peasants, their sense of self was confined to an evaluation in terms of material, rather than psychological, well-being. This is perhaps not surprising in a preliterate society where the daily struggle for physical survival was the foremost consideration.

The absence of a psychological sense of self has also been observed in a literate and rapidly industrialising country: present-day China. We in the West believe that each individual has a private self which is not necessarily available to change by outside intervention; we recognise that people sometimes behave in ways contrary to their private thoughts and feelings and we respect this privacy. In complete contrast, the Chinese concept of man has no room for a private self (Munro, 1977). Since all thoughts are regarded as being promptings to act, thoughts are inevitably made public through behaviour. Since behaviour has social consequences, the State is responsible for both behaviour and thought and hence an individual's sense of self is public and available for change. It is difficult for someone socialised in a Western culture, for whom the sense of a private, inaccessible sense of self seems an inevitable consequence of being human, to appreciate that this sense is absent for the modern-day Chinese. Thus, for a Chinese student, this whole chapter on the private self would seem a baffling misconception.

The Three Perspectives on Personality

Over the present and preceding chapters three perspectives on personality have been presented: that of the personality theorist, the lay person and the self. It has been argued that none of these perspectives may be regarded as more accurate than the others and therefore the most complete representation of personality is likely to be obtained by combining all three views. The description obtained by the personality theorist from a personality test may be modified by a person's own assessment of their personality (self-perspective) and the opinions of others (lay perspective). Unfortunately, owing to the discipline boundaries drawn around each perspective, it is rare to find studies which have attempted to construct a view of personality using all three kinds of information and which would therefore support this argument. However, one such example of the use of the constructivist approach is the study of the cross-situational consistency of traits by Bem and Allen (1974). This study has already been mentioned in Chapter 4 but it is appropriate to introduce it again to illustrate the power of the constructivist approach.

Bem and Allen studied the cross-situational consistency of friendliness and conscientiousness by correlating several different measures which they regarded as measuring the traits in different situations. These measures included self-assessment, questionnaire scores, parental and peer ratings. The important aspect of the self-assessment was that it included an assessment by the subjects of how cross-situationally consistent they believed themselves to be. They were asked 'How much do you vary from one situation to another in how friendly/conscientious you are?' The subjects were then divided into a high variability group (i.e. not consistent) and a low variability group (i.e. consistent) on the basis of the self-assessments. It was found that for the low variability group, who perceived themselves to be cross-situationally consistent, the correlations between the different measures of the traits were high. In contrast, for the high variability group, who perceived themselves as inconsistent, the corresponding correlations were low. If Bem and Allen had not looked at self-perceived consistency but had analysed the group as a whole they would have obtained generally low correlations suggesting that people are not consistent on these traits.

Bem and Allen viewed parental and peer ratings as measures of the traits in different situations. An alternative view, in line with the present argument, is to regard them as measures from another perspective, the lay perspective. For the trait of friendliness Bem and Allen had data available from all three perspectives because, in addition to the ratings and to the self-assessments of consistency, they also obtained extraversion scores on the EPI which may be regarded as an index of the personality theorist's perspective on friendliness. Bem and Allen report the correlations for the high and low variability groups between their extraversion scores and the overall self-assessment on the trait, the parental and peer ratings. Here we have a direct comparison of the three perspectives. The correlations (see Table 7.1) demonstrate that without the input from the self-perspective (the distinction between low and high self-perceived variability) the correlations between the personality theorist's perspective (the EPI scores) and the lay perspective (parental and peer ratings) would have been lowered substantially.

Table 7.1 Correlations between high and low variability subjects' extraversion scores and other measures of extraversion obtained from other perspectives (from Bem and Allen, 1974)

Extraversion versus:	Self-rated variability	
	Low	High
Self-report (overall)	0.77	0.65
Mother's report	0.54	0.37
Father's report	0.26	0.24
Peer's report	0.71	0.41

Thus by making use of all three perspectives, a considerably more accurate assessment of personality was obtained in the sense that it was predictive of actual behaviour. In the next two chapters, we shall examine how far a constructivist approach is helpful in the understanding and prediction of personality over the life-span (Chapter 8) and deviant personality (Chapter 9).

8 Personality over the Life-Span

In the preceding chapters three perspectives on personality have been presented: that of the personality theorist, the lay person and the self. The present chapter is concerned with the application of these three perspectives to the study of personality over the life-span. So far it has been shown how these three perspectives are used to study personality at one particular moment in time; but personality, like any other psychological or physical characteristic, cannot be assumed to be static. The main concern of life-span research in personality has been to try to establish how much personality changes over a person's life and to what extent it remains stable. While we would all agree that the personality of a man of 50 will be different from his personality as a 5-year-old boy, we would also acknowledge that the child is father to the man. There is both continuity and change.

The three perspectives have been applied both separately and in combination in life-span research. Each perspective may be likened to a film camera recording personality from its own particular angle. Let us imagine that the three cameras are filming constantly and, at any point in time, we can stop any or all of the cameras and study a still photograph from each, or even a composite photograph built up from a combination of two or three perspectives. Such has been the case in the previous chapters where only what may be described as personality stills from one time point have been studied. In the investigation of personality over the life-span, a series of stills from one or more cameras taken at different time points may be used; or, more dramatically, the cameras may be left to roll and the continuous moving picture may be studied. Most life-span research may be categorised as either the product of the personality theorist's perspective or as the product of a combination of all three; there is little work which may be viewed as representing the self perspective and even less that could be categorised as making sole use of the lay perspective. Accordingly, this chapter will concentrate primarily on the personality theorist's research and on studies involving a combination of perspectives.

From the personality theorist's perspective (e.g. Eysenck, Cattell) the aim of life-span research has been to demonstrate continuity in its strongest form: that personality, once formed, remains stable. The stability of traits over time and across situations is the central assumption of the personality concept, as we saw in Chapter 4. To demonstrate intra-individual consistency over time intervals as long as years or even decades would be a real triumph. Life-span studies which have adopted a more constructivist approach by making use of data obtained from a combination of perspectives have tended to be less committed to continuity and are more willing to countenance change. In particular, the constructivist approach has favoured the view that personality proceeds through a series of developmental stages which continues right through the life-span and which may necessitate change in order to be negotiated (e.g. Erikson, 1963). Instead of focusing on particular personality traits, the constructivist approach considers the whole person as perceived from two or more perspectives.

Life-span research, irrespective of its ruling perspective, has a choice of three main classes of research designs: longitudinal, cross-sectional or sequential. Each type of design raises its own particular methodological problems (Nunnally, 1973; Schaie, 1965, 1973) and therefore, in order to be in a position to evaluate the studies to be described later in the chapter, the first section will describe these designs and their attendant advantages and disadvantages.

Research Designs in Life-Span Psychology

Life-span psychology is concerned with mapping the changes that occur in psychological characteristics, particularly intellectual and personality variables, as individuals grow older (Baltes, Reese and Lipsitt, 1980). It is therefore a forward extension of developmental psychology, which has traditionally only been concerned with development during childhood and adolescence and has regarded the biologically mature adult as of no further interest. Life-span psychology, with its stress on the adult years, may also be seen as a backward extension of gerontology which has picked up the developmental story in old age to study the decline of physical and psychological powers. Life-span psychology does not regard development as a journey towards an end state of maturity in the biological sense beyond which, like the fading of a prize bloom, it is downhill all the way. Instead, no distinction is made between development and ageing: life-span psychology regards the human being as continually developing from birth to death.

The purpose of life-span psychology is to study developmental change, the aims being to describe the changes and to explain them. Usually the investigator wants to explain developmental change in terms of age, but often there are methodological weaknesses in the research design which prevent a confident explanation in terms of age alone (Nunnally, 1973; Schaie, 1965, 1973). There are three factors which could explain developmental change (Schaie, 1965): ageing, the nature of the cohort and time of measurement. Ageing refers to the amount of time elapsed from the birth of the organism to the point in time of the investigation. The term 'cohort' refers to the total population of individuals born at approximately the same point in time, which is usually taken to mean born during the same calendar year, e.g. everyone born in 1960 belongs to the 1960 cohort. Time of measurement refers to the total environmental impact acting on the individuals being investigated at the time of the study. Time of measurement is, probably, the most difficult of the three factors to grasp. As time goes by two things may be said to be happening: people are growing older (the age factor) and the world they experience, their environment, is changing. At any moment in time a particular constellation of environmental factors will impinge upon the individual: the world in 1980 is different from the world in 1970, it will be different tomorrow from the way it is today. Time of measurement is a shorthand term suggested by Schaie (1965) to sum up this notion of the impact of the current environment.

The difficulty facing life-span researchers is to sort out which of these three factors is the source of an observed developmental change. Before a change may be attributed to age the effects of cohort and time of measurement must be ruled out. None of the research designs are entirely successful in this respect and hence it is important to know where each succeeds and fails. The strategy adopted by longitudinal and cross-sectional designs is to keep one of the factors constant thus leaving the other two free to vary. As a result, the explanation of an observed developmental change is always problematic because of the confounding of two of the three factors. Confounding is the primary methodological problem of these two designs. In addition, they each also suffer from a secondary problem created by holding the third factor constant. In each case, by ruling out the effects of one factor these effects remain unexplored and therefore the findings cannot be generalised beyond the one condition investigated in the study.

Longitudinal designs

In longitudinal studies the same group of individuals is studied over an extended period of time. Generally the group is not studied continuously but is measured on the variables under investigation at various points in time. The group may be established initially at any age and studied for as short or as long a time as is appropriate for the variables in question. For example, in the longitudinal research carried out at the Fels Institute (Kagan and Moss, 1962), the subjects were contacted in their first year of life and studied through to their mid 20s; in the longitudinal research carried out by the Institute for Human Development, Berkeley (Block, 1971) the subjects have been followed up from school to mid life. Longitudinal designs are represented by the rows in Table 8.1.

Table 8.1 Age of cohorts measured at six ages with annual measurement intervals indicating the variety of life-span research designs (adapted from Schaie, 1973)

Cohort		Time of measurement				
		A 1975	B 1976	C 1977	D 1978	E 1979
1954	1	21	22	23	24	25
1955	2	20	21	22	23	24
1956	3	19	20	21	22	23
1957	4	18	19	20	21	22
1958	5	17	18	19	20	21
1959	6	16	17	18	19	20

Row 1 represents a group of subjects all born in 1954 who are studied over a period of five years between the ages of 21 to 26. Because the subjects were all born in the same year they may be said to be members of the same cohort. To illustrate, imagine that row 1 represents a longitudinal study of locus of control. The 1954 cohort were measured in 1975 when they were aged 21 and then every year for five years until they were aged 26. Assume that the results indicated a steady increase in external locus of control over this 5-year period. Is it possible to conclude from this study that people typically become more external as they grow older? It is impossible to draw this conclusion with any confidence because of the potential influence of another factor on the sample's locus of control scores, namely the prevailing environmental influences at the times of measurement. It could be that the 1970s, as a decade of rising inflation and world recessions, provided a climate to which people responded with increasing feelings of powerlessness, thus causing the steady increase in externality in the same individuals over this period.

The problem of interpretation of age changes is rooted in the fact that longitudinal designs confound age changes with time of measurement. Not only is the sample growing older over the period but also the times are changing. If the 1954 cohort could be allowed to age naturally and yet to look every day at a world identical to the one which existed in the year they were born, then we could confidently attribute any change in locus of control to age. Of course, such an experiment is impossible; as time passes people grow older and the world they live in changes. Any age changes observed in a longitudinal study could be due to environmental changes (i.e. time of measurement) rather than the process of ageing.

A secondary problem in longitudinal designs is that since only one cohort has been sampled, it may be that the developmental changes are specific to this particular cohort and would not generalise to other cohorts. In terms of Table 8.1, the scores in row 1 might be different from the scores for rows 2, 3 and 4, etc. Unless other cohorts are studied, it is invalid to assume that the results are applicable to people from earlier or later cohorts who have lived through a different set of environmental experiences.

Cross-sectional designs
One way of extricating the influences of age and time of measurement is to use cross-sectional designs. Here, several groups of different ages are studied at the same point in time: age is varied while the time of measurement, and hence the environment, is held constant. This design is represented by the columns of Table 8.1. Thus column A represents a study conducted in 1975 in which, let us imagine, locus of control was measured in groups of subjects born in 1954, 1955, 1956, 1957, 1958 and 1959 who were aged 21, 20, 19, 18, 17 and 16. Any differences in the scores between the various age groups could not be attributed to the time of measurement factor as was the case in longitudinal designs because the time of measurement factor had been held constant. All the subjects looked out on the same world on the day they were tested even though they were of different ages. The cross-sectional design thus solves the problem inherent in longitudinal research by deconfounding age change and environmental change; however, it brings with it another and equally serious confounding. Imagine that the cross-sectional investigation of locus of control demonstrated that the older

subjects were more external than the younger ones. Would such an observation be conclusive support for the hypothesis that people become more external as they grow older? Again, the answer is not straightforward. Cross-sectional designs confound age and cohort. Each of the different age-groups tested at the same point in time have been drawn from different cohorts. Thus if persons aged 21 are more external than persons aged 16 when both are tested in 1975, the older group may be more external as a result of the accumulated environmental impact experienced by the cohort born in 1954 rather than as a result of being older. For example, an adolescence dominated by the Vietnam war may have had a unique influence on the 1954 cohort, rendering this group more external than a group born in 1959 who were still children in the late 1960s and early 1970s. Age differences in cross-sectional research cannot be attributed to the process of ageing because of the confounding of age and cohort. The psychological differences between the groups could be due to differences in age or to the difference in cohort.

The secondary problem in cross-sectional designs is that the observed age differences may be due to the particular environmental impact at the point in time the investigation was conducted. Thus, different cohorts may react differently to the time of measurement and this possibility makes it invalid to conclude that if the investigation were to be repeated at another time of measurement, e.g. as represented by columns B, C or D etc., the same age differences would emerge.

Neither longitudinal nor cross-sectional designs are satisfactory. Both hold one of the three factors in life-span research constant leaving the effects of the other two confounded. Longitudinal designs hold the cohort constant leaving age and time of measurement confounded; cross-sectional designs hold time of measurement constant leaving age and cohort confounded. In addition, both designs do not permit generalisation of their findings because of the secondary problems created by leaving the effects of one factor unexplored.

Sequential designs
There are three varieties of sequential designs that may be

seen as extensions of the straightforward longitudinal and cross-sectional designs. Essentially, sequential designs involve carrying out simultaneously either a sequence of longitudinal studies, or a sequence of cross-sectional studies, or a sequence of both longitudinal and cross-sectional studies. The advantage of sequential designs is that they permit the investigation of two of the factors determining developmental change within the same study and thus they are able to overcome the secondary problems encountered in the conventional designs although, unfortunately, the primary problems still remain.

In the cohort-sequential design, two or more longitudinal studies are carried out simultaneously. Thus cells 2B, 2C, 3C and 3D of Table 8.1 represent the minimal case of this design. The same age sequence is studied in two cohorts. The advantage of the cohort-sequential design is that it allows developmental changes observed in one cohort to be compared with those observed in another cohort, thus permitting both the factor of age and cohort to be investigated in the same study. As a result, the investigator can discover whether the developmental change observed in one cohort generalises to other cohorts in a straightforward way or whether age and cohort interact. For example, the 1955 and 1956 cohorts may both show increases in externality with age but the 1955 cohort may be consistently more external than the 1956 cohort at both times of measurement. Such a result would suggest that while externality probably does increase with age, the environmental experiences unique to a given cohort are liable to enhance or diminish this age change. The disadvantage of the cohort-sequential design is the same as that of a regular longitudinal design, namely that time of measurement remains confounded. Thus it should only be used where the investigator is confident that the impact of the environment is irrelevant to the psychological variable under study.

The sequential design which involves running two or more cross-sectional studies simultaneously is known as the time-sequential design. Thus an investigation represented by cells 4B, 5B, 5C and 6C of Table 8.1 would give the minimum condition for a time-sequential design. This design permits the investigator to make a comparison between groups with the same differences in age at several different points in time.

It will be recalled that a single cross-sectional study only allows for differences between age-groups to be observed at one point in time. The time-sequential method permits the comparison to be made across at least two points in time, thus allowing for the impact of time of measurement to be assessed in addition to observing developmental change between the age-groups. The disadvantage of the time-sequential design is the same as that of the conventional cross-sectional design, namely that the effects of cohort have not been controlled. Thus developmental change could be due to cohort differences and not to the influence of age and time of measurement which have been assessed by the design. The time-sequential design is therefore only appropriate in those circumstances where the investigator can be confident that cohort effects are unimportant.

The final research design to be described is the cross-sequential design. The minimal case of this design is represented by cells 4D, 4E, 5D and 5E in Table 8.1. The two factors investigated here are cohort and time of measurement: several cohorts are studied over several times of measurement. The cross-sequential design is a mixture of both the conventional longitudinal design and the conventional cross-sectional design. Each cohort is measured on several occasions (longitudinal) and, additionally, different age-groups are measured at the same point in time (cross-sectional). The cross-sequential design also incorporates the advantages of the cohort-sequential and the time-sequential designs by studying several cohorts at several times of measurement. Cross-sequential designs allow the investigator to tease out the relative contributions of cohort and time of measurement to developmental change. However, while this design has a certain logical appeal, it is probably the least satisfactory so far as the life-span psychologist is concerned because it does not allow for the age factor. Notice that cells 4D, 4E, 5D and 5E contain different ages. Thus it is only suitable where the investigator can be certain that age is irrelevant. It is possible that cross-sequential designs would be appropriate in studies of adulthood where biological development is no longer important for the variable under study but cohort and time of measurement may be critical.

In all the research designs described so far, age has been treated as an independent variable: it is regarded as one of the factors that can explain developmental change. In other words, researchers have been trying to obtain results such as that people aged 25 are more external than people aged 21, or children aged 12 have a larger digit span than children aged 8. There is one developmental psychologist who disagrees with this approach and has proposed a radical alternative. Wohlwill (1970, 1973) has argued that age should not be regarded as an independent variable but, instead, as a dependent variable. The consequence of adopting Wohlwill's view of age is that age differences are not the object of investigation but are regarded as inherent characteristics of behaviour. There are other areas in psychology where change is not studied for its own sake but is regarded as an inherent aspect of the behaviour in question, e.g. the processes of habituation, adaptation and forgetting and Wohlwill argues that developmental change should be regarded in the same light. Thus, instead of studying different age-groups to discover differences in locus of control or digit span, age changes in these variables are assumed and the influence of other factors, such as environmental conditions, should be investigated. The application of Wohlwill's approach to personality involves studying developmental functions of personality variables: instead of comparing different age-groups, the variables' patterns of change over the life-span are studied. The developmental function of a personality variable may be estimated using the research designs described above.

Life-Span Research and the Personality Theorist's Perspective

The stability model
Life-span psychology has been characterised by three contrasting models of development: the stability model, the ordered change model and the dialectical model (Gergen, 1977). In the main, the personality theorist's perspective has adopted the stability model which assumes that, once formed, personality will not undergo major changes and hence long-term predictions may be made on the basis of personality

measurement. The most prominent example of a personality theorist operating with a stability model is Freud. He proposed that the experiences of the first six years of life leave an indelible mark on an individual and lay the foundations of the adult personality. The adult's career choice, sexual preferences, eating habits, hobbies and indeed any behaviour of social significance are all determined by early childhood experiences.

Freudian theory proposes that there are three adult personality types: the oral, anal and phallic types corresponding to the three early stages of development centred on each of the erotogenic zones, the oral, anal and phallic stages. There are three ways in which the adult's personality reflects the infant's experiences of oral, anal and phallic gratification: the gratification may be perpetuated into adulthood, e.g. the adult who smokes is perpetuating oral gratification; it may be sublimated, e.g. socially unacceptable anal gratification may be sublimated into an adult passion for collecting things (equivalent to retention of faeces); or it may be subject to reaction formation such as the hatred of waste which could be a reaction formation against gratification associated with the expulsion of faeces.

The Freudian theory of psychosexual personality syndromes has been summarised by Kline (1972). The oral personality is believed to be formed as a result of the frustration or satisfaction of two sorts of oral gratification: sucking and biting. Thus, impatience is an adult oral trait believed to be the result of frustrated sucking whereas sociability is the result of satisfied sucking. Since oral eroticism is permissible in Western society, few oral traits are the result of sublimation or reaction formation. The anal personality is characterised by the three key traits of obstinacy, parsimony and orderliness. Anal characteristics are believed to derive from the act of expulsion of faeces and from interest in the faeces themselves. Anal eroticism, being less acceptable, is prone to sublimation and reaction formation in the adult. The phallic personality is said to be characterised by recklessness, self-assurance and resolute courage often accompanied by intense pride and vanity.

Kline (1972) has indicated two major hypotheses which

may be derived from the theory: first, that adult personality will be characterised by clusters of traits corresponding to the psychosexual syndromes described by Freud; and second, that the occurrence of these adult clusters can be related to childhood experiences during these stages. The research investigating these hypotheses provides some evidence for the existence of the oral and anal personality syndromes (Kline, 1969, 1972; Kline and Storey, 1977, 1980) but the phallic syndrome has received no support. Attempts to relate the adult syndromes to early childhood, particularly weaning and toilet training, have not proved illuminating. Kline (1972) comments on the methodological weaknesses of many of these studies, e.g. information on child-rearing practices is often obtained retrospectively by asking adults to recall how they themselves were brought up or how they brought up their own children, and these data are prone to distortions and inaccuracies. The hypothesised relation between childhood experience and adult personality has not been disproved since there remains the possibility that methodologically superior studies would provide the necessary evidence.

While Freud's theory is an excellent example of one in which personality is assumed to remain stable over the lifespan, much of the life-span research investigating stability has been conducted within the framework of trait theories such as Cattell's or Eysenck's, presumably because of the reliable personality measures associated with these theories. This research will be presented according to the type of design employed: longitudinal, cross-sectional or sequential.

Longitudinal research

Prior to 1940 there were virtually no longitudinal studies concerned specifically with personality. The emphasis of the pre-1940 work was on intelligence, which is not surprising given that reliable and valid measures of IQ were available in those days whereas personality measures were not. An example of this early work is the study of gifted children by Terman and his colleagues (e.g. Terman and Oden, 1959) in which it was discovered, contrary to popular belief, that high IQ (135–200) does not 'burn itself out' but that the gifted child grows up into the gifted and successful adult. It was also found that the person blessed with a high IQ also tends to be well endowed in other ways such as by having good physical health, artistic talents, being of good character and popular. This all-round superiority was retained in comparison with a normal IQ control group throughout the length of the study from the first testing when the subjects were aged eleven years to the last testing when they had reached their mid 40s.

Another of the early studies, with more relevance for the present discussion, was the longitudinal research carried out at the Fels Institute (Kagan and Moss, 1962). The Fels workers, unlike Terman, were not primarily interested in intellectual development but instead wanted to study the development of social behaviours such as dependence, aggression and achievement. They were particularly interested to see if it is possible to track down early signs in the child which would predict the way that child would behave when he or she grew up. Thus they were operating a stability model in assuming that there is continuity between the child and the adult. It could be extremely useful, for example, to be able to spot the warning signs of adult aggression in a 2-year-old because it would leave plenty of time for preventive action to be taken.

Kagan and Moss present the data collected on forty-five girls and forty-four boys studied from the first year of life through to their mid 20s. The data gathered in the early stages consisted of observations and ratings made during home visits and included the mother's behaviour towards the child as well as the child's behaviour. Assessment at later stages was predominantly via ratings of social behaviour, e.g. dependence, aggression, heterosexual behaviour, fear of physical harm, passivity and withdrawal. One of the ways the rating data were analysed was by correlating ratings obtained when the children were young with the same ratings made when they were older. If there was a high correlation between the two sets of ratings, then the behaviour in question had shown no marked change from child to adult, but if the correlation was low, it suggested that the developmental path had taken a dramatic twist or turn. These analyses were carried out separately for males and females and some interesting differences emerged. It was found that for males, measures of aggression taken when they were aged 6 to 10 years did correlate with adult measures, whereas early measures of dependency and passivity did not correlate with later measures. For females, the reverse pattern emerged: aggression did not remain stable across the two measuring points whereas dependency and passivity did. These findings suggest that the developmental paths taken by males and females diverge fairly early on in childhood, resulting in adult sex differences in social behaviour. What this study cannot tell us is whether these diverging paths are the result of biological maturation, the intervention of socialisation or a combination of the two.

Another interesting finding in the Fels study was the emergence of what Kagan and Moss describe as 'sleeper effects'. These were discovered in the investigation of predictor variables and the term refers to situations where an early characteristic is a better predictor of adult behaviour than a characteristic at an intermediate stage. For example, Kagan and Moss reported that a critical maternal attitude towards girls in the first three years of life was a better predictor of adult achievement in adulthood than similar measures of maternal attitude when the girls were aged 3-6 years or 6-10 years.

The Fels study is subject to several of the criticisms that may be levelled at many longitudinal studies (Block, 1971; Honzik, 1965). As mentioned already in the description of research designs, longitudinal designs only sample one cohort and therefore the generality of the findings is limited to that particular cohort. The generality will be further restricted if the sample cannot be claimed as representative of the cohort. The Fels sample, which was relatively small, was limited by the fact that many of the subjects were siblings (nineteen families supplied forty-five of the eighty-nine subjects and only sixty-three families were involved in total). Thus the study described the development of children drawn from a particular group of families that were not necessarily representative of the cohort. A second criticism concerns the length of follow-up. Longitudinal designs typically follow the same sample through the age-span deemed appropriate for the aims of the study. The Fels study has been criticised for stopping too soon; the subjects were last tested in their mid 20s and more recent life-span research suggests that this may have been too early for the accurate assessment of mature characteristics (e.g. Block, 1971). It should be pointed out, however, that the immense practical problems involved in sustaining a longitudinal study over the major portion of the sample's life-span often outweigh the original aims of the study.

In addition to criticisms of the design, the Fels study has been criticised for the quality of its measurements. Many of the data were ratings for which inadequate checks of rater reliability were made. Each subject was rated by the same rater on each of the occasions that ratings were obtained during childhood and adolescence. This policy, adopted deliberately, was most unfortunate because it means that any agreement between ratings obtained at the different times could be attributed either to the continuity in the subject's behaviour or to the continuity of the rater's perception of the subject.

A further problem in the ratings lay in the definition of the variables to be rated. For example, the indices of aggression in an 8-month-old baby are necessarily different from the indices of aggression in a 16-year-old adolescent. How can the investigator be sure that these two measures assess the same variable? The problem of equivalence of measures of the same variable over a wide age-range is present in any longitudinal research. It can be overcome if the same measuring instrument such as an IQ test or personality questionnaire is used at each time of testing, but this is not always practicable, e.g. where the subject is too young to complete a self-administered test.

The Kagan and Moss study is typical of much longitudinal research in that it was concerned with the continuity between childhood and adulthood. Far less attention has been paid to the issue of continuity between young adulthood and middle or old age. One such study is Kelly's longitudinal inquiry into the personality of married couples (E.L. Kelly, 1955). Three hundred engaged couples were contacted between 1935 and 1938 and each person was given extensive interviewing and testing, including measures of interests, values, personality and intelligence. The subjects were followed up annually until 1941 and seen finally in 1953-4. The intra-individual correlations between scores obtained at initial testing and scores twenty years later showed a marked consistency in values and vocational interests (which correlated around 0.50), rather less consistency in personality as measured on the Beunreuter Personality Inventory and self-ratings on various traits (correlations for these measures were all around 0.30), and the least consistency was observed in attitude measures (which correlated around 0.10).

Reviews of the longitudinal studies of personality tend to conclude that there is, in general, considerable evidence for the consistency of adult personality, but detailed inspection of the studies will reveal substantial variability in consistency between different traits (Bloom, 1964; Livson, 1973). As yet the definitive study in which reliable personality measures have been obtained across the whole range of the life-span has not been carried out. Now that versions of the 16PF and EPI are available for testing very young children such a study is feasible, although the enormous practical limitations on such a project still remain. A more realistic solution is to use cross-sectional or sequential designs to estimate the developmental functions of personality traits since these designs do not require waiting for the completion of a particular individual's life-span.

Cross-sectional research

A considerable amount of cross-sectional research has been carried out using the personality measures derived from Eysenck's and Cattell's personality theories with the intention of validating these theories by demonstrating their applicability to all age-groups. These theories are based on a stability model of personality in which it is assumed that the structure of adult personality will demonstrate continuity with that of the child. Cross-sectional studies of this kind are not concerned with finding high correlations between trait scores of different age-groups but rather the concern is to demonstrate similarity in factor structure in personality studies of different age-groups. Thus, while young people may, for example, be considerably more extraverted than old people, the important finding would be that extra-version emerged as a major factor in studies of both old and young people.

Within the framework of Eysenck's theory the personality of children has been investigated and appears to be similar to that of adults. Both extraversion and neuroticism have been assessed in children using a special form of the Eysenck Personality Inventory, the Junior Personality Inventory (S.B.G. Eysenck, 1965) which is reliable for use with children as young as 8 years (S.B.G. Eysenck, 1969). In his review Rachman (1969) concluded that extraversion remains stable during childhood and early measures reliably predict ado-lescents' scores. Neuroticism is less stable and boys tend to have lower scores than girls. Cross-sectional studies within the adult age-range (S.B.G. Eysenck and H.J. Eysenck, 1969) have demonstrated that extraversion, neuroticism and psy-choticism may be measured in young, middle-aged and old people. Young people (below 30) were more extraverted, neurotic and psychotic than middle-aged (30–49) and old people (over 50). These differences were not so large as to imply a discontinuity but large enough to be significant given the big samples (see Table 8.2).

Table 8.2 Mean scores on extraversion (E), neuroticism (N) and psychoticism (P) for three age-groups shown separately for males and females (from S.B.G. Eysenck and H.J. Eysenck, 1969)

		E	N	P
under 30	M	13.46	8.34	2.60
	F	13.02	9.71	1.92
30–49	M	11.81	6.68	2.15
	F	11.72	7.62	1.73
over 50	M	11.55	5.79	2.90
	F	11.40	6.50	2.33

The same pattern of continuity between childhood and adult personality factors has been observed within the frame-work of Cattell's personality theory (Cattell, 1973; Dreger, 1977). There are versions of the 16PF for three school ages:

the High School Questionnaire, the Children's Personality Questionnaire and the Early School Personality Questionnaire. In addition there is even a questionnaire for pre-school children now available. The results of studies of children of various age-groups using these different questionnaires indicate that nearly all the adult personality factors are to be found in children (Cattell and Kline, 1977). At present there remain eight adult factors which have not been identified and it has yet to be established whether they are genuinely not present in children or whether, once suitable items have been constructed, they will emerge.

While cross-sectional research from the personality theorist's perspective has tended to confirm that there is continuity in the structure of personality across age-groups it has also suggested that there may be fairly substantial differences between the scores of different age-groups. In contrast longitudinal research has tended to suggest stability of adult personality. Owing to the inherent limitations of longitudinal and cross-sectional designs the question of personality stability is best resolved by conducting sequential research.

Sequential research
Sequential designs have been adopted widely in the study of intelligence (e.g. Schaie, 1973, 1974) but they are still comparatively rare in personality. The most extensive personality investigation to date based on sequential designs is that conducted by Schaie and Parham (1976). In his investigation of intelligence Schaie had already succeeded in dispelling one myth (that intelligence declines with age) and in investigating personality he hoped to dispel another: that adult personality remains stable.

Schaie and Parham hypothesised that there would be three types of trait each characterised by a particular form of developmental change: biostable traits, which either through genetics or learning remain relatively stable throughout life and therefore show systematic sex differences but no age differences; acculturated traits, which are primarily determined by the environment and may therefore show age differences related to cohort and time of measurement effects but no sex differences; and biocultural traits, which are determined by genetics, yet are susceptible to environmental influences, and hence show no age differences but cohort differences and time of measurement effects. Personality measures were obtained using a questionnaire constructed specially for the study which measured thirteen of Cattell's personality factors and six attitudes. The data were obtained in such a way as to permit a cross-sequential repeated measures analysis, a cross-sequential analysis with independent samples and a time-sequential analysis with independent samples. This was achieved by testing two independent samples of subjects, one in 1963 (sample A) and the other in 1970 (sample B). In addition, the sample tested in 1963 was also retested in 1970 (sample A_1). In each sample the subjects ranged in age from their early 20s to their late 70s and were grouped into eight cohorts (a cohort being defined broadly as a 7-year span). The youngest cohort was aged 21–28 and the oldest 71–77 years. The design is represented in Table 8.3.

Table 8.3 The design used by Schaie and Parham (1976)

Cohort (mean time of birth)	Samples		
	A	A_1	B
1 1889	a	a_1	b
2 1896	a	a_1	b
3 1903	a	a_1	b
4 1910	a	a_1	b
5 1917	a	a_1	b
6 1924	a	a_1	b
7 1931	a	a_1	b
8 1938	a	a_1	b
Time of measurement	1963	1970	1970

The scores obtained for samples A and A_1 provided the data for the cross-sequential repeated measures analysis; scores obtained for samples A and B provided the data for the cross-sequential analysis with independent samples and for the time sequential analysis. The results of this study, as can be imagined, are exceedingly complex. At the risk of over-simplification, the conclusion that may be drawn from the three sequential analyses is that within cohorts there was considerable evidence for the stability of personality traits despite some differences between cohorts and across the two times of measurement. These findings are particularly impressive in view of the various sequential analyses employed which all confirmed the overall trend of stability.

In addition to reporting the main findings Schaie and Parham also discussed how far their results supported the threefold model of personality traits which they had proposed initially. In the light of their findings they extended this model to a total of thirteen different subtypes of adult personality traits: four types of biostable traits, six types of acculturated traits and three types of biocultural traits. However, it is difficult to see how this highly complex extension of the model of adult personality development will be helpful for future investigators.

Schaie and Parham's study has demonstrated that even with the benefit of the more rigorous sequential designs adult personality traits appear, on the whole, to remain stable over the life-span. Stability proved, after all, to be more fact than fantasy. Support for stability was also obtained in a more recent study by Siegler, George and Okun (1979). In this study 16PF scores were obtained from men and women ranging in age from 46 to 69. A cross-sequential design was used and each cohort was assessed four times over an 8-year period. The average correlation for all the trait scores between different times of measurement was around 0.50 which is as stable as the short-term test-retest reliability of the 16PF. The more complex analyses of the results confirmed the overall pattern of stability and also showed greater similarity between cohorts than had been observed by Schaie and Parham.

The final study to be described in this section (Woodruff and Birren, 1972) is representative of the personality theorist's perspective insofar as a personality inventory was used to assess the subject's personality, but it could also be said to illustrate the self perspective because a measure of the subjects' self-perceived personality stability was also obtained. In the late 1960s Woodruff and Birren obtained access to some data which at first sight could not have looked very promising. The data consisted of a group of 19-year-olds' scores on the California Test of Personality (CTP), the time of testing being over twenty years earlier in 1944. However, Woodruff and Birren used these scores as the basis of a sequential design. By following up the group tested in 1944 and giving them the same test in 1969 they were able to obtain some valuable longitudinal data and by testing a group of contemporary 19-year-olds they were able to make cross-sectional comparisons. Only a portion of the rather complex study will be described here and the relevant part of the design is set out in Table 8.4 below.

Table 8.4 Age of cohorts measured at one or more times of measurement by Woodruff and Birren (1972)

Time of measurement	Cohort	
	1924	1948
1944	19	—
1969	45	19

Woodruff and Birren were fortunate in being able to trace eighty-five members of the original sample of 485 and to retest them on the same form of the CTP as the one used initially. This group was referred to as the 1924 cohort. When retested in 1969 the 1924 cohort filled out the CTP twice: first they were asked to respond as they saw themselves now and then they were asked to respond in the way they thought they had responded when they were 19-year-olds. Thus there were three sets of CTP scores available for the 1924 cohort: their scores when 19-year-olds in 1944; their scores when in their 40s obtained in 1969 and their retrospective perceptions of themselves as 19-year-olds also obtained in 1969.

The CTP is primarily a measure of personal and social adjustment and although it contains several subscales, it yields a single composite score (higher scores represent better adjustment). When the 1924 longitudinal data were analysed there were no significant differences for either men or women between their 1944 and 1969 test scores: their responses had remained stable over the twenty-five year interval. Interestingly the retrospective scores showed that the subjects' self-perceptions lacked this stability. The 1924 cohort remembered themselves as being less well adjusted at 19 than they actually were. It is rather alarming to think that we could have such inaccurate views of what we were like twenty-five years ago: however, recent research confirms that we do have remarkably poor memories for our past lives. For example, Linton (1978) argues that we have forgotten the majority of the significant events that happened to us only six years ago and Nisbett and Wilson (1977) cite evidence suggesting that attitudes are recalled inaccurately over intervals amounting to no more than a few weeks.

Where had the 1924 cohort picked up such a negative and inaccurate view of themselves as 19-year-olds? A possible answer is that they were describing themselves according to their accurate perception of what current 19-year-olds in 1969 were like: alternatively, they were responding on the basis of the prevailing 19-year-old stereotype. Woodruff and Birren were able to provide a partial answer to this question because they had obtained a set of CTP scores from a group of young people aged 19 in 1969. They were selected to be as similar as possible in background to the 1924 cohort and were referred to as the 1948 cohort. The 1948 cohort turned out to have significantly lower adjustment scores than the 1924 cohort at 19 years. Young people in 1969 saw themselves more negatively than did young people in 1944. The negative self-view that emerged in the 1924 retrospective scores was more similar to the self-view of the 1948 cohort than to the actual self-view of the 1924 cohort obtained at 19 years. One interpretation of these findings is that adults in 1969 were remembering themselves at 19 as being more like the 19-year-olds they saw around them than they really were. Another interpretation which cannot be ruled out is that both the 1924 cohort and the 1948 cohort were responding in 1969 on the basis of a widely held stereotype of what 19-year-olds are like.

Woodruff and Birren concluded from the longitudinal aspect of their study that there is personality stability, and from the cross-sectional element that there was a marked generation gap with the 1948 cohort seeing itself as less well adjusted than the 1924 cohort. The difference between the 1924 cohort's actual and retrospective scores is intriguing and could be interpreted as adaptive, for while objectively there were marked differences between the two generations, subjectively the gap was narrower.

The results of longitudinal, cross-sectional and sequential research conducted from the personality theorist's perspective generally support a stability model of personality. Longitudinal studies support stability by indicating that individuals' personality scores do not undergo marked changes over the course of their adult lives and cross-sectional studies support continuity by demonstrating that the structure of personality remains essentially the same from childhood to adulthood. Sequential designs have supported the overall pattern of stability although some traits appear to be more susceptible to change than others. In contrast, the studies to be discussed in the next section conducted from the constructivist viewpoint have stressed the evidence for personality change as opposed to stability.

Life-Span Research and the Constructivist Approach

The studies to be described in this section have made use of a combination of two or more of the three perspectives on personality, those of the personality theorist, the lay person and the self, in the investigation of personality over the life-span. The personality theorist's perspective is represented by the use of psychometric tests and the conceptualisation of the studies within the framework of a personality theory. The lay perspective is represented by the data collected from the subjects' peers and family. The self perspective is given more prominence than the other two as is evidenced by the stress on long and detailed interviews with the subjects in which they are asked to give their own account of their personality development.

Two of the studies to be described used conventional longitudinal designs following up the same group of subjects for time-spans of twenty to thirty years or more. Block (1971) has data from the junior high school years through to mid-life and Vaillant (1977) followed his subjects from their college years through to mid life. The third study (Levinson, 1978) may also be described as longitudinal with the qualification that the data were obtained retrospectively in a series of interviews with subjects in their mid life. Levinson's study is therefore based primarily on the self perspective.

The change model

The most striking feature of all three studies is the stress on personality change, in contrast to personality stability of the kind discussed in the previous section. The ordered change model is one of the three models in life-span psychology (Gergen, 1977), the stability and dialectical models being the other two. The ordered change model regards development as involving a sequence of changes over time. These changes may be regarded as qualitative or quantitative in nature. Where change is regarded as quantitative there is continuity between earlier and later stages in the sequence and there is a sense in which a quantitative, orderly change is a weak form of the stability model since the early stages may be used to predict the later stages. Freud has already been introduced as exemplifying the stability model and yet he, like so many major figures, defies precise categorisation since he may also be used to represent the quantitative, orderly change model. We have already seen how he believed personality to develop over a series of clearly defined stages during early childhood and that the experiences during these stages will determine the personality of the adult.

The Freudian model has been used by Overton and Reese (1973) in their discussion of models of development to exemplify the mechanistic model, which is a version of the quantitative, orderly change model. Mechanistic models set out to describe the state of the organism which, like a machine, is inherently at rest. It only begins to operate when it is acted upon by external forces. Since complete description of the organism at any stage is believed possible, if the nature of the external force is understood then the prediction of future states of the organism is also possible. Another example of the mechanistic or quantitative, orderly change model would be the behaviouristic approach of developmentalists such as

Baer (1970) in which it is assumed that change is the consequence of learning and present behaviour can be explained in
terms of previous learning.

Overton and Reese also discuss their equivalent of the
qualitative orderly change model which they call the organismic model. Here the living organism serves as the guiding
metaphor: the organism is regarded as an organised whole
which is in continuous transition from one state to another.
The organism is active; its behaviour is the consequence of
internally generated purpose rather than the consequence of
the action of external forces. Because of this teleological
element, complete description and prediction is impossible.
Overton and Reese cite Piaget's theory of cognitive development as exemplifying the organismic model, but of more
relevance here is the personality theorist Erik Erikson since
his ideas have strongly influenced the three studies to be
described.

Erikson's (1963) view of personality is an extension of
Freudian theory for while Erikson makes use of many Freudian concepts, he regards personality as subject to change
right through the life-span whereas Freud regards the adult as
a puppet being controlled by strings which reach back into
childhood. According to Erikson there are eight developmental stages:

1 Trust *v.* basic mistrust		
2 Autonomy *v.* shame and doubt	early childhood	
3 Initiative *v.* guilt		
4 Industry *v.* inferiority		
5 Identity *v.* role diffusion	adolescence	
6 Intimacy *v.* isolation		
7 Generativity *v.* stagnation	adulthood	
8 Ego identity *v.* despair		

The stages' bipolar titles indicate that each stage contains a
conflict which has to be resolved. At any point in the life-
span the personality is the product of the way these conflicts
have been resolved. As a result of the way each stage is resolved the personality undergoes qualitative change. With
Erikson as with Freud we have to contend with a major
theory which defies categorisation, since Erikson's theory is

not only illustrative of the ordered change model but it also contains the essential feature of the dialectical model in which development is seen as the product of the resolution of thesis and antithesis. This takes place in the context of the developmental task confronting the person in each stage.

The first three stages are akin to the Freudian oral, anal and phallic stages. During the first stage (oral) the infant's task is to learn that the mother may be trusted to return as the source of comfort. The second stage (anal) is centred on the task of anal muscular control and learning when it is appropriate to hold back and when to let go. Like Freud, Erikson regarded the task of the third stage (phallic) as the development of conscience. The title of the third stage implies Erikson's view that a child may acquire too strict a conscience at this time which will result in excessive guilt and a corresponding crippling of initiative. During the two adolescent stages the tasks involve learning to win recognition by producing things and the integration of experience and expression into a career. During the first adult stage the task involves establishing an intimate relationship with another person, which requires having enough confidence to be able to lose a part of the self in the merging with another. If achieved, such a relationship will foster the release of creative and productive powers and in stage 7 these powers can be directed towards establishing and guiding the next generation. The task of the final stage is one of reviewing life's successes and failures and preparing for death. Erikson believes that these stages are pan-cultural: the conflicts remain the same although every culture will have its own particular ways of resolving them.

The work of Block, Vaillant and Levinson has been influenced by several aspects of Erikson's ideas. First, these investigators all believe that personality changes take place during the adult years. Second, they conceptualise development as a series of tasks which may be executed successfully or unsuccessfully. This second point is the basis for the third more general point that development is viewed as the process of adaptation to life. The way a person resolves the conflicts of each stage is the major determinant of that person's psychological adjustment. Their work is therefore not only about the development of personality but is also about the origins of mental illness and mental health as seen within the context of the life-span.

Popular interest in life-span research has been growing of late (e.g. Sheehy, 1976). Adults are eager to read about the developmental stages they are supposed to be experiencing and those which lie ahead. An explanation for this current interest is the enthusiasm, particularly in the United States, for the idea that adults can change themselves. Encounter and T groups, meditation, jogging, the Reverend Moon and the like are all believed to hold the key to positive change. More than ever before, we seem to be fascinated with the malleability of human nature. However, the research described so far in this chapter has generally supported the stability model rather than a change model. The constructivist approach appears to have identified changes ignored by the personality theorist's perspective.

Longitudinal research

The first study to be described is the work reported in Block's book *Lives Through Time* (Block, 1971). This report is based on data obtained in two studies carried out at the Institute for Human Development, Berkeley, one of which began in 1929, the other in 1932. Together they involved five hundred subjects, approximately half male and half female. By now these subjects have been studied from childhood to their mid 40s although *Lives Through Time* only reports the findings up to and including the testing at the mid 30s.

When Block began to tackle the job of making sense of the data mountain amassed over the years, he was confronted by a series of virtually overwhelming problems typical of longitudinal research. He had not been involved with the research from its inception and there had been no continuity in the personnel concerned. As a result the data had been collected without a guiding hypothesis or theory in mind. A bewildering mass of varied information had built up over the years on each subject including such diverse materials as school reports, personality test scores, parents' reports, college records, unstructured interviews with the subjects and even newspaper cuttings referring to the subject's exploits. Each subject's file contained a unique conglomeration of information.

Block approached his daunting task with two goals in view. He believed that adolescence is a critical time in personality development so he wanted to see how personality at adolescence demonstrated continuity or change when compared with personality at an earlier or later point in life. Adolescence has long been regarded by psychologists as a period of rapid change and accompanying difficulties of adjustment and Block hoped that a longitudinal analysis would show how this period of apparent upheaval made sense in terms of a longer time perspective. A second goal of Block's work was to see if there were groups of subjects each characterised by their own particular form of development. We have already had a hint of the importance of different paths of development in the Kagan and Moss study where males and females showed different development of certain social behaviours. Block wanted to see if in addition to sex differences within the male and female groups there would be subgroups which could be distinguished from one another. For example, it could be that some individuals go through a stormy adolescence but emerge as well-adjusted adults whereas others have an easy passage into a disturbed adulthood. There may be several different routes all leading to the same end point, or there may be as many end points as paths. His interest in individual differences in developmental paths is unusual; most longitudinal studies have been aimed at describing a single, generally applicable course of development. However the range of developmental paths we can imagine if we simply compare some of our own friends and acquaintances suggests that the many end points, many paths model is nearer to the truth.

Block's first decision concerned which points in time to choose for comparison. Since he was particularly interested in adolescence he chose one time point during the subjects' senior high-school years and compared this with two other time points: the junior high school years and the mid 30s. In this way he was able to compare pre-adolescence, adolescence and adulthood. His next problem was to decide which parts of the mass of data available at these time points to actually use and how best to compare them. He hit on an excellent solution which reduced the bulk of the data without losing too much of the detail contained within it. The solution was to use a Q sort. As was outlined in Chapter 7, a Q sort consists of a series of personality statements such as 'Is a popular person', 'Is dominant' or 'Quick to become angry' which a judge places in rank order from the most to the least applicable to the subject in question. Where there are many statements the judge may be asked to sort them into a small number of categories ranging from very characteristic to very uncharacteristic with a fixed number to be allocated to each category. For example, in one of the Q sorts used in Block's study there were one hundred statements which had to be sorted into nine categories according to the following distribution:

$$5 \quad 8 \quad 12 \quad 16 \quad 18 \quad 16 \quad 12 \quad 8 \quad 5$$
very characteristic   very uncharacteristic

The advantage of using Q sorts in this particular study was that the mass of varied data available for each subject could be boiled down to a description consisting of a particular sorting of a series of statements. Exactly the same procedure could be applied to all the subjects, who could then be compared. Comparisons within subjects at different time points could also be made. It was a brilliant solution to the problem created by the fact that for no subject had exactly the same set of data been collected and anyway the sheer bulk of the material prevented its detailed analysis.

The Q sorts became the basic data for all subsequent analyses so it was essential that they were obtained in a methodologically sound manner. A file of raw data for each subject for each of the three time points was prepared. A Q sort was then obtained for each subject at each of these time points. Three judges read the data file and made their own Q sorts; no judge performed more than one Q sort for the same subject. The agreement between the three judges' sorts was assessed and if it was between 0.72 and 0.78 a composite Q sort consisting of the average of the three was constructed. Where judges did not agree a fourth judge would be called in and if agreement could still not be reached then that subject would be dropped from the study. Checks were made to

make sure that judges were not basing their Q sorts on stereotypes of hypothetical persons of the three ages. As a result
of this elaborate judging process each subject was described
by three Q sorts, one for their junior high-school years, one
for their senior high-school years and one for their mid 30s.

Block proceeded to analyse the Q sorts in two ways. First,
in keeping with most longitudinal research, he looked for
general trends. He wanted to find out if there were any clear
patterns in male and female development. Second, he looked
at the data more closely to see if there were any subgroups
which could be described by distinct developmental paths
which differed from the other subjects.

In order to analyse the data for general trends he looked in
particular at the continuity or change between the junior and
senior high-school Q sorts and the senior high-school and
adult Q sorts. The broad picture which emerged was not very
informative. For both males and females the Q sorts for the
two time points during the school years were highly similar,
but there was considerably less correspondence between the
senior high-school and adult Q sorts. No clear sex differences
emerged from this general analysis.

The general analysis had hinted at personality change
between adolescence and the mid 30s but the details of this
change were unclear. Block's second analysis involved looking
for groups of subjects characterised by particular developmental paths. It could be that the differences between subgroups were cancelling each other out in the general analysis
and hence blurring the overall picture. The technique he used
to locate subgroups characterised by similar developmental
paths was inverted or Q factor analysis (Stephenson, 1953).
So far we have seen how factor analysis may be used to
identify clusters of highly intercorrelating *variables*; in Q
factor analysis clusters of highly intercorrelating *subjects* are
identified. The initial correlation matrix is composed of
measures of similarity between each subject and every other.
In Block's analysis the measure of similarity consisted of the
correlations between pairs of subjects' combined adult and
adolescent Q sorts. The factors obtained in Q factor analysis
identify subgroups of highly similar subjects which in Block's
analysis were subjects who had followed similar developmental

paths as indexed by their profiles on their combined adolescent and adult Q sort.

Q factor analysis of the males resulted in five subgroups, whereas six were found for the females. In order to get a full picture of the characteristics of each group he used other data available on the subjects such as their pre-adolescent Q sorts and material not used in the Q sorting process. The five male and six female types revealed the diversity of developmental paths which had been obscured hitherto when the sample was considered as a whole. For example, the best-adjusted male type was the 'Ego Resilient', of whom there were nineteen instances. They were characterised by intelligence, good health and good family background. They showed maturity even in their junior high-school years and this developed steadily over the next two time points. Their development was untroubled, predictable and continuous. In contrast there were eleven 'Anomic Extraverts'. These men had bad family backgrounds with dominant mothers and weak fathers. They conformed to the adolescent stereotype, being gregarious, vigorous, self-confident and rebellious. However this early vigour had burnt out by adulthood leaving tense, anxious and repressive men who were surprisingly empty after such a promising adolescence.

The female types were entirely different from the male types with no equivalent to the successful and positively-evaluated male Ego Resilients. The largest subgroup consisted of nineteen Female Prototypes. These women are described by Block as having led smoothly progressive and satisfying lives. They had been poised and pretty as teenagers and had matured into replicas of the All-American House-wife. The greatest change was observed in fourteen Cognitive Copers. As adolescents these women were maladjusted but by adulthood they had grown into mature, well-educated and well-adjusted women. The least well adjusted of the female types were the ten Hyper-feminine Repressives. These women had been moderately inadequate as adolescents but by adulthood Block describes them as being in a shambles. The father played more of a part in their upbringing than their working mothers (which Block regarded as a bad start). These women were physically voluptuous as adults, trying to be conventional but displaying all the symptoms of a hysterical personality: preoccupied with their health, complaining, devious and whiny.

The major difficulty with producing a typology is making sense of the individual types. Unavoidably a subjective bias will invade the interpretations in the effort to produce a meaningful picture. Early on, Block acknowledges a debt to psychoanalytic thinking and this becomes apparent at the final stage of the book when he presents the subtypes. He stresses the importance of parental characteristics for future development and he uses psychoanalytic terms such as 're-pression' and 'ego strength' to portray the qualities of the types. As well as introducing a subjective element, the typo-logical findings can also be criticised for being limited to the particular sample studied. Only 83 males and 86 females were available at the end of the follow-up period for the typological analysis and it is doubtful whether subgroups composed of 10-20 individuals will be replicated in sub-sequent samples.

How do the results of Block's analyses relate to the two main goals he set at the outset, namely to examine the im-portance of adolescence in the life-span and to see if develop-ment followed distinct paths for different subgroups? The two goals became fused in the actual analysis since the dis-tinctive developmental paths adopted by the subgroups were frequently characterised by the nature of the continuity or change between adolescence and adulthood. Block's research has certainly demonstrated that within his particular sample there were distinctive subgroups characterised by particular developmental pathways. His work deserves praise for the ingenuity and care with which the wealth of data was moulded into shape. However, despite all the efforts the en-tire enterprise was questionable, as Block readily admitted in the conclusion of the book. It was a biographical study of a particular cohort of individuals moving through their own unique experience of environmental events. The character-istics of development which Block described for his sub-groups may be typical for other cohorts, but his study can-not tell us that and must remain therefore a severely limited contribution to our understanding of development. The fault does not lie with the researcher, the method of analysis, the theoretical slant or any other aspect of the inquiry: it is inherent in the longitudinal approach.

The same fundamental criticism may be levelled against the Grant study reported by Vaillant (1977). While Vaillant has charted the developmental progress of certain characteristics and has looked for stages of adult development, these activities have all served a specific purpose: to further the understanding of the nature of human adjustment. He was not interested merely in how adults develop, but how they develop successfully to be fully-adjusted, psychologically healthy adults.

The subjects of the study were ninety-five men from each of the classes of '42, '43 and '44 from Harvard University. (It is rumoured that one of the subjects may have been J.F. Kennedy.) When they were at college they participated in intensive testing and interviewing amounting to about twenty hours in all. After they had graduated they completed a questionnaire every year until 1955 when the frequency of the questionnaire was reduced to every two years. They were then reinterviewed in 1955 and Vaillant himself interviewed forty-four of them in 1967. Vaillant discusses the findings from two viewpoints: first he was interested in seeing to what extent these men's biographies revealed a series of developmental stages through which they had all passed, and second he was interested to see if any characteristics at an early stage predicted the sorts of outcomes at later stages.

In assessing the data for evidence of stages Vaillant was influenced by Erikson's theory of the eight stages of man. In the years immediately following college the men were concerned with establishing intimate relationships in the form of marriage and friends (Erikson's stage 6: Intimacy *v.* isolation). They were also working hard, particularly between the ages of 25 and 30 years. During this time they were very conforming and in Vaillant's words had lost their capacity to play. When they were in their forties the men went through a kind of second adolescence: a period of questioning and reappraisal which led either to a more relaxed attitude towards their work and a new-found nonconformity leading to a more adventurous approach to life, or to depression and an inability to grow in new directions. This period is equivalent to Erikson's stage of generativity *v.* stagnation.

Since Vaillant was primarily interested in the nature of human adjustment he compared the men who by 1967 had the best outcomes with those who had the worst outcomes (as assessed by his adult adjustment scale). He then explored their past histories to discover the characteristics of successful and unsuccessful lives. There were a number of surprises and some old beliefs were challenged. For example, the Worst Outcomes were not predicted by the symptoms of maladjustment at college: shyness, ideational thinking, introspection, inhibition and absence of purpose. The characteristics of the college student that were found in the Best Outcomes were: being well-integrated, practical and organised. These are not features of the stereotype of the adolescent. The Best Outcomes were found to have achieved stable marriages before the age of 30 and to have remained married until 50. The Worst Outcomes had either married very young, after 30, or were separated before 50. The men who by mid life had become company presidents (a recognised index of success in the United States) had the best marriages and friendships.

In his careful study of the biographies of these men, Vaillant came to the conclusion that they had all had to cope with experiences which were enough to precipitate a mental breakdown even though only a small proportion had actually become mentally ill. He believes adult adjustment to be the result of experiencing trials as well as blessings. Using Erikson's terminology he regards varied experience of positive and negative kinds as an aid to ego development. In Terman's longitudinal study of intellectually superior individuals it turned out that they were better adjusted than a normal IQ control group. Vaillant would not agree that intelligence alone is enough to guarantee adjustment. He argues that adjustment is achieved by developing healthy defence mechanisms as exemplified by one of his subjects who was a bomber pilot during the war and now writes poetry as an outlet for his feelings of guilt. A critical assessment of Vaillant's contribution will be postponed until Levinson's study has been presented because these two studies share a number of similar limitations.

The final study to be described is the retrospective longitudinal study conducted by Levinson (1978). In contrast to Block who was particularly interested in adolescence, Levinson was motivated to carry out his research by his fascination with the difficulties of middle age, partly inspired, as he acknowledges, by his own experiences during this period. Levinson like Vaillant was interested in charting the stages of adult development and was influenced by Erikson's views on adult personality development.

Levinson studied forty males all born between 1923 and 1934 and therefore aged between 35 and 45 years at the time the study was carried out in 1969. They were drawn from four different occupational groups: industrial workers, business executives, university biologists and novelists. Levinson and his colleagues spent many hours with each subject obtaining an extensive biography. They then sifted through these biographies to see if a general developmental pattern emerged. Levinson was impressed by the similarity between all his subjects' biographies despite their varied economic, racial, religious and educational backgrounds. Although the particular events differed from person to person, Levinson claimed that all his subjects went through periods of major upheaval and transition at remarkably similar ages. On the basis of his observations he proposed that everyone passes through a sequence of developmental periods and transitional stages which can be depicted as a series of steps, as is shown in Figure 8.1.

On the right of the staircase there are the eras which Levinson likens to the seasons of spring, summer, autumn and winter. On the left there are the transitional periods between eras. These are the periods of life crisis. During a transitional period one era has to be terminated and another begun. This process always took about five years in Levinson's subjects and occurred within specific age-limits. Each era and its associated transitions, Levinson argued, is characterised by a series of tasks. For example, in the young adult era a young man has to carry out four tasks: form a dream of what he wants out of life, form a mentor relationship to aid in the realisation of that dream, form an occupation and

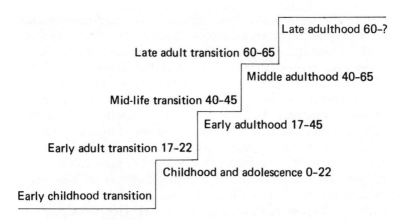

Figure 8.1 *Levinson's theory of developmental periods and transitional stages*

form love relationships, marriage and a family. Around the middle of the young adult era comes the crucial transitional period. It is not a step between eras, it occurs within the same era: nevertheless Levinson regarded it as the most traumatic of all the transitional phases. He called it the Age Thirty transition and it occurs between the ages of 28 and 33 years. It is a period of upheaval because it is the time when the initial experimentation with young adult life draws to a close and a man settles down to making a variety of commitments which will shape his future life; commitments in his occupation and his family. The next time of upheaval after the Age Thirty transition is the mid-life transition. It is not always as chaotic as the Age Thirty transition and some fortunate people will hardly notice it slip by, but for others it too can be a period of exceptional difficulty.

The sources of difficulty in these transitional periods are different for everyone, but they will be centred on the significant areas in the person's life which are usually work, family and relationships and for some a hobby or spare-time activity. For example a young man may have married during his early adult transition when he was busy rejecting his parents and all they stood for. His wife may have represented the alternative set of values he wanted to identify with and yet, at the same time, provided a form of mother substitute to ease the separation-anxiety induced by the transition. Such a marriage may well founder when it hits the Age Thirty transition, argues Levinson. The man has finished his period of exploration and experimentation and now seeks real commitment. He is a different person from the rebellious youth of ten years ago and it will be an elastic marriage that can accommodate this change and development. Marital difficulties are often the symptoms of a mid life transition too when a man is forced to reflect on his successes and failures. How far has he realised his dream? How is he going to face the fact that he has not won the Nobel prize or not written a best-selling yet profound novel? How is he going to face the fact that his marriage has slowly dissolved from the early closeness and passion to a business partnership between acquaintances?

A radical solution to the mid life crisis may require cutting out aspects of the previous era in order to come to terms with what lies ahead. Erikson referred to adulthood as a period of generativity versus stagnation and Levinson regards middle adulthood as a time to accept your successes and failures and give way to a younger generation, serving them as a source of wisdom via mentor and parental relationships. One reason why the mid life transition can be so difficult to accept is that it involves stepping out into another generation. The man of 45 is no longer one of the boys and must accept and find rewards in being a member of the older generation.

Levinson's book is absorbing and non-technical and makes excellent reading. He describes in detail the biographies of four of his subjects, one from each of the occupational groups he studied, showing how they conform to his stages of development. He does not present any quantified analysis of his findings and as a piece of psychological research his work may be faulted in many respects. The sample is small (N = 40) and was drawn from the Boston area of the United States which is highly unrepresentative in that it attracts a large proportion of intelligent and talented people. (The same criticism may be levelled against Vaillant's study.) The data were retrospective and therefore subject to the biases of a selective memory. Not only will people forget and distort events that occurred twenty years ago, they will also imbue their past with a meaning and organisation that was absent at the time. Levinson commented that it was only by looking back over long time periods that the structure of an individual's life became apparent, but with the aid of hindsight it is easy to make the course of an individual's life appear purposeful and directed. Since there was no attempt to derive the sequence of developmental stages in an objective and quantifiable fashion it is impossible to evaluate Levinson's claim that all his subjects passed through these stages. They did in Levinson's eyes, but would another researcher have reached the same conclusion? (Again the same criticism may be levelled against Vaillant's work.) Levinson includes little theoretical discussion about the status of these stages but he does propose that they are universal and that they are the product of biological maturation and environmental pressures produced by a complex social system.

Throughout the book Levinson seems to be confused about the origin of the developmental tasks. For example, when commenting on the fact that most people get married during their twenties, the period of early adulthood, he says: 'It is astonishing that nature's timing is so bad: we must choose a partner and start a family before we quite know what we are doing or how to do it well' (Levinson, 1978, p.107). To attribute the age of marriage in Western society to the force of nature is unconvincing since the typical age of marriage varies culturally and historically. It would be more appropriate to blame the pressure of Western society for expecting people to marry in their 20s. A similar confusion arises in his discussion of young adulthood when he describes the young man as experimenting with life and not really settling down until he reaches his 30s. Such experimentation is surely a luxury restricted to certain privileged groups in industrialised society; it is certainly not found in more primitive cultures or in earlier periods of our history where usually an individual's occupation is not a matter of choice and there is no room for experimentation.

In both Levinson's and Vaillant's books there is inadequate discussion of the extent to which adult development is due to the way society is structured, thus imposing a series of tasks on its members as they grow older and the extent to which the tasks are the inevitable products of maturation. If the developmental stages of adult life are the consequence of the way careers and relationships are structured in a particular society or section of society then they are less interesting than if they can be shown to be true universally.

Stability or change?
Of these three studies, Block's is the only one to conform to acceptable standards of quantitative, empirical research and for this reason it would be unwise to give the findings as a whole too much weight. Nevertheless it is worth considering why these studies, particularly Vaillant's and Levinson's, have stressed change: they studied the development of personality during adulthood showing how the personality at mid life can be traced back through a series of transitions to the personality of the young person. Why should these studies find evidence of personality change while the studies from the personality theorist's perspective have stressed stability?

The material collected in the studies by Block, Vaillant and Levinson covered a wide range, including data from the lay perspective, i.e. parental and peer reports, and the self perspective as well as conventional test data of the type used by the personality theorist's perspective. This suggests that while test data may yield evidence of stability, a person's self-perceptions and others' perceptions of that person indicate personality development and change. This change is not inexplicable but appears reasonable in the light of the developmental tasks that have been tackled. Ask yourself whether you think you are the same as you were ten years ago and it is likely that you will perceive yourself to have changed in some ways since then, although the changes will make sense to you in the light of your experiences. However, self-perceived change and change perceived by others can be misleading because it may be wrongly attributed to the person when in fact it should be attributed to the situation. Perhaps perceived change is yet another example of the fundamental attribution error (Ross, 1977): the tendency to overestimate the importance of personality dispositions at the expense of situation variables.

Both Vaillant and Levinson imply that there are periods of particularly intense personality change and these are during the major transitional periods, e.g. from adolescence to adulthood, from young adulthood to middle age. These transitory periods are marked by specific developmental tasks such as breaking away from the ties of the family and establishing an independent identity or switching from the younger to the older generation. It could be that in carrying out the tasks more or less successfully our personalities are actually changed. Alternatively, it could be that our personalities remain the same but we have to apply ourselves to a different set of tasks and this gives a spurious sense of change in ourselves. Other people see us behaving in the necessary ways to adapt to a new stage and perceive us as having changed. For example, the novice parent is the subject of comments such as 'I never knew he could be so good with babies', and personality changes are attributed when it may only be the circumstances which have changed.

According to this argument life-span research carried out with a constructivist approach in which the subjects' personalities are assessed from all three perspectives will be likely to yield evidence of personality change because the material obtained from the subjects themselves and from the subjects' families and peers will contain assertions of change. In contrast, research carried out from the personality theorists's perspective in which personality test data are obtained will produce a more stable picture of personality. It is of course impossible to answer the question: which view is the more accurate, stability or change? It may be more objective to argue on the basis of the personality theorist's studies that personality remains stable, but if this view contradicts the beliefs and intuitions of the lay person and the self-perceiver it will not be particularly helpful in the understanding of life-span development to ignore these contradictory views. Personality is the construction of all three perspectives.

9 Criminal Personality

Particularly in Western industrialised society we value individuality and cherish the fact that everyone is unique. However,
there is a limit to our tolerance and admiration for idiosyncrasies and there comes a point at which eccentricity
becomes abnormality. This point is extremely difficult to
define. Despite our implicit understanding of the concept of
deviant personality attempts at making it explicit are only
partially successful. Nevertheless it is valuable to consider
some of the attempts at an explicit definition of deviance
because they give a greater awareness of the conditions
under which a person or a behaviour is branded as having
passed the limit of acceptability. In achieving a greater understanding of those conditions perhaps we learn as much about
ourselves and the society we live in as we do about the concept of deviance itself. After considering the problems of
defining deviance the rest of this chapter will focus on one
form of deviance, criminality, and discuss it from each of the
three perspectives on personality.

Defining Deviance

Deviance as non-conformity
Attempts at defining deviance by concentrating on the qualities of the person or the behaviour identified as deviant are
generally unsuccessful. Thus deviance has been defined as
that which is statistically rare, but rarity alone does not
guarantee deviancy. Having red hair, playing the bagpipes and

being a cross-channel swimmer are all relatively rare qualities but a person would not be branded as deviant for possessing one of them (although being characterised by all three might raise an eyebrow). Deviance has been defined as that which causes distress to the deviant or to the victim, but psychopaths are capable of highly deviant behaviour which causes them no distress and deviant behaviour does not always distress those at the receiving end. Indeed, sometimes it is quite the reverse: the musical genius's deviant ability to play the piano exquisitely may give pleasure to millions. Behaviour with which others cannot empathise has been defined as deviant but non-deviants can empathise with the person found guilty of speeding or driving over the alcohol limit: 'There but for the grace of God go I.' The deviant has been defined as someone who causes a problem for society. Thus in the Soviet Union political dissidents present a problem for society and are labelled mentally ill (deviant), which solves the problem by allowing the removal of the dissident to a mental hospital (Lader, 1977). However, dissidence itself cannot be said to be deviant since in other societies critical appraisal of existing social structures is tolerated if not encouraged.

Searching for the hallmark of deviance within the person or the behaviour is continually hampered by the unavoidable fact of cultural relativism and all its implications. Cultural relativism refers to the fact that different societies place different values on the same behaviour. For example, we abhor the killing of new-born babies but it has been reported by anthropologists that certain societies regard infanticide as an acceptable form of population control. A person who claims to be able to see and hear things unseen and unheard by others is regarded in our society as suffering from hallucinations and may well end up in mental hospital, whereas the same person in another social context could well become the most revered member of the group. Societies do not only differ on what forms of behaviour are to be regarded as antisocial deviance: they also vary in the definition of pro-social deviance. For example, independence and individuality are cultivated in the United States, while dependence and the submerging of the self beneath the State is expected in modern-day China (Munro, 1977).

The inevitable consequence of acknowledging cultural relativism is that no behaviour or person may be regarded as inherently deviant in the pro- or anti-social sense. There will always be a society somewhere in the world today or one that has existed in the past capable of invalidating a claim for the universal evaluation of a behaviour as deviant. However, the significance of cultural relativism should not be exaggerated for it must be acknowledged that societies show a considerable degree of consistency in outlawing certain behaviours such as murder, rape and theft (Lemert, 1972; Welford, 1975). Does this mean that after all certain behaviours are inherently deviant? Not necessarily, since such behaviours may be universally proscribed because they are disruptive of human social life which although capable of superficial variation is restricted by certain biological limitations. Despite the similarities between many societies we can never arrive at a satisfactory definition of deviance. We are forced to end up by saying that deviance is that which a particular society has chosen to evaluate as such, be it positive or negative deviance, at a particular point in time. The definition of deviance does not depend upon some quality inherent in a person or a behaviour but on the rules of society which determine the boundary between deviance and conformity. Recognising the importance of social rules in defining deviance has resulted in a shift in attention away from the person and the behaviour on to the conditions under which a person or behaviour comes to be regarded as deviant.

Given that deviance must be defined in terms of the social context in which it occurs it follows that deviance may be defined as non-conformity to accepted social norms. When a given culture has categorised a particular behaviour as deviant then, generally speaking, the performance of that behaviour is usually fairly rare. We do not typically commit infanticide, have more than one spouse and steal the weekly groceries. However, these behaviours do occur and when they do they are regarded as deviant. In other words, most people most of the time conform to society's explicit and implicit rules and when people fail to conform they are labelled as deviant. Defining deviance as non-conformity is illuminating because it incorporates the idea that deviant behaviour is frequently unexpected or unpredictable: it is not the way most people would behave in the circumstances.

The three perspectives on deviance
Deviance may be studied from any of the three perspectives on personality. From the personality theorist's perspective deviance is primarily the result of internal characteristics of the person which cause him or her to behave in a deviant fashion. From the lay perspective the interesting questions about deviance are not how it is caused but which behaviours and people come to be evaluated as deviant by others and under what circumstances and why. The subject-matter of the lay perspective is the process by which some members of society attribute deviance to others. The self perspective is concerned with self-attributions of deviance. Here the focus of attention is on the deviant's self-perceptions, in particular on how a deviant identity is acquired and its effects on subsequent behaviour.

Deviance may work to the benefit or the detriment of society and therefore be encouraged or discouraged accordingly. In this chapter the focus will be on criminality which is generally considered to be a form of anti-social deviance although, as we shall see below, it has been argued that it has beneficial effects. Criminality will be considered from each of the three perspectives.

The Personality Theorist's Perspective on Criminality

Attention throughout the following discussion will be on the person who commits crimes as opposed to the actual criminal behaviours themselves, which are the special interest of the criminologist and sociologist. Some psychologists (e.g. Feldman, 1977) have chosen to focus on criminal behaviours, arguing that they are learned in the same way that non-deviant behaviours are learned and that the best way to arrive at an explanation of criminality is to understand the contingencies controlling the performance of criminal activities. I have chosen to focus on the person rather than the behaviour because while virtually all of us have engaged in a technically criminal activity at some time, only a few of us have become hardened criminals in the sense that we are continually engaged in criminality as a way of life. The hardened criminal commits hundreds or even thousands of crimes in his lifetime and is extremely resistant to any attempts at therapeutic change. Only the male personal pronoun will be used in this chapter. Although there are signs that female criminality is on the increase (Radzinowicz and King, 1977), at present it is still the case that the vast majority of apprehended criminals are male and there is a regrettable paucity of research data on female criminality (but see Cowie, Cowie and Slater, 1968; Wadsworth, 1979).

The personality theorist's perspective emphasises the role of person variables at the expense of situational variables in the determination of behaviour and in theories of criminal personality this bias is strongly apparent. The aim of theories of criminal personality is to demonstrate that people who commit crimes are characterised by a particular constellation of personality traits which differentiate them from people who do not commit crimes. Implicit in this aim is the view that these traits are the underlying cause of the criminal behaviour. The research from this perspective falls into two categories: studies either compare criminals with non-criminals or they look for different criminal subtypes within the criminal population. In most of these studies the criminal subjects are drawn from the population of 'official' criminals: those who have been apprehended by the police and subsequently found guilty of an offence and entered into the criminal statistics.

There are two important disadvantages associated with the use of official criminals. First, official criminal statistics not only grossly underestimate the amount of crime that actually takes place (Wootton, 1959) but they are also unrepresentative of the total population of criminals and their crimes (Box, 1971; Feldman, 1977). The incarcerated criminal, while providing the ideal captive subject, cannot be said to be representative of criminals in general. Investigators who limit themselves to studying official criminals are in danger of developing theories which are only applicable to the highly atypical criminal: the one who gets caught. Although attempts to make statements about criminals in general on the basis of findings obtained from such a biased sample must be highly speculative, the findings may be generalised with reasonable confidence to other official criminals. The criminal statistics do not vary dramatically from year to year, which indicates the official criminal population remains fairly constant. However, research on unofficial criminals such as self-reported offenders is essential in order that the generality of these theories may be tested.

The second disadvantage of studying the official criminal is that any personality characteristics found to distinguish the apprehended criminal may be the result of his present imprisonment and recent experiences rather than indications of enduring qualities which were present before arrest and were causally related to the criminal behaviour. While this possibility cannot be excluded it does seem rather tenuous in connection with the relatively enduring personality traits such as those measured by Cattell and Eysenck's questionnaires which, as longitudinal studies have shown, remain relatively stable over the adult life-span. The point is more relevant where measures of less stable characteristics such as attitudes are involved.

Criminals versus non-criminals
In general the results of studies in which criminals have been compared with non-criminals on personality measures have suggested that the differences between the two are less clear-cut than the personality theorist's perspective would have assumed. In 1950 Schuessler and Cressey reviewed all the investigations of the previous twenty-five years and of the 113 studies only 42 per cent obtained results differentiating between criminals and non-criminals. A review of the 94 studies conducted between 1950 and the mid 1960s (Waldo and Dinitz, 1967) indicated an improvement with 81 per cent of the studies differentiating between criminals and non-criminals, which could well be due to the increased sophistication of personality assessment techniques during this period.

Multi-trait theories have featured in particular in the more recent studies of criminals versus non-criminals. As was described in Chapter 4, Eysenck has elaborated a theory of criminal personality in which criminals are believed to have failed to acquire the constraints of a conscience as a result of defective learning. He predicts that criminals are characterised by high scores on all his three personality factors: extraversion, neuroticism and psychoticism. Since psychoticism is a recent addition to the theory most of the studies only provide data on extraversion and neuroticism. In two comprehensive reviews (Cochrane, 1974; Passingham, 1972) it has been concluded that while there is some support for the hypothesis that criminals are highly neurotic, the evidence for the hypothesis that they are also highly extravert is inadequate. Cochrane reviewed twenty studies and in five of these the results were actually in the reverse direction with criminals scoring significantly lower than non-criminals on extraversion (reported in Hoghughi and Forrest, 1970; S.B.G. Eysenck and H.J. Eysenck, 1971). In defence Eysenck has pointed out that some of the items on the extraversion scale may be unsuitable for a prison population (e.g. an item referring to whether the respondent likes going to parties is inappropriate in a context where parties do not take place). The presence of unsuitable items could lead to the artificial lowering of the prisoners' extraversion scores. Eysenck was also critical of the control groups used in some studies and stressed the importance of matching the criminals and non-criminals on variables such as age, sex, social class and intelligence, all of which are themselves related to extraversion.

Burgess (1972) proposed that an appropriate test of Eysenck's theory must take account of extraversion and neuroticism scores simultaneously. This is done by dividing the subjects into four groups on the basis of their scores corresponding to the four quadrants formed by the two orthogonal dimensions of extraversion (E) and neuroticism (N), i.e. high E, high N; high E, low N; low E, high N; low E, low N. He demonstrated that although there may be no significant differences between the two groups when the means for the two dimensions were analysed separately, if the number of criminals appearing in the high E high N quadrant was compared with the corresponding number in the non-criminal group, significant differences may be obtained. However, a study by Shapland and Rushton (1975) which met all the necessary methodological requirements, including quadrant analysis, failed to support Eysenck's theory. Using self-reported delinquency a high delinquency group and an appropriately-matched low delinquency group were compared for the frequency of highly extraverted and neurotic subjects. The results showed no tendency for the highly delinquent group to contain an excess of neurotic extraverts.

In sum, there is no conclusive support for Eysenck's theory that criminals are highly neurotic and extraverted. The evidence as regards psychoticism is limited but does support the theory (H.J. Eysenck, 1970, 1974). In view of the criticisms of Eysenck's theory concerning the relations between personality and learning (see Chapter 3), it is not surprising that the hypothesised personality characteristics of criminals which are intended to account for their supposed defective learning ability have failed to emerge.

The other major multi-trait theorist who has been concerned in the investigation of differences between criminals and non-criminals is Cattell. Unlike Eysenck, Cattell did not develop a specific theory of criminal personality. However, given that his representation of the structure of personality is relatively complex it is possible to compare criminals and non-criminals on Cattell's personality tests to see if criminals emerge with a distinctive profile. As with Eysenck's theory, the results using Cattell's theory are inconclusive. Cattell, Eber and Tatsuoka (1970) reported the personality profile derived from a sample of eight hundred prisoners. They were found to be below average in superego and ego strength (low G and low C) and low on self-sentiment (low Q3). They were also characterised by desurgency (low F) and guilt-proneness (high O). They were not dominant (low E) and they had high autistic imagination (high M). Other studies have obtained different results even on such presumably key factors as G, superego strength (e.g. Warburton, 1965, found that a sample of highly dangerous psychopaths had near-average scores on G), which makes it impossible to draw any firm conclusions.

The reviews of earlier studies using a variety of personality measures and the more recent studies using Eysenck's and Cattell's questionnaires indicate that clear-cut personality differences between criminals and non-criminals are not easy to find. Perhaps the lack of evidence in the personality domain can be offset by greater success in other areas of psychological functioning. Two other dimensions of individual variation, neither of which are strictly regarded as personality variables but which would seem likely candidates, are intelligence and moral reasoning.

It might be expected that official criminals would be less intelligent than non-criminals. Such a hypothesis could be based on the assumption that all criminals are less intelligent than non-criminals or that only the less intelligent criminals are likely to get caught. The evidence however does not provide strong support for the hypothesis, whatever its basis. Caplan (1965) reviewed the evidence from studies of delinquents and concluded that the typical finding was that delinquents scored around eight points lower than non-delinquents. There was also some evidence for a discrepancy between delinquents' performance versus their verbal subtest scores in the direction of higher performance scores. The evidence, such as there is, suggests that the differences in intelligence are small and could be due to the effects of institutionalisation as opposed to being a significant precursor to criminality. Caplan recommended that more studies be carried out on unofficial, self-reported criminals. In just such a study West and Farrington (1973, 1977) found slightly lower scores in their high delinquent group and poorer educational achievement as compared with the low delinquency group. Thus there is some evidence for an association between marginally lower intelligence and delinquency but the difference in intelligence is smaller than expected and has yet to be thoroughly investigated in the adult criminal.

Theories of moral development (Piaget, 1932; Kohlberg, 1964) propose that children and adults pass through a series of developmental stages beginning with a stage characterised by egocentricity in which morally right behaviour is regarded as that which avoids breaking rules, and the motivation to behave correctly is a desire to avoid punishment. The end point of moral development will vary between individuals with some attaining a higher level of moral maturity than others. In Kohlberg's theory the highest stage, stage six, is characterised as one in which a person governs his or her behaviour according to a set of self-chosen ethical principles which are universal principles in the sense that they transcend culture-specific legal rules and regulations. Kohlberg's six stages are divided into three levels: the preconventional (stages one and two), conventional (stages three and four) and postconventional (stages five and six). Most adults reach the conventional level of moral reasoning in which the individual is recognised as being part of a social system which has to be preserved by following rules and regulations. Only about 10 per cent of adults are believed to attain stage six. Research into moral reasoning involves presenting subjects with moral dilemmas which the subjects have to resolve giving a full account of their reasoning. Their responses are then categorised as indicative of one of the six stages.

Criminal behaviour typically involves violating society's rules and regulations and hence also involves violating most individuals' moral principles, since stage-four morality is composed of a respect for authority and avoidance of censure. Hence it could be expected that official criminals would be at a lower stage of moral development than their non-criminal counterparts. This possibility is discussed by Feldman (1977) who cites two studies investigating the association between morality and criminal behaviour. Kohlberg (1969) argued that prisoners demonstrated a morality at levels one and two in their statements about the morality of criminal behaviour. Fodor (1972) found that official delinquents were significantly lower than matched non-delinquents on a quantitative measure of morality even though both groups fell within the range of level-four moral reasoning. More recently Griffore and Samuels (1978), using Rest's defining issues test (Rest, 1974), found that residents of a maximum security prison in the United States were predominantly at Kohlberg's stage four.

As with intelligence, the evidence for differences in moral reasoning between criminals and non-criminals does not appear substantial enough to provide an adequate explanation of criminality. While more research might be helpful there are a number of limitations to the study of moral development. When people are asked to give their opinions about moral dilemmas in a paper-and-pencil task it is their moral attitudes which are being assessed, and attitudes are notorious for not correlating with behaviour. A person may respond in a level-five manner on Kohlberg's task but when confronted with a real-life moral dilemma behave at level two. Further studies of the correspondence between moral reasoning ability and actual moral behaviour are needed. Another series of problems is concerned with the degree to which a person will apply the same level of moral reasoning to different aspects of his or her life. For instance, a person may have worked out and adhere to certain level-six universal ethical principles but still behave in a stage-two way in certain contexts. The extent to which moral development proceeds uniformly in different domains requires further investigation. This point will be developed later in the chapter when we come to take a closer look at the criminal mind.

The search for distinguishing characteristics, be they personality traits or other psychological dimensions of individual variation has not proved particularly successful, with very few clear-cut findings to be reported. One possible explanation for the absence of results is the heterogeneity of official criminals. A sample of incarcerated criminals will be a mixture of people of different ages with different criminal records. It is possible that there are homogeneous subgroups within the broad category of official criminals which are similar with respect to personality variables but the differences between these subgroups may be of such an order as to cancel out any characteristics for the category as a whole. The importance of heterogeneity has been recognised by Eysenck, Rust and Eysenck (1977) who recommend that subgroups be studied.

Criminal subgroups

The most striking source of heterogeneity within the criminal population is the variety of offences for which criminals have been convicted. There has been a tendency for investigators to assume that criminals specialise in particular sorts of offences, e.g. the property offender is generally non-violent, the child molester is law-abiding in all other respects, and hence offence-based typologies have been developed (e.g.

Gibbons and Garrity, 1962; Hayner, 1961). Such typologies are based on intuition and past experience and, although they can be applied to criminal groups to see how well they account for the heterogeneity, they are not as satisfactory as empirically derived typologies.

Using multivariate techniques such as factor analysis or cluster analysis it is possible to feed in a profile of information on each subject and discover which subgroups of subjects share similar profiles and thus arrive at an empirical typology. We have already come across an example of this approach in Block's longitudinal study where Q factor analysis was used to identify subgroups who had undergone similar long-term personality development. These techniques have been applied with some success to criminal groups. The main disadvantage of empirically based typologies is that they are limited by the nature of the sample from which they were derived. Thus if the sample contained no violent offenders then no indication as to whether violent offenders form a subgroup could be obtained. Ideally, empirically derived typologies should be tested out on additional samples to check on their generality. Additionally, the results from different studies can be compared to see if the same subgroups have been found by different investigators. Studies of heterogeneous prison samples of adult offenders in Britain and America have produced some consistent findings on criminal subtypes. The two most reliable types appear to be the active aggressive type characterised by a long history of impulsive violence, and the inadequate type characterised by passivity and lack of social skills (Carlson, 1972; Marcus, 1960; Sinclair and Chapman, 1973; West, 1963).

In view of the immense variety of individuals to be found in the prison population, some researchers have turned their attention to studying subgroups within a specific subsection of official criminals. In particular, the subsection of violent offenders has attracted considerable interest. Much of this work has been stimulated by Megargee's theory of two types of aggressive person: overcontrolled and undercontrolled (Megargee, 1966). He proposed that the most extreme acts of violence were performed by overcontrolled people without any history of violence; they keep all their hostility bottled up and when they eventually allow it to escape the effects are disastrous. Undercontrolled people commit numerous but relatively minor violent acts. Megargee (1966) obtained moderate support for this typology in a study of delinquents, but Blackburn's work on Broadmoor patients provided more conclusive evidence (Blackburn, 1968a, 1968b, 1970). The MMPI profiles of patients convicted for extremely violent acts were different from those of patients convicted for moderately violent offences, the differences being on scales relating to overcontrol such as Repression (R), Ego control (Eo) and Mania (Ma).

In Britain violent offenders are sometimes sent to special hospitals such as Broadmoor, as opposed to prison, because they have been deemed mentally abnormal by the courts and hence regarded as in need of custodial treatment rather than imprisonment. Not all mentally abnormal offenders have committed violent crimes and the less dangerous offenders will be sent to regular psychiatric hospitals for their treatment. For a criminal to be deemed mentally abnormal the court must be satisfied that he is either mentally ill, of subnormal intelligence or psychopathic. Mentally abnormal offenders are therefore a legally created subsection of official criminals based on a psychological rationale. They are particularly worthy of investigation because they are supposed to be receiving treatment and yet very little is known about the nature of their problems or the best way to help them.

One subtype of mentally abnormal offender to receive considerable attention from both professionals and the public is the psychopath. The validity of this diagnostic category is dubious (Wootton, 1959) and it has been described as a wastepaper-basket category which is used to dispose of patients who do not fit into any other category. Clinical descriptions of the psychopath are varied but usually include references to an abnormal absence of guilt for antisocial behaviour, an inability to form lasting bonds of affection and a failure to learn by experience (Cleckley, 1964; Craft, 1966; McCord and McCord, 1964). Some studies of criminal subtypes have generated a type resembling the clinical description of a psychopath and the MMPI is able to locate those diagnosed as psychopathic by their distinctive 4-9 profile (high scores on the Psychopathic deviate and Mania scales).

In my own investigations of the subtypes within mentally abnormal offenders (Hampson, 1975; Hampson and Kline, 1977) criminals and matched non-criminals were analysed together to see if subtypes would emerge which both differentiated within the criminal group and between the criminals and non-criminals. The subjects were given a battery of tests including personality questionnaires, objectively scored projective tests and variables were derived from lengthy interviews and the subjects' life histories. Subjects' profiles based on the projective test and interview data were Q factor analysed and, in three separate analyses of three different samples of mentally abnormal offenders and appropriately matched non-offender controls, subgroups composed exclusively of offenders were obtained. These subtypes were identified with the aid of the questionnaire and life history data which had not been used in the Q factor analyses. While the subtypes found within each offender sample did not replicate there were many points of similarity. In the first two samples, which were both drawn from the same institution and contained a high proportion of mentally subnormal abnormal offenders, two offender subtypes per sample were obtained. Within each sample the subtypes distinguished between inadequate, immature offenders with authoritarian attitudes and the more insecure, egocentric and aggressive offenders. These subtypes are reminiscent of the inadequate and aggressive subtypes found in other studies. The third sample was drawn from Broadmoor patients who are typically of around average intelligence and the two offender subtypes which emerged contrasted those who were impulsive and psychopathic against the more anxious and pessimistic individuals. The investigations demonstrated that with the use of highly detailed personality data it is possible to differentiate certain criminals from non-criminals and to draw distinctions within a criminal sample.

In conclusion, the research on criminal personality characteristics indicates that it is unlikely that any single personality trait will unerringly differentiate between criminals and non-criminals. Such a conclusion is not particularly surprising in view of the opening discussion of the definition of deviance which implied that crimes are defined by society rather than inherent properties of behaviour, and in view of the evidence that official criminals are a highly biased sample of the criminal population as a whole (to be discussed below). The research indicates that criminals are a heterogeneous group and that the study of offender subgroups is a more promising approach, particularly when a wide variety of personality measures are used. However, any studies of official criminals' personality characteristics are circumscribed by the uncertainty of their general applicability to the non-official criminal population.

Conclusions

Viewed from the personality theorist's perspective the criminal is expected to be characterised by distinguishing personality traits. The perspective is based on the assumption that personality determines behaviour so, since criminals engage in forms of antisocial behaviour, they should demonstrate personality differences when compared with non-criminals. These differences may be the result of genetic factors, environmental factors, or a combination of both. The evidence for a 'Mark of Cain' is far from convincing. Certainly there are no straightforward differences between criminals and non-criminals but it may be that there are complex combinations of personality measures which will yield differences within official criminals and between criminals and non-criminals. The aetiology of such refined and complex differences has yet to be explored.

The personality theorist's perspective cannot claim much success in the prevention of crime or the treatment of criminals. This failure has been one of the reasons for the shift in emphasis in criminology away from the criminal, who appears to be much the same sort of person as the rest of us, to the processes by which some people come to be labelled as criminals while others do not. Under what conditions is a criminal attribution made and what effect will it have on the person so labelled? These are questions which have been asked mainly by sociologists and criminologists but they are relevant here because they may be viewed as representative of the lay and self perspectives.

The Lay and Self Perspectives on Criminality

The lay and self perspectives refer to people's perceptions of the personalities of other people and themselves. In the context of criminality, the lay perspective refers to the study of the processes by which people come to be regarded as criminals by others and the self perspective is concerned with how people come to perceive themselves as criminals. Investigations from these points of view are comparatively recent developments in sociology and criminology and the approach is known as social labelling theory.

Social labelling theory
Social labelling theory (Becker, 1963; Box, 1971; Schur, 1971) is composed of four major propositions.
    1 No behaviour is inherently deviant.
    2 The official criminal statistics give a biased and unrepresentative impression of crimes and criminals.
    3 The processes by which certain people are selected and labelled as official criminals serve the function of maintaining social order.
    4 People labelled as official criminals may as a result acquire a criminal identity and continue to commit crimes.
    The first proposition of social labelling theory states that no behaviour is inherently deviant. In other words, a behaviour is neither pro- nor anti-social until society has evaluated it as such.
    The labelling theorists' claim that no behaviour is inherently deviant has been challenged in the light of the evidence that crimes such as murder, rape and theft are considered antisocial by virtually all societies (Lemert, 1972; Welford, 1975). However, just because a behaviour is regarded as antisocial by most societies this does not make it 'inherently deviant'; indeed it is difficult to appreciate what precisely is meant by the concept of 'inherent deviance' since it is impossible to distinguish operationally between a behaviour which is universally regarded as antisocial and one which is inherently deviant. Since the concept of inherent deviance is unsatisfactory, arguments about whether or not it exists are unhelpful. Fortunately, even though social labelling theorists

have insisted on the proposition that no behaviour is inherently deviant, the other elements of the theory do not appear to depend critically on this confused concept.

The second point, that official criminals are unrepresentative of those who commit crimes, is well substantiated (Feldman, 1977). Official criminal statistics include figures on both crimes and criminals and both are probably highly inaccurate. For a crime to appear in the official statistics it has to be reported, which means it must either be observed by the police or reported to them by a witness or the victim. It follows that crimes which are not reported are those which are invisible to the police or witnesses, such as drug abuse in the home, and those in which the victim is unaware of his or her victim status, as in a confidence trick, or where there is no obvious victim as in tax embezzlement. Additionally, victims may not report crimes because they fear embarrassment and distress as in the case of sexual assaults.

Some idea of the amount of unreported crime can be obtained by asking people whether they have been the victim of an unreported crime and whether they have committed crimes which have not come to official attention. Winslow's (1969) survey in Boston revealed that three times as many serious crimes had been committed as were actually reported by their victims and Wallerstein and Wyle (1947) found that 99 per cent of New Yorkers admitted to undetected offences. Belson's study of self-reported delinquency in London revealed that virtually every member of a random sample of 1,445 boys admitted to some form of prosecutable offence (Belson, 1975). Recently, Radzinowicz has confirmed his estimate that only approximately 15 per cent of the total number of crimes actually committed (the 'dark figure') are ever brought to police notice and a culprit convicted (Radzinowicz and King, 1977).

The statistics on the people who commit crimes are misleading because they imply that the majority of criminals are male members of the lower classes and minority ethnic groups. Investigations into the 'dark figure' using self-report techniques have shown that the proportion of people from the lower classes and ethnic minorities appearing in the official statistics is far higher than is representative of the actual distribution of social class and race in the criminal population as a whole (Belson, 1975; Box, 1971; Gold, 1966; Wadsworth, 1975; Wolfgang, Figlio and Sellin, 1972).

While the evidence supports the claim that working-class people and ethnic minorities are discriminated against, social labelling theory does not specify how this discrimination comes about. Do the police actively seek out these people, ignoring middle-class white criminals? Perhaps they have their own lay perspective on criminality, a 'police theory' (Rock, 1973), which determines where they look. Or does the bias occur after the alleged criminal is apprehended and the middle-class white is better equipped in social skills and general knowledge of the 'system' to extricate himself before a prosecution takes place? These two questions were recently investigated by Bennett (1979) in the London Metropolitan Police District. He studied the operations of the Juvenile Bureau and found that significantly more middle-class than working-class children were let off with a caution and thus avoided being sent to court.

On interviewing the officers concerned, Bennett was satisfied that they were not operating with a stereotype of working-class delinquency. In order to test the other hypothesis, that the middle classes are better able to negotiate their way out of a prosecution, Bennett studied the reports of home visits made routinely in these juvenile cases. The reports suggested that middle-class families were able to create a considerably more favourable impression on the officer than did the working-class families. Bennett concluded that the police should not be blamed for the unrepresentativeness of official criminals and implied it is the result of the inferior interactional skills of working-class people. Clearly considerably more research of a more precise nature is needed before this conclusion can be accepted.

The third and fourth propositions of labelling theory may be presented in terms of the three perspectives on personality. The personality theorist's perspective has been rejected in the first two propositions by saying that there is nothing special about criminals, particularly official ones, since they are victims of a biased labelling process. Instead, in proposition three, the lay perspective is advocated. What is it that causes one group of people to single out another as deviant and put them through an elaborate labelling process? What functions does labelling serve for those who engage in it? The self perspective is also regarded as important because labelling theorists are interested in the effects of the label (see proposition four). Does it serve to reduce deviance or, paradoxically, could labels actually enhance the very qualities they were designed to eradicate?

The lay perspective: the function of labels
According to social labelling theory, the process of apprehending and punishing criminals makes little impact on the bulk of criminal activity and therefore the interesting question to ask is why the process continues. Sociologists have challenged the traditional view that crime is mainly dysfunctional and disruptive and instead propose that crime acts to preserve social order and is useful and desirable to those in control over society (Box, 1971; K.T. Erikson, 1962; Quinney, 1970). The process of apprehending and punishing criminals serves to clarify and maintain the boundaries between unacceptable and acceptable behaviour: it serves to remind us of the rules and hence bind society together. It is therefore not the criminal behaviour itself that is of importance but the response in others to that behaviour. This means that information about crime and the consequences of criminality must be made salient. In the past this was done by visible punishments such as public hangings; today it is achieved by the media. For example, even the relatively serious-minded newspaper the *Guardian* gave front-page coverage to an account of the execution by electric chair of the convicted murderer John Spenkelink. It included a step by step description of the entire procedure and such graphic details as the singe to the right calf produced by the first surge of shock (*Guardian*, 26 May 1979).

Box (1971) has argued that it is not only those in power who feel uncertain about the nature of social reality and strive to find ways of preserving their particular definition. He believes insecurity afflicts us all. We need to impose order on the chaos of life by clinging to our definitions of what is normal, right and good. By being sanctimonious about the deviance of others we can suppress the nagging doubts we may have about ourselves. The public labelling of criminals helps to preserve the consensus about social reality. Theorists like Box and Quinney argue that the scapegoats who are legally 'processed' are likely to be the least powerful members of society, which explains the bias towards the working class and ethnic minorities. Those in control are unlikely to label themselves as criminal. In order to function effectively as scapegoats official criminals should not be portrayed as being different from the rest of us. It follows that those in power would be resistant to the idea that criminals have distinguishing psychological characteristics. If criminals are different from non-criminals then the latter would not have anything to learn from the former.

Socially labelling theory is generally seen as sensitising us to the evils of capitalist society which makes scapegoats out of innocent victims. In contrast the personality theorist's perspective on criminality is regarded as an attempt to divert the responsibility for crime onto the criminal's shoulders and away from the evils of society. However, the personality theorist's perspective is a potentially powerful means of attacking the use of crime for social control. By demonstrating that criminals are different from non-criminals the non-criminal population would have no need to be anxious about their own normality and would not see themselves as having a lesson to learn from the criminal scapegoats.

Previous chapters have indicated ways in which the personality theorist's perspective and the lay perspective have been shown to be compatible; but the lay perspective on the criminal personality cannot be reconciled with the personality theorist's perspective. The lay perspective rests on the assumption that official criminals are scapegoats serving positive functions for society. The personality theorist's perspective assumes that criminals are different from non-criminals and that their behaviour is dysfunctional for both themselves and society. Before considering this incompatibility further it is necessary to see what the self perspective can contribute.

The self perspective: the effect of labels
The self perspective encompasses the final proposition in labelling theory: the effects of labelling on the recipient of the label. The theory argues that persons labelled as criminals, either officially by the authorities or unofficially by their family and peers, will commence on a process of identification with that label which will eventually result in the adoption of the criminal identity and its accompanying life style (Box, 1971; Matza, 1969). It is assumed that the imposition of a label is likely to raise identity doubts and the processes of conviction, imprisonment and the return to society are all likely to increase rather than decrease these doubts (Goffman, 1961). As a result the person acquires a new identity, that of being a criminal, and behaves in ways consistent with this new identity. The irony is that the label was intended to reduce criminality and yet it may actually increase it.

The proposition is highly speculative and the psychological processes by which identity changes take place have not been spelled out by social labelling theorists. However, there are a number of studies in the psychological literature on the effects of labels which are relevant here although they were conducted in laboratory settings and used non-deviants. One such study by Snyder and Swann (1978) investigated whether labelling someone results in that person living up to their label by studying the perseveration of a behaviour induced originally by the application of a label.

The experiment involved a competitive interaction between two subjects referred to as the target and the perceiver. The two subjects performed a reaction time task in which the faster of the two was the winner on each trial. They could interfere with each other's performance by using a noise weapon which consisted of blasting white noise down the opponent's head phones. The weapon was available alternatively for the perceiver and the target on successive trials. The dependent variable was the level of the noise weapon the subjects chose to use. There were two target conditions and two perceiver conditions. The targets were either told that the level of the noise weapon they chose depended on their personalities or on the level selected by their opponent, i.e. was situational. The perceivers were told either that the person they would be playing against (the target) was hostile or non-hostile. After playing against the perceiver, the target played a second game against another opponent who had not been informed about the target's hostility.

The results showed that perceivers who had been led to expect hostile targets used higher levels of the noise weapon which in turn resulted in hostile responses from their targets. When these same targets played a second game with naive opponents, those targets who had been led to believe that their choice of noise level was a product of their personalities continued to use high levels (i.e. be hostile) whereas those who had been told their hostility was situationally determined did not maintain their hostility in the second game. Snyder and Swann concluded that the former targets 'had become truly hostile persons, whose behaviour reflected the cross-situational consistency and temporal stability that are the hallmarks of personality traits' (1978, p.57). While such a conclusion is possibly something of an overstatement, the experiment does show that people who are convinced that their behaviour is the result of the sort of person they are, are more likely to continue behaving in such a fashion.

Although Snyder and Swann found that negative labels result in behaviour consistent with the label, other studies have found that negative labels cause people to behave in ways which disconfirm the label (e.g. Steele, 1975). Gurwitz and Topol (1978) ran both a naturalistic and a laboratory study to attempt to unravel the effects of negative labels. In both studies people were negatively labelled by the experimenter and then given an opportunity to behave in a way consistent with the label. Two additional factors were introduced into the design. Some subjects were told that the negative label applied to their peer group (e.g. students were told that they, like their peers, made inadequate use of the amenities provided by the nearby city) whereas for the other subjects their peers were not mentioned. Also, some subjects had provided evidence consistent with the label before the accusation was made whereas others had not (e.g. some students were asked how often they had visited the city before being accused of not making enough use of it). When subjects had provided evidence consistent with the label and the label was applied to their peers they subsequently behaved in such a way as to confirm the label. When no evidence had been provided, subjects disconfirmed the label more if their peers had been mentioned than if they had not.

Since the results were unexpected, Gurwitz and Topol came up with a *post hoc* explanation. Subjects who had provided evidence of the negative behaviour and had been told the label applied to their peer group did not regard the negative behaviour as so bad and hence were able to confirm it. When subjects had provided no evidence of the negative behaviour and the label had been applied to their peers, they had an opportunity to disassociate themselves from their peers or prove that their peers were not so bad by disconfirming the label. In relation to criminal identity, this study suggests that official criminals, who have provided evidence of criminal behaviour to justify the criminal label, will be more likely to conform to the label if they also see themselves as part of a similarly labelled peer group.

While studies have succeeded in demonstrating that labels can affect subsequent behaviour, there is no evidence for the key theoretical proposition: that the person acquiring the identity which goes with the label comes to see him or herself as that sort of person. Labelling theory implies that people attribute to themselves all the characteristics believed to go with the label and, as a result of their self-perceptions, they proceed to behave in ways consistent with the label. What is needed is a study in which people's self-perceptions are measured in addition to their behaviours to see if behaviour change is preceded by corresponding changes in self-perception.

An integration of the three perspectives
There is an inconsistency between the last proposition of labelling theory and the earlier ones. Labelling theorists are adamant that there is nothing special about the criminal and argue that the focus of attention should be directed away from the criminal to the labelling process. However, in proposing that one of the effects of labelling is that criminals acquire deviant identities which cause them to continue behaving deviantly, the theorists are now arguing that there is something distinctive and special about people who adopt

crime as a way of life. The distinction between primary and secondary deviance is useful here (Matza, 1969). Primary deviants are those who do not acquire a criminal identity and for whom crime does not become a way of life. They return to the fold of law-abiding society after a brief spell of deviancy. Secondary deviants are those who adopt criminal identities and the associated lifestyle.

Early on in this chapter it was stated that the focus of attention would be on the 'hardened criminal' or secondary deviant. As a result of working through the lay and self perspectives incorporated in social labelling theory we can now see that labelling theory is not incompatible with the personality theorist's perspective insofar as secondary deviants are concerned, even though the theory is internally inconsistent. Labelling theory proposes that the way secondary deviants see themselves will be different from the way both primary deviants and non-criminals see themselves.

A combination of the three perspectives on criminality suggests that the place to look for psychological characteristics which will differentiate reliably between criminals and non-criminals and within the criminal population is in the area of self-perception. There has been very little work adopting such a point of view but there is one extensive clinical study which contains much relevant material (Yochelson and Samenow, 1976). Another source of information is the accounts of criminality given either by criminals themselves or by their biographers. Both sources will be drawn upon in the next section.

Another Look at Criminal Personality

It is puzzling that studies from the personality theorist's perspective have failed to locate differences between criminals and non-criminals with respect to self-perception if, as the lay and self perspectives suggest, this is the best area in which to look for such differences. A possible solution to the puzzle is provided by Yochelson and Samenow (1976), who have proposed a new approach to criminality every bit as revolutionary as that put forward by the social labelling theorists. They argue that criminals, particularly 'hard-core' ones (i.e. secondary deviants), are psychologically distinct from non-criminals, but not in the ways explored in the previous, inconclusive studies. What distinguishes the hard-core criminal are his typically criminal thinking patterns. Yochelson and Samenow use the term 'thinking patterns' to include emotions and attitudes as well as styles of information processing. They believe these patterns are central in aiding the criminal in his pursuit of crime. Yochelson and Samenow argue that a criminal is totally immersed in criminality in the same way that an alcoholic is immersed in drinking. As a consequence of this view, they are convinced that the only way to change a hard-core criminal is to eradicate every last vestige of those criminal thinking patterns and replace them with normal ones. The criminal must be persuaded to abandon every aspect of criminality; even a stray thought about crime is as dangerous to the criminal as one drink can be for the alcoholic.

At the outset it must be acknowledged that Yochelson and Samenow's theory of criminality is based on research flawed by numerous methodological weaknesses. Therefore in presenting their ideas it would be foolish to claim any strong scientific validity for them, but I do consider their arguments compelling, despite the conspicuous absence of material evidence. For those who find the ideas repugnant or ill-founded as well as for those who find them fascinating and insightful, the conclusion is the same: the theory needs translating into testable hypotheses and the appropriate research conducted.

Yochelson and Samenow's views of criminal personality are the result of fourteen years' investigations of criminal subjects in the United States. Over two hundred and forty male official criminals were involved, many of whom were detained in psychiatric hospitals as the US equivalent of the mentally abnormal offender. Most of the subjects were hard-core adult criminals with histories of repeated violations. The method of study was intensive interviewing amounting to considerable periods of time with each subject, e.g. twelve received five thousand hours of interviewing each. The aim of the study was to gain some understanding of criminal personality in order that an effective treatment could be evolved. The treatment programme which emerged from the study is novel in its approach and Yochelson and Samenow claim, on the basis of the ten-year follow-up of some subjects, to be 100 per cent effective in some cases. The critical reader will have already noticed the major design flaws: no control group, a total reliance on interviewing and no attempt at controlled assessment of the treatment programme. Suspending our critical faculties for a while, let us look at what emerged from this fourteen-year-long enterprise.

Yochelson and Samenow called the first chapter of their book 'The reluctant converts'. Contrary to expectation, the title does not refer to the criminal subjects of the study but to the investigators. They had started out on the project with an extensive knowledge of the psychological and sociological literature and therefore were committed to the belief that criminals are the victims of their psychological defects and sociological deprivations. Through their prolonged and intense contact with criminals, the investigators were reluctantly forced to come to the conclusion that the model of the criminal as victim is a subversive myth cultivated by the machinations of the criminal mind and nurtured by the gullibility of social scientists.

Social labelling theory argues that the official criminal is liable to acquire a deviant identity and hence see himself and his behaviours as deviant: he tells himself he is a 'bad' person and proceeds to live up to his expectations about himself. Yochelson and Samenow's findings are entirely the reverse. They argue that the criminal does not see himself as a criminal but as an exceptionally superior and good person. 'The apprehended criminal believes that, although he broke the law, he is inherently not criminal. He thinks he is a good person who should not be punished' (Yochelson and Samenow, 1976, p.486). They believe that criminals are totally lacking in any kind of insight into the immorality of their way of life. No wonder the personality theorist's perspective failed to find evidence to support the labelling theorist's view that criminals would have negative self-perceptions — they do not! The criminal views himself in a particularly positive light.

If Yochelson and Samenow are right, how can the criminal reconcile himself to the unavoidable fact that he has behaved in ways which society deplores? Yochelson and Samenow argue that this mental somersault is achieved with the aid of criminal thinking patterns. These patterns help him to commit crimes and yet maintain a positive self-image. Yochelson and Samenow compiled their description of criminal thinking patterns on the basis of their clinical experience and they provide no quantitative evidence to support their identification of these patterns. While the patterns must therefore be regarded as speculations it is interesting to note that several have been identified independently in autobiographical and biographical accounts of criminality, as will be indicated by drawing on the accounts of the lives of crime led by McVicar, the Kray twins and Mackay.

John McVicar was a professional thief with a reputation for violence. He became widely known to the general public in 1968 when he made a sensational escape from the notorious maximum security wing of Durham Prison. He was at large for two years and when finally recaptured he faced a cumulative sentence of twenty-six years' imprisonment. He was released on parole in 1978, having spent the previous eight years studying for A-levels and a degree. McVicar (1979) gives an account of his escape and a brief autobiography in which he attempts to explain his criminality. Ronald and Reginald Kray were also professional criminals but on a much larger scale than McVicar. During the 1950s and 1960s they contrived to build up a network of control over the criminal activity in London akin to the operations of the Mafia (Pearson, 1972). Eventually they were convicted and sent to prison to serve life sentences for murder. Patrick Mackay was labelled as a dangerous psychopath when only a teenager, and at 23 was sentenced to life imprisonment for three murders. His is a disturbing story of lack of communication between the police, medical and social services to whom he had been well known since childhood (Clark and Penycate, 1976).

Criminal thinking patterns
The first cluster of criminal thinking patterns to be described by Yochelson and Samenow are those concerned with the criminal's emotional life. Providing a basis for everything else

is the criminal's tremendous supply of energy which gets translated into both physical and mental activity. His continual need for excitement is charged by these seemingly limitless energy reserves. Next most important is the cluster of emotions associated with what McVicar (1979) called 'machismo', although Yochelson and Samenow do not use the term. Central to the concept of machismo is fear. In particular, the criminal finds the fear of being humiliated the most hard to tolerate and yet humiliations, referred to by Yochelson and Samenow as 'putdowns', large and small, loom in every aspect of his life. 'For the criminal, emerging from all situations on top is an overriding concern. Both in everyday situations and fantasy, the criminal must be a winner every time' (Yochelson and Samenow, 1976, p. 281). When a criminal experiences a major putdown he is in what Yochelson and Samenow describe as a zero state. From being a mega success he becomes a mega failure and sinks into a deep depression centred on intense feelings of worthlessness. Putdowns must be avoided in order that machismo be maintained.

The preoccupation with maintaining machismo is illustrated in McVicar's autobiography, which reveals that even as a child he considered it his number one priority. His only fear when first going to primary school was that he might not be tough enough to win the fights. 'I believed not only that fighting was the best method of settling any dispute, but that courage and success in showing aggression provided the only true basis for self-esteem' (McVicar, 1979, p. 145). A similar pattern is revealed in the biography of the Kray twins. As children they ruled over their own gang and kept rival gangs at bay by fighting. As teenagers the Krays trained to become professional boxers and McVicar considered seriously the idea of making a career out of sport.

Physical superiority remains a way of maintaining machismo in adulthood although by then it is enhanced in other ways such as through sexual conquests, money and possessions. Also associated with machismo are the emotions of anger (when it is threatened) and pride (when it is enhanced), both of which are present in excess in the criminal. According to Yochelson and Samenow, the criminal's pride in his self-image as all-powerful and self-determining prevents him from accepting any form of authority.

In contrast to the aggressive and fiercely masculine self-image associated with machismo the criminal is characterised by another set of emotions relating to sentimentality. Yochelson and Samenow claim to have found sentimentality in every hardened criminal they have worked with. It is often directed towards helpless objects such as the elderly, the disabled and animals; in addition criminals are prone to excessive sentimentality about their mothers. Certainly this appeared to be true of McVicar and the Krays. It would seem contradictory for the criminal to be both sentimental and to cultivate machismo but he accommodates these apparently conflicting clusters of emotions because being sentimental conforms with his self-image of being a good person. For example, one of Ronnie Kray's favourite books was *Boys' Town*, an account of a work of charity for homeless boys.

The turbulent emotional life of the criminal is only part of the syndrome of deviant thinking patterns identified by Yochelson and Samenow. Just as important are the deviant cognitive processes they have ascribed to the criminal mind, for these essential processes could underlie a wide range of criminal activity. Of these, two seem crucial: the criminal's vivid imagination and the fragmentation of his thinking.

According to Yochelson and Samenow, the criminal's energies are liable to be directed to mental activity as well as physical. His mind is continuously fantasising about crime and rehearsing criminal escapades; it is 'a reservoir of criminal ideas' (1976, p.411). It is difficult for a non-criminal to imagine what this must be like but Yochelson and Samenow insist that the criminal is constantly weighing up the criminal potential of every situation he is in and fantasising about the rewards and costs of committing crime. Singer (1976) has described how one significant function of fantasy is to prepare the individual for action by mental rehearsal and the criminal is apparently well versed in this piece of psychology. One of the most powerful fantasies for the professional thief is that of the 'big score'. One day he will carry out a robbery of such proportions that he will be able to retire for ever on the proceeds. The imagination of the criminal, including the concept of the 'big score', is portrayed expertly in one of Ed McBain's novels, *Doors* (1978). More direct evidence that criminals are characterised by vivid imaginations is to be found in Cattell's studies where criminals have been found to be high scorers on factor M (autistic imagination) (Cattell, Eber and Tatsuoka, 1970).

It is because of the criminal's fertile imagination that Yochelson and Samenow argue that there is no such thing as a crime of passion. The criminal has repeatedly thought about the act he eventually commits: 'In our experience, no criminal has ever suddenly done something that he has not *repeatedly* considered before' (Yochelson and Samenow, 1976, p.450, their italics). However, there are probably many people who engage in fantasies they would never translate into reality, so what makes the criminal different? The answer, say Yochelson and Samenow, lies in the fragmented nature of the criminal mind and his ability to operate a 'cut-off'. Fragmentation is present to some extent in us all: it refers to the inconsistency between attitudes and behaviours. However, it occurs on a massive scale in criminals. We have seen signs of fragmentation already: criminals revere their mothers and yet they cause them grief; they are sentimental about the helpless and yet they exploit them ruthlessly when it suits them; they believe they are morally superior and yet they engage in acts of gross immorality. Fragmentation permits the maintenance of a positive self-image in the face of contradictory evidence.

Fragmentation, along with all the other deviant thinking patterns, becomes most relevant when the criminal is engaged in committing a crime. His fertile imagination aids in planning the crime and fragmentation and cut-off prevent him from dwelling on the long-term consequences and the short-term fear associated with the criminal activity. The successful execution of a crime is tremendously rewarding, confirming the criminal's high opinion of himself and enhancing his machismo. Criminals describe the experience of excitement and pleasure associated with criminality as a 'charge' and it is graphically portrayed in Mackay's account of his horrific killing of an elderly priest. Although the murder had been planned in advance, when Mackay began to hack at the priest's head with knives and an axe he became possessed by a frenzy of excitement.

While Yochelson and Samenow have discussed many other aspects of supposed criminal thinking, the essentials have been summarised here. The criminal's emotional life is believed to be dominated by machismo and his thought processes are at the mercy of his vivid imagination and ability to cut out the unwanted. Yochelson and Samenow do not attempt to explain how it is that the criminal comes to be characterised by these patterns; they dismiss purely genetic or environmental explanations. Indeed, they go so far as to dismiss the whole enterprise of searching for causes because they believe that it detracts from the responsibility of the individual criminal. They argue that the only way to change the criminal is to alter his criminal thinking patterns and this can only be achieved if he is made to feel responsible for his behaviour.

The approach to rehabilitation advocated by Yochelson and Samenow is based on the assumption that the criminal has to undergo an entire change in identity if he is to give up criminality. Telling him he is like he is because of his unhappy childhood, or his position in society, or analysing the reinforcement contingencies for a specific criminal act, will all bypass the critical problem. The criminal has to be persuaded to abandon criminal values and adopt the ethical standards of normal society. It is a question of moral education. Yochelson and Samenow demanded a total abstinence from all criminal activity, be it fantasy or reality, and required a rigid adherence to conventional morality. In their own rehabilitation programme they have worked with criminals individually and in groups with these goals in view. They used what they described as a phenomenological approach in which criminals were required to report comprehensively on their thoughts during the previous day and the therapists pointed out where these thoughts were deviant and constituted evidence of criminal thinking patterns. Before being allowed to begin the programme the criminal gave an undertaking that all his current criminal activity would cease. (It is a sobering thought that incarcerated offenders are frequently engaged in as much criminal activity while in prison or hospital as they are outside.)

It is interesting to note that McVicar (1979) recommends

a form of rehabilitation on much the same lines as that proposed by Yochelson and Samenow. He argues that criminals require ethical indoctrination to bring about what amounts to an identity crisis as the way to jolt them out of their criminal life-styles. He writes bitterly of his wasted youth and the complete failure of any 'punishment' he has received:

> at almost any time anyone who understood the psychodynamics of crime, who could relate them to my own life, who commanded my respect and attention in conditions that were designed to promote them, could have exposed my criminality for what it was and crushed it. (McVicar, 1979, p. 140)

Conclusions on Criminal Personality

Yochelson and Samenow's ideas are provocative and remain essentially speculative requiring empirical investigation rather than wholesale rejection or acceptance. Their theory of the criminal mind is worthy of careful consideration because it seems to solve a number of riddles and is consistent with both biographical and clinical data.

The theory resolves the contradictions between the personality theorist's perspective, the lay and self perspectives. The personality theorist's perspective hypothesises that differences between the personalities of criminals and non-criminals will be found, and yet the evidence is far from conclusive. The lay perspective, as presented within social labelling theory, hypothesises that hard-core criminals will be characterised by negative or deviant identities whereas the self perspective, as suggested by Yochelson and Samenow, indicates that the criminal's self-image is highly positive. As yet there is no direct evidence to support the hypothesis of the self perspective and it would be difficult to obtain by conventional testing methods. The criminal would probably not be fooled into responding honestly on self-esteem questionnaires and instead would conform to the image he perceived as expected by the investigator, which would be one of low self-esteem. By taking the self perspective into account it looks as though the social labelling theorists have been misled into thinking that criminals acquire deviant identities and the personality theorist's perspective might concentrate on investigating the criminal's possibly distorted and inflated self-perceptions.

The self perspective also resolves the contradictions posed by the findings on criminals' moral development. Although more studies are needed, it is likely that criminals are not less moral than non-criminals since they are capable of average moral thinking. Nevertheless, there is a discrepancy between their moral thinking and actual behaviour. This discrepancy can be accommodated by Yochelson and Samenow's theory by the concept of fragmentation. While the criminal shows normal moral development in some respects, e.g. he may be a model father and husband, he is able to cut out any ethical considerations when he carries out a crime because of the fragmentation which characterises his thinking patterns.

The power of the theory to resolve the riddles associated with criminal personality suggests that it would be a worthwhile basis for future research. Instead of focusing on personality traits or other psychological characteristics, investigators should look for differences between criminals and non-criminals with respect to the criminal thinking patterns hypothesised by Yochelson and Samenow.

10 The Construction of Personality

Overview

This book has been organised around three perspectives on personality: the personality theorist's perspective, the lay perspective and the self perspective. Throughout, it has been argued that each perspective alone is incomplete, and personality is best regarded as a construction made up of contributions from all three perspectives.

The perspectives refer to three vantage points from which personality has been studied by psychologists. In Chapters 2 and 3 some examples of the study of personality from the personality theorist's perspective were presented. The personality theorist regards personality as being a characteristic residing within the individual which is a major determinant of the individual's behaviour. The study of personality therefore involves inferring the structure of personality from observations of overt behaviour. Personality theories arising from the personality theorist's perspective are of two kinds: single-trait theories, which concentrate on one aspect of personality (for example, Field Dependence–Independence); and multi-trait theories, which are concerned with describing the entire personality structure (for example, Eysenck's personality theory). Personality assessment is central to the personality theorist's perspective. Since personality theorists believe that personality is a major determiner of behaviour, one of the major contributions of this perspective has been the development of methods of personality measurement which are intended for the prediction of behaviour.

The personality theorist's perspective has been seriously challenged. The concept of personality utilised by this perspective relies on the existence of behavioural consistency. Personality is inferred from some forms of behavioural consistency and is used to predict other forms of behavioural consistency. Chapter 4 discussed the evidence for and against behavioural consistency. Mischel, in his earlier work (Mischel, 1968), claimed that the evidence for behavioural consistency was inadequate and advocated *situationism* in place of personality theory. Mischel's social learning theory assumes that behaviour is primarily determined by situational factors, not personality, and hence the same person could be expected to behave inconsistently as a result of changes in situational contingencies. However, the weaknesses of a pure situationist position soon became apparent (see Bowers, 1973), and *interactionism* became the most influential alternative to either personality theory or situationism.

Interactionism regards behaviour as the product of both personality traits and situational variables: personality and situation *interact* to produce behaviour. Taking both personality and situation into account has resulted in better explanation and prediction of behaviour than relying on either personality or situation alone. However, the superiority of the interactionist approach does not pose a threat to the personality theorist's perspective. Interactionism demonstrates the value of the personality concept when used in conjunction with situational variables. It has also helped to clarify the question of behavioural consistency. Experiments have demonstrated that consistency may be found in particular people in relation to particular situations, i.e. that consistency is the product of an interaction between personality and situation rather than due to the main effects of either personality or situation alone (e.g. Bem and Allen, 1974).

Thus, while the concept of personality needs to be expanded to take serious account of the role of situational variables, it nevertheless remains an important factor in the explanation and prediction of behaviour. With the modification, as opposed to the invalidation, of the personality concept, the personality theorist's perspective remains a legitimate viewpoint from which to study personality.

Chapters 5 and 6 presented the second perspective from which personality can be studied: the lay perspective. Here, the subject-matter for investigation by psychologists is the theories people as lay persons hold about other people's personalities. These lay or implicit personality theories are important because they influence interpersonal behaviour. In the same way that a psychologist explains and predicts behaviour with the aid of a formal personality theory such as that of Freud or Eysenck, a lay person will use his or her own set of beliefs about personality to understand the behaviour of others. Therefore, in order to understand social behaviour we, as psychologists, need to know something about the everyday theories of social behaviour upon which people base their social interactions.

In Chapter 5 evidence was presented to demonstrate that most people hold similar theories about personality: we share a set of beliefs about the interrelations between personality traits. This belief system allows us to communicate about personality and to make additional inferences about personality on the basis of limited information.

Chapter 6 presented the complex issue of how far these commonly held beliefs about personality correspond to reality. The main difficulty in considering this issue lies in the fact that there is no truly objective measure of personality against which to compare people's beliefs. This difficulty may be overcome by proposing that personality traits be regarded as categorising concepts which are applied to clusters of behavioural and situational characteristics which do exist in the real world. Trait categories function like any other perceptual categories to help us impose organisation and structure on the mass of information on the real world. The accuracy of such categories can be assessed by considering how useful they are in understanding and predicting the events to which they refer. Lay theories of personality, while not resulting in 100 per cent accuracy of prediction, correspond closely enough to be useful.

A similar approach may be taken with regard to the question of the epistemological status of the personality traits making up the structure of personality as described from the personality theorist's perspective. The trait categories used by lay persons and personality theorists are broadly similar. Both use between three to five dimensions to characterise the main aspects of variation between individuals. In the case of personality theory, these dimensions are inferred from systematic observations of behaviours which are subjected to statistical analyses. The resulting dimensions are hypothetical constructs and, as such, are useful for categorising behavioural consistencies.

The view that traits are categorising concepts has resulted in a shift towards a more cognitive approach to the study of lay personality theories. A number of experiments have been conducted where the effects of trait categories on the processing of personality-related information have been explored (e.g. Cantor and Mischel, 1977; Berman and Kenny, 1976). These experiments have shown that beliefs about personality form part of our general knowledge and can be investigated in the same way as beliefs about other aspects of the world.

In Chapter 7 the third and final perspective on personality was presented: the self perspective. In addition to having lay theories about the personalities of others, we also have theories about our own personalities. We are capable of describing ourselves and we use our self-knowledge to understand and predict our own behaviour. Psychologists have studied two aspects of self-knowledge: its origins and its effects on behaviour.

We construct our self-knowledge from information derived from three sources: our appraisal of other people's views of us; observations of our own behaviour, and consideration of our private thoughts, feelings and memory of past experiences — privileged information to which only we have access. The consequences of self-perception for behaviour have been studied from both a motivational and a cognitive standpoint. In motivational terms, self-perception is seen as producing a drive state causing a person to behave in such a way as to change the self-perception; for example, a person with low self-esteem will be motivated to raise it. In cognitive terms, self-knowledge may be conceptualised as being organised in schemata (Markus, 1977) which, like other cognitive categories, control the processing of self-related information.

The studies presented under the three perspectives have,

traditionally, been regarded as belonging to non-overlapping areas in psychology. However, it has been the intention here to show how they may all be interrelated. All three perspectives make their own contribution to the understanding of personality and by considering all three a more complete account of personality is achieved. Chapters 8 and 9 were intended to illustrate this argument by showing how a greater understanding of the issues encountered in the study of personality over the life-span and of criminal personality is reached when these topics are considered from all three perspectives.

Consideration of the three perspectives, separately and together, leads to the conclusion that personality should not be regarded simply as an entity existing within individuals but rather as a cognitive construction. Behaviours and situations occur in the real world but their significance is created by those who observe, and personality refers to the set of categories we use to organise these observations.

Conclusions

In describing personality from all three perspectives, the material presented has been drawn from a wide range of psychological research. Personality, like a number of other headings in psychology such as 'emotion' or 'learning', is more usefully thought of as a topic which may be approached from a number of theoretical and methodological standpoints rather than as a distinct subject area in its own right. With the inclusion of the lay and self perspectives, much of the work presented here may be broadly classified as belonging to social psychology.

Social psychology today is characterised by an increasingly strong cognitive emphasis (Eiser, 1980; Mower White, this series). Social psychologists are studying how people think about social behaviour as well as how they actually behave. The study of cognitive factors has developed along two theoretically and methodologically distinct lines: cognitive social psychology has adopted traditional experimental techniques, whereas the 'new' social psychology rejects them.

In cognitive social psychology, models and techniques have been borrowed from cognitive psychology and laboratory experiments are designed which are relatively far removed from the experiences of everyday life. In the personality domain, this approach is exemplified by the work of investigators such as Cantor and Mischel (1979a) who have used cognitive models to study how people store and process their beliefs about personality. The view of traits as categories (see Chapter 6) represents an extension of cognitive psychology into the social domain. The cognitive experimental approach to personality is a promising development: it provides illuminating ways of approaching existing problems in addition to opening up new areas for investigation.

The alternative to experimental cognitive social psychology is the so-called 'new' social psychology (Mower White, this series). Three schools within the new social psychology may be identified: ethogeny, ethnomethodology and symbolic interactionism (Billig, 1977). While ethnomethodology and symbolic interactionism have been developed primarily within sociology, ethogeny has been heralded as a new paradigm in social psychology (Harré and Secord, 1972).

Ethogeny is concerned with the meaning of behaviour. Instead of trying to predict and control behaviour, Harré and Secord advocate that psychologists should aim to *understand* behaviour. Controlled experiments are rejected because they assume a mechanistic as opposed to a dynamic model of man. Researchers are encouraged to involve themselves in the real-life expression of the interpersonal behaviour under investigation. In particular, serious attention should be paid to the way participants themselves understand their behaviour and to this end Harré and Secord recommend the study of people's accounts of their actions. As yet, there has not been a great deal of research conducted from an ethogenic approach. One example is the work on understanding football hooliganism (Marsh, 1978; Marsh, Rosser and Harré, 1978). Here it was found that by establishing rapport with the fans and obtaining their accounts of their behaviour, it was possible to render their apparently senseless behaviour meaningful and rule-governed.

The ethogenic approach offers a promising alternative to

cognitive social psychology for some aspects of the study of personality. In particular, the lay and self perspectives have drawn attention to the importance of the way people think about their own and other people's personalities. Experimental techniques can tell us about the cognitive processes involved in constructing the perception of personality, but these processes may not seem of any great significance to the subjects of such experiments. For example, subjects would probably not regard as meaningful to *them*, the findings in Harris and Hampson's (1980) study that they can process two traits as rapidly as they can process one (see Chapter 5). In contrast, the subjects in Levinson's research into personality over the life-span found it a significant and insightful experience to go over their biographies (Levinson, 1978).

While some of the life-span research may be seen as having adopted an ethogenic approach unwittingly, the ethogenic approach to personality has been explicitly articulated by De Waele and Harré (1976). They argue that the concept of personality needs reconsidering. Personality is conceived of as the 'social resources of a human being' (De Waele and Harré, 1976, p. 193), which are manifested through the enactment by the individual of a series of personas. Of particular interest here is the method of personality assessment advocated by the ethogenic approach to personality. Great stress is placed on the uniqueness of the individual and this uniqueness is believed to be best understood by obtaining a detailed autobiography from the individual. The authenticity of the individual's account of his or her life history and present state can be verified from direct observation, asking informants, and presenting the individual with contrived problem and conflict situations and observing the response.

There is room for an ethogenic approach and a rigorous experimental approach in the study of personality. It is necessary to study people's understanding of their own and others' personalities, even if this understanding can be shown experimentally to be erroneous or incomplete (Nisbett and Wilson, 1977), because the way people think about personality will have implications for their behaviour. By regarding personality as a cognitive construction, the way people *think* about personality (either other people's or their own) becomes

the prime object of investigation. Therefore, future personality research needs to be concerned with these personality
cognitions. The two approaches to the study of cognitive
factors in social psychology have both been applied already
to personality cognitions and should be pursued further in
future research.

Bibliography

Adorno, T.W., Frenkel-Brunswick, E., Levinson, D.J. and Sanford, R.N. (1950), *The Authoritarian Personality*, New York, Harper & Row.

Alker, H.A. (1972), 'Is personality situationally specific or intraphysically consistent?', *Journal of Personality*, vol. 40, pp. 1–16.

Alker, H.A. (1977), 'Beyond ANOVA psychology in the study of person-situation interactions', in D. Magnusson and N.S. Endler (eds), *Personality at the Crossroads: Current Issues in Interactional Psychology*, Hillsdale, New Jersey, Lawrence Erlbaum Associates.

Allport, G.W. (1937), *Personality: A Psychological Interpretation*, New York, Holt, Rinehart & Winston.

Allport, G.W. and Odbert, H.S. (1936), 'Trait names: A psycholexical study', *Psychological Monographs*, vol. 47, whole no. 171.

Anastasi, A. (1976), *Psychological Testing*, 4th edn., New York, Macmillan.

Anderson, N.H. (1962), 'Application of an additive model to impression formation', *Science*, vol. 138, pp. 817–18.

Anderson, N.H. (1965), 'Averaging versus adding as a stimulus-combination rule in impression formation', *Journal of Experimental Psychology*, vol. 70, pp. 394–400.

Anderson, N.H. (1974), 'Cognitive algebra', in L. Berkowitz (ed.), *Advances in Experimental Social Psychology*, vol. 7, pp. 1–101, New York, Academic Press.

Anderson, N.H. (1976), 'Equity judgments as information integration', *Journal of Personality and Social Psychology*, vol. 33, pp. 291–9.

Anderson, N.H. (1978), 'Progress in cognitive algebra', in L. Berkowitz (ed.), *Cognitive Theories in Social Psychology*, New York, Academic Press.

Anderson, J.R. and Reder, L.M. (1974), 'Negative judgments in and about semantic memory', *Journal of Verbal Learning and Verbal Behaviour*, vol. 13, pp. 664–81.

Argyle, M. (1976), 'Personality and social behaviour', in Rom Harré (ed.), *Personality*, Oxford, Blackwell.

Argyle, M. (1977), 'Predictive and generative rules models of P x S interaction', in D. Magnusson and N.S. Endler (eds), *Personality at the Crossroads: Current Issues in Interactional Psychology*, Hillsdale, New Jersey, Lawrence Erlbaum Associates.

Argyle, M. and Little, B.R. (1972), 'Do personality traits apply to social behaviour?', *Journal for the Theory of Social Behaviour*, vol. 2, pp. 1–35.

Asch, S.E. (1946), 'Forming impressions of personality', *Journal of Abnormal and Social Psychology*, vol. 41, pp. 258–90.

Asch, S.E. (1956), 'Studies of independence and conformity: I. A minority of one against a unanimous majority', *Psychological Monographs*, vol. 70, whole no. 416.

Averill, J.R. (1973), 'The dis-position of psychological dispositions', *Journal of Experimental Research in Personality*, vol. 6, pp. 275-82.

Baer, D.M. (1970), 'An age-irrelevant concept of development', *Merrill-Palmer Quarterly of Behaviour and Development*, vol. 16, pp. 238–46.

Bales, R.F. (1951), *Interaction Process Analysis*, Cambridge, Massachusetts, Addison-Wesley.

Bales, R.F. (1970), *Personality and Interpersonal Behaviour*, New York, Holt, Rinehart & Winston.

Baltes, P.B., Reese, H.W. and Lipsitt, L.P. (1980), 'Lifespan developmental psychology', *Annual Review of Psychology*, vol. 31, pp. 65–110.

Bandura, A. (1977), 'Self-efficacy: Toward a unifying theory of behavioral change', *Psychological Review*, vol. 84, pp. 191–215.

Bannister, D. and Mair, J.M.M. (1968), *The Evaluation of Personal Constructs*, London, Academic Press.

Becker, H.S. (1963), *Outsiders*, New York, Free Press.

Belson, W. (1975), *Juvenile Theft: The Causal Factors*, New York, Harper & Row.

Bem, D.J. (1965), 'An experimental analysis of self-persuasion', *Journal of Experimental Social Psychology*, vol. 1, pp. 199–218.

Bem, D.J. (1967), 'Self-perception: An alternative interpretation of cognitive dissonance phenomena', *Psychological Review*, vol. 74, pp. 183–200.

Bem, D.J. (1972), 'Self-perception theory', in L. Berkowitz (ed.), *Advances in Experimental Social Psychology*, vol. 6, pp. 1–62, New York, Academic Press.

Bem, D.J. and Allen, A. (1974), 'On predicting some of the people some of the time: the search for cross-situational consistencies in behaviour', *Psychological Review*, vol. 81, pp. 506–20.

Bem, D.J. and Funder, D.C. (1978), 'Predicting more of the people more of the time', *Psychological Review*, vol. 85, pp. 485–501.

Bem, S.L. (1974), 'The measurement of psychological androgyny', *Journal of Consulting and Clinical Psychology*, vol. 42, pp. 155–62.

Bennett, T. (1979), 'The social distribution of criminal labels: Police, "proaction" or "reaction" ', *British Journal of Criminology*, vol. 19, pp. 134–45.

Berg, I.A. (ed.) (1967), *Response Set in Personality Assessment*, Chicago, Aldine Press.

Berman, J.S. and Kenny, D.A. (1976), 'Correlational bias in observer ratings', *Journal of Personality and Social Psychology*, vol. 34, pp. 263–73.

Berry, J.W. (1966), 'Temne and Eskimo perceptual skills', *International Journal of Psychology*, vol. 1, pp. 207–29.

Billig, M. (1977), 'The new social psychology and "fascism" ', *European Journal of Social Psychology*, vol. 7, pp. 393–432.

Blackburn, R. (1968a), 'Personality in relation to extreme aggression in psychiatric offenders', *British Journal of Psychiatry*, vol. 114, pp. 821–8.

Blackburn, R. (1968b), 'Emotionality, extraversion and aggression in paranoid and nonparanoid schizophrenic offenders', *British Journal of Psychiatry*, vol. 115, pp. 1301–2.

Blackburn, R. (1970), 'Personality types among abnormal homicides', *Social Hospitals Report*, no. 1.

Blass, T. (ed.) (1977), *Personality Variables in Social Behaviour*, Hillsdale, New Jersey, Lawrence Erlbaum Associates.

Block, J. (1971), *Lives Through Time*, Berkeley, California, Bancroft Books.

Block, J. (1977a), 'Advancing the psychology of personality: paradigmatic shifts or improving the quality of research?', in D. Magnusson and N.S. Endler (eds), *Personality at the Crossroads: Current Issues in Interactional Psychology*, Hillsdale, New Jersey, Lawrence Erlbaum Associates.

Block, J. (1977b), 'Correlational bias in observer ratings: Another perspective on the Berman and Kenny study', *Journal of Personality and Social Psychology*, vol. 35, pp. 873–80.

Block, J., Weiss, D.S. and Thorne, A. (1979), 'How relevant is a semantic similarity interpretation of personality ratings?', *Journal of Personality and Social Psychology*, vol. 37, pp. 1055–74.

Bloom, B.S. (1964), *Stability and Change in Human Characteristics*, New York, Wiley.

Boakes, R.A. (in press), *An Introduction to Animal Psychology*, London, Routledge & Kegan Paul.

Borgatta, E.F., Cottrell, L.S. and Mann, J.H. (1958), 'The spectrum of individual interaction characteristics: An inter-dimensional analysis', *Psychological Reports*, vol. 4, pp. 279-319.

Bower, G.H. (1976), 'Experiments on story understanding and recall', *Quarterly Journal of Experimental Psychology*, vol. 28, pp. 511-34.

Bowers, K.S. (1973), 'Situationism in psychology: an analysis and critique', *Psychological Review*, vol. 80, pp. 307-36.

Box, S. (1971), *Deviance, Reality and Society*, London, Holt, Rinehart & Winston.

Brand, E.S., Ruiz, R.A. and Padilla, A.M. (1974), 'Ethnic identification and preference: A review', *Psychological Bulletin*, vol. 81, pp. 860-90.

Bransford, J.D. and Johnson, M.K. (1972), 'Contextual prerequisites for understanding: Some investigations of comprehension and recall', *Journal of Verbal Learning and Verbal Behaviour*, vol. 11, pp. 717-26.

Bruner, J.S. (1957), 'Going beyond the information given', in H. Gruber *et al.* (eds), *Contemporary Approaches to Cognition*, Cambridge, Massachusetts, Harvard University Press.

Bruner, J.S., and Tagiuri, R. (1954), 'The perception of people', in G. Lindzey (ed.), *Handbook of Social Psychology*, Cambridge, Massachusetts, Addison-Wesley.

Bruner, J.S., Shapiro, D., and Tagiuri, R. (1958), 'The meaning of traits in isolation and in combination', in R. Tagiuri and L. Petrullo (eds), *Person Perception and Interpersonal Behaviour*, Stanford University Press.

Burgess, P.K. (1972), 'Eysenck's theory of criminality: A new approach', *British Journal of Criminology*, vol. 12, pp. 74-82.

Buros, O.K. (ed.) (1975), *Personality Tests and Reviews II. Seventh Mental Measurements Year Book*, New Jersey, Gryphon Press.

Burton, R.V. (1963), 'Generality of honesty reconsidered', *Psychological Review*, vol. 70, pp. 481-99.

Butler, J.M. and Haigh, G.V. (1954), 'Changes in the relation between self-concepts and ideal concepts consequent upon client-centered counseling', in C.R. Rogers and R.F. Dymond (eds), *Psychotherapy and Personality Change: Co-ordinated Studies in the Client-centered Approach*, University of Chicago Press.

Byrne, D. (1964), 'Repression–sensitization as a dimension of personality', in B.A. Maher (ed.), *Progress in Experimental Personality Research*, vol. 1, New York, Academic Press.

Cantor, N. and Mischel, W. (1977), 'Traits as prototypes: Effects on recognition memory', *Journal of Personality and Social Psychology*, vol. 35, pp. 38-48.

Cantor, N. and Mischel, W. (1979a), 'Prototypes in person perception', In L. Berkowitz (ed.), *Advances in Experimental Social Psychology*, vol. 12, pp. 3–52, New York, Academic Press.

Cantor, N. and Mischel, W. (1979b), 'Prototypicality and personality: Effects on free recall and personality impressions', *Journal of Research in Personality*, vol. 13, pp. 187–205.

Caplan, N.S. (1965), 'Intellectual functioning', in H.C. Quay (ed.), *Juvenile Delinquency Research and Theory*, Princeton, New Jersey, Van Nostrand.

Carlson, K.A. (1972), 'Classes of adult offenders: a multivariate approach', *Journal of Abnormal Psychology*, vol. 79, pp. 84–93.

Cattell, R.B. (1946), *Description and Measurement of Personality*, London, George Harrap.

Cattell, R.B. (1947), 'Confirmation and clarification of primary personality factors', *Psychometrika*, vol. 12, pp. 197–220.

Cattell, R.B. (1957), *Personality and Motivation Structure and Measurement*, Yonkers-on-Hudson, World Books.

Cattell, R.B. (1966), 'The meaning and strategic use of factor analysis', in R.B. Cattell (ed.), *Handbook of Multivariate Psychology*, Chicago, Rand McNally.

Cattell, R.B. (1973), *Personality and Mood by Questionnaire*, San Francisco, Jossey-Bass.

Cattell, R.B. and Child, D. (1975), *Motivation and Dynamic Structure*, London, Holt, Rinehart & Winston.

Cattell, R.B. and Kline, P. (1977), *The Scientific Analysis of Personality and Motivation*, New York, Academic Press.

Cattell, R.B. (1973), *Supplement to the 16 PF Handbook*, Champaign, Illinois, Institute for Personality and Ability Testing.

Cattell, R.B. and Scheier, I.H. (1961), *The Meaning and Measurement of Neuroticism and Anxiety*, New York, Ronald Press.

Cattell, R.B. and Warburton, E.W. (1967), *Objective Personality and Motivation Tests*, Urbana, Illinois, University of Illinois Press.

Cattell, R.B., Eber, H.W. and Tatsuoka, M.M. (1970), *Handbook for the Sixteen Personality Factor Questionnaire*, 3rd edn, Champaign, Illinios, Institute for Personality and Ability Testing.

Child, D. (1970), *The Essentials of Factor Analysis*, London, Holt, Rinehart & Winston.

Child, I.L. (1968), 'Personality in culture', in E.F. Borgatta and W.W. Lambert (eds), *Handbook of Personality Theory and Research*, Chicago, Rand McNally.

Claridge, G.S. (1967), *Personality and Arousal*, Oxford, Pergamon Press.

Clark, T. and Penycate, J. (1976), *The Case of Patrick Mackay*, London, Routledge & Kegan Paul.

Cleckley, H. (1964), *The Mask of Sanity*, 4th edn, St Louis, Missouri, Mosby.

292   *Bibliography*

Coates, S.W. (1972), *Preschool Embedded Figures Test*, Palo Alto, California, Consulting Press.

Cochrane, R. (1974), 'Crime and personality: theory and evidence', *Bulletin of the British Psychological Society*, vol. 27, pp. 19–22.

Collins, A.M. and Loftus, E.F. (1975), 'A spreading-activation theory semantic processing', *Psychological Review*, vol. 82, pp. 407–28.

Collins, R.W. and Dmitruk, V.M. (1979), 'Personal validation: Some effects and non-effects of persons, personality tests, and personality descriptions', Unpublished manuscript.

Collins, R.W., Dmitruk, V.M. and Ranney, J.T. (1977), 'Personal validation: Some empirical and ethical considerations', *Journal of Consulting and Clinical Psychology*, vol. 45, pp. 70–7.

Comrey, A.L. (1970), *The Comrey Personality Scales*, San Diego, Educational and Industrial Testing Service.

Cooley, C.H. (1902), *Human Nature and the Social Order*, New York, Scribner.

Couch, A. and Keniston, K. (1960), 'Yeasayers and naysayers: agreeing response set as a personality variable', *Journal of Abnormal Social Psychology*, vol. 60, pp. 151–74.

Cowie, J., Cowie, V. and Slater, E. (1968), *Delinquency in Girls*, London, Heinemann.

Craft, M. (ed.) (1966), *Psychopathic Disorders and their Assessment*, London, Pergamon.

Craig, G. and Boyle, M. (1979), 'The recognition and spontaneous use of psychological descriptions by young children', *British Journal of Social and Clinical Psychology*, vol. 18, pp. 207–8.

Crandall, V.C., Katkovsky, W. and Crandall, V.J. (1965), 'Children's beliefs in their control of reinforcements in intellectual-academic achievement situations', *Child Development*, vol. 36, pp. 91–109.

Cronbach, L.J. (1957), 'The two disciplines of scientific psychology', *American Psychologist*, vol. 12, pp. 671–84.

Cronbach, L.J. (1975), 'Beyond the two disciplines of scientific psychology', *American Psychologist*, vol. 30, pp. 116–27.

Cronbach, L.J. and Snow, R.E. (1977), *Aptitudes and Instructional Methods: A Handbook for Research on Interactions*, New York, Irvington.

Crowne, D.P. and Marlowe, D. (1960), 'A new scale of social desirability independent of psychopathology', *Journal of Consulting Psychology*, vol. 24, pp. 349–54.

D'Andrade, R.G. (1965), 'Trait psychology and componential analysis', *American Anthropologist*, vol. 67, pp. 215–28.

D'Andrade, R.G. (1974), 'Memory and the assessment of behaviour', in H.M. Blalock Jr (ed.), *Measurement in the Social Sciences*, Chicago, Aldine-Atherton.

De Waele, J.-P. and Harré, R. (1976), 'The Personality of individuals', in R. Harré (ed.), *Personality*, Oxford, Blackwell.

Dmitruk, V.M., Collins, R.W. and Clinger, D.L. (1973), 'The "Barnum effect" and acceptance of negative personal evaluation', *Journal of Consulting and Clinical Psychology*, vol. 41, pp. 192-4.

Dreger, R.M. (1977), 'Developmental structural changes in the child's personality', in R.B. Cattell and R.M. Dreger (eds), *Handbook of Modern Personality Theory*, New York, Halsted.

Dubin, R. and Dubin, E.R. (1965), 'Children's social perceptions: A review of research', *Child Development*, vol. 36, pp. 809-38.

Duval, S. and Wicklund, R.A. (1972), *A Theory of Objective Self Awareness*, New York, Academic Press.

Eaves, L.J. and Eysenck, H.J. (1975), 'The nature of extraversion: a genetical analysis', *Journal of Personality and Social Psychology*, vol. 30, pp. 102-12.

Ebbesen, E.B. and Allen, R.B. (1979), 'Cognitive processes in implicit personality trait inferences', *Journal of Personality and Social Psychology*, vol. 37, pp. 471-88.

Edwards, A.L. (1957), *The Social Desirability Variable in Personality Assessment and Research*, New York, Dryden.

Eiser, J.R. (1979), 'Attitudes', in K. Connolly (ed.), *Psychology Survey* no. 2, London, George Allen & Unwin.

Eiser, J.R. (1980), *Cognitive Social Psychology: A Guidebook to Theory and Research*, London, McGraw-Hill.

Ekehammar, B. (1974), 'Interactionism in personality from a historical perspective', *Psychological Bulletin*, vol. 81, pp. 1026-48.

Endler, N.S. (1973), 'The person versus the situation — a pseudo issue? A response to Alker', *Journal of Personality*, vol. 41, pp. 287-303.

Endler, N.S. (1975), 'A person-situation interaction model for anxiety', in C.D. Speilberger and I.G. Sarason (eds), *Stress and Anxiety* vol. 1, Washington D.C., Hemisphere.

Endler, N.S. and Edwards, J. (1978), 'Person by treatment interactions in personality research', in L.A. Pervin and M. Lewis (eds), *Perspectives in Interactional Psychology*, New York, Plenum Press.

Endler, N.S. and Magnusson, D. (1976), 'Toward an interactional psychology of personality', *Psychological Bulletin*, vol. 83, pp. 956-74.

Epstein, S. (1979), 'The stability of behaviour: I. On predicting most of the people much of the time', *Journal of Personality and Social Psychology*, vol. 37, pp. 1097-1126.

Erikson, E.H. (1963), *Childhood and Society*, 2nd edn., New York, Norton.

Erikson, K.T. (1962), 'Notes on the sociology of deviance', *Social Problems*, vol. 9, pp. 307-14.

Eysenck, H.J. (1944), 'Types of personality – a factorial study of 700 neurotic soldiers', *Journal of Mental Science*, vol. 90, pp. 851-961.

Eysenck, H.J. (1947), *Dimensions of Personality*, London, Routledge & Kegan Paul.

Eysenck, H.J. (1953), *The Structure of Personality*, London, Methuen.

Eysenck, H.J. (1954), *The Psychology of Politics*, London, Routledge & Kegan Paul.

Eysenck, H.J. (1967), *The Biological Basis of Personality*, Springfield, Illinois, C.C. Thomas.

Eysenck, H.J. (1970), *Crime and Personality*, 2nd edn., London, Granada Press.

Eysenck, H.J. (1974), 'Crime and personality reconsidered', *Bulletin of the British Psychological Society*, vol. 27, pp. 23-4.

Eysenck, H.J. (1977), *Crime and Personality*, London, Paladin.

Eysenck, H.J. and Eysenck, S.B.G. (1964), *Manual of the Eysenck Personality Inventory*, University of London Press.

Eysenck, H.J. and Eysenck, S.B.G. (1968), 'A factorial study of psychoticism as a dimension of personality', *Multivariate Behaviour Research*, All-clinical special issue, pp. 15-31.

Eysenck, H.J. and Eysenck, S.B.G. (1969), *Personality Structure and Measurement*, London, Routledge & Kegan Paul.

Eysenck, H.J. and Eysenck, S.B.G. (1975), *Manual for the Eysenck Personality Questionnaire*, London, Hodder & Stoughton.

Eysenck, H.J. and Eysenck, S.B.G. (1976), *Psychoticism as a Dimension of Personality*, London, Hodder & Stoughton.

Eysenck, S.B.G. (1965), 'A new scale for personality measurement in children', *British Journal of Educational Psychology*, vol. 35, pp. 362-7.

Eysenck, S.B.G. and Eysenck, H.J. (1963), 'On the dual nature of extraversion', *British Journal of Social and Clinical Psychology*, vol. 2, pp. 46-55.

Eysenck, S.B.G. and Eysenck, H.J. (1967), 'Salivary response to lemon juice as a measure of introversion', *Perceptual Motor Skills*, vol. 24, pp. 1047-53.

Eysenck, S.B.G. and Eysenck, H.J. (1968), 'The measurement of psychoticism: a study of factor stability and reliability', *British Journal of Social and Clinical Psychology*, vol. 7, pp. 286-94.

Eysenck, S.B.G. and Eysenck, H.J. (1969), 'Scores on three personality variables as a function of age, sex and social class', *British Journal of Social and Clinical Psychology*, vol. 8, pp. 69-76.

Eysenck, S.B.G. (1969), 'Personality dimensions in children', in H.J. Eysenck and S.B.G. Eysenck (eds), *Personality Structure and Measurement*, San Diego, California, Knapp.

Eysenck, S.B.G. and Eysenck, H.J. (1971), 'A comparative study of criminals and matched controls on three dimensions of personality', *British Journal of Social and Clinical Psychology*, vol. 10, pp. 362–6.

Eysenck, S.B.G., Rust, J. and Eysenck, H.J. (1977), 'Personality and the classification of adult offenders', *British Journal of Criminology*, vol. 17, pp. 164–74.

Feldman, M.P. (1977), *Criminal Behaviour: A Psychological Analysis*, London, Wiley.

Flavell, J.H. (1963), *The Developmental Psychology of Jean Piaget*, Princeton, New Jersey, Van Nostrand.

Fodor, E.M. (1972), 'Delinquency and susceptibility to social influence among adolescents as a function of moral development', *Journal of Social Psychology*, vol. 86, pp. 257–60.

Fodor, J.A., Bever, T.G. and Garrett, M.F. (1974), *The Psychology of Language*, New York, McGraw-Hill.

Forer, B.R. (1949), 'The fallacy of personal validation: A classroom demonstration of gullibility', *Journal of Abnormal Social Psychology*, vol. 44, pp. 118–23.

Franks, C.M. (1956), 'Conditioning and personality: a study of normal and neurotic subjects', *Journal of Abnormal Social Psychology*, vol. 52, pp. 143–50.

Franks, C.M. (1957), 'Personality factors and the rate of conditioning', *British Journal of Psychology*, vol. 48, pp. 119–26.

Frederiksen, N. (1972), 'Toward a taxonomy of situations', *American Psychologist*, vol. 27, pp. 114–23.

Gale, A. (1973), 'Individual differences: Studies of extraversion and EEG', in P. Kline (ed.), *New Approaches in Psychological Measurement*, London, Wiley.

Gallup, G.G. (1970), 'Chimpanzees: Self-recognition', *Science*, vol. 167, pp. 86–7.

Gardner, R.A. and Gardner, B.T. (1969), 'Teaching sign language to a chimpanzee', *Science*, vol. 165, pp. 664–72.

Gergen, K.J. (1973), 'Social psychology as history', *Journal of Personality and Social Psychology*, vol. 26, pp. 309–20.

Gergen, K.J. (1977), 'Stability, change and chance in understanding human development', in N. Datan and H.W. Reese (eds), *Life-span Developmental Psychology: Dialectical Perspectives on Experimental Research*, New York, Academic Press.

Gibbons, D.C. and Garrity, D.L. (1962), 'Definition and analysis of certain criminal types', *Journal of Criminal Law and Police Science*, vol. 53, pp. 27–35.

Gibbons, F.X. (1978), 'Sexual standards and reactions to pornography: enhancing behavioural consistency through self-focused attention',

Journal of Personality and Social Psychology, vol. 36, pp. 976-87.

Goffman, E. (1961), *Asylums*, New York, Anchor Books.

Gold, M. (1966), 'Undetected delinquent behaviour', *Journal of Research in Crime and Delinquency*, vol. 3, pp. 27-46.

Golding, S. (1975), 'Flies in the ointment: methodological problems in the analysis of the percentage variance due to persons and situations', *Psychological Bulletin*, vol. 82, pp. 278-88.

Gollin, E.S. (1958), 'Organizational characteristics of social judgements – a developmental investigation', *Journal of Personality*, vol. 26, pp. 139-54.

Goodenough, D.R. (1978), 'Field dependence', in H. London and J.E. Exner (eds), *Dimensions of Personality*, New York, Wiley.

Gray, J.A. (1970), 'The psychophysiological basis of introversion-extraversion', *Behaviour Research and Therapy*, vol. 8, pp. 249-60.

Gray, J.A. (1972), 'The psychophysiological nature of introversion-extraversion: A modification of Eysenck's theory', in V.D. Neblitsyn and J.A. Gray (eds), *Biological Bases of Individual Behaviour*, New York, Academic Press.

Green, S.E. (in press), *Physiological Psychology*, London, Routledge & Kegan Paul.

Gregg, V.H. (in press), *Memory*, London, Routledge & Kegan Paul.

Griffore, R.J. and Samuels, D.D. (1978), 'Moral judgment of residents of a maximum security correctional facility', *The Journal of Psychology*, vol. 100, pp. 3-7.

Guilford, J.P. and Zimmerman, W.S. (1956), 'Fourteen dimensions of temperament', *Psychological Monographs*, vol. 70, no. 10, pp. 1-26.

Gurin, P., Gurin, G., Lao, R.C. and Beattie, M. (1969), 'Internal-external control in the motivational dynamics of Negro youth', *Journal of Social Issues*, vol. 25, no. 3, pp. 29-53.

Gurwitz, S.B. and Topol, B. (1978), 'Determinants of confirming and disconfirming responses to negative social labels', *Journal of Experimental Social Psychology*, vol. 14, pp. 31-42.

Hall, C.S. and Lindzey, G. (1978), *Theories of Personality*, 3rd edn, New York, Wiley.

Hammond, S.B. (1977), 'Personality studied by the method of rating in the life situation', in R.B. Cattell and R.M. Dreger (eds), *Handbook of Modern Personality Theory*, New York, Halsted.

Hampson, S.E. (1975), 'The personality characteristics of certain groups of mentally abnormal offenders', Unpublished PhD thesis, University of Exeter.

Hampson, S.E. and Kline, P. (1977), 'Personality dimensions differentiating certain groups of abnormal offenders from non-offenders', *The British Journal of Criminology*, vol. 17, pp. 310-31.

Hampson, S.E., Gilmour, R. and Harris, P.L. (1978), 'Accuracy in self-perception: the "fallacy of personal validation" ', *British Journal of Social and Clinical Psychology*, vol. 17, pp. 231-5.

Harman, H.H. (1967), *Modern Factor Analysis*, University of Chicago Press.

Harré, R. and Secord, P.F. (1972), *The Explanation of Social Behaviour*, Oxford, Blackwell.

Harris, P.L. and Hampson, S.E. (1980), 'Processing information within implicit personality theory', *British Journal of Social and Clinical Psychology*, vol. 19, pp. 235-42.

Hartshorne, H. and May, M.A. (1928), *Studies in the Nature of Character*, vol. 1, *Studies in Deceit*, New York, Macmillan.

Hartshorne, H. and May, M.A. (1929), *Studies in the Nature of Character*, vol. 2, *Studies in Service and Selfcontrol*, New York, Macmillan.

Hartshorne, H., May, M.A. and Shuttleworth, F.K. (1930), *Studies in the Nature of Character*, vol. 3, *Studies in the Organisation of Character*, New York, Macmillan.

Hayner, N.S. (1961), 'Characteristics of five offender types', *American Sociological Review*, vol. 21, pp. 96-102.

Hays, W.L. (1958), 'An approach to the study of trait implication and trait similarity', in R. Tagiuri and L. Petrullo (eds), *Person Perception and Interpersonal Behaviour*, Stanford University Press.

Heider, F. (1958), *The Psychology of Interpersonal Relations*, New York, Wiley.

Hermstein, R.J. (1973), *I.Q. in the Meritocracy*, London, Allen Lane.

Hoghughi, M.S. and Forrest, A.R. (1970), 'Eysenck's theory of criminality: an examination with approved-school boys', *British Journal of Criminology*, vol. 10, pp. 240-54.

Hollan, J.D. (1975), 'Features and semantic memory: set-theoretic or network models', *Psychological Review*, vol. 82, pp. 154-5.

Honess, T. (1979), 'Children's implicit theories of their peers: A developmental analysis', *British Journal of Psychology*, vol. 70, pp. 417-24.

Honess, T. (1980), 'Reference to self in children's descriptions of their peers: Egocentricity or collaboration?', *Child Development*, vol. 51, pp. 476-80.

Honzik, M. (1965), 'Review of Kagan and Moss', *Merrill-Palmer Quarterly of Behaviour and Development*, vol. 11, pp. 77-88.

Immergluck, L. and Mearini, M.C. (1969), 'Age and sex differences in response to embedded figures and reversible figures', *Journal of Experimental Child Psychology*, vol. 8, pp. 210-21.

Jackson, D.N., Chan, D.W. and Stricker, L.J. (1979), 'Implicit Personality theory: Is it illusory?', *Journal of Personality*, vol. 47, pp. 1-10.

Jackson, D.N., Messick, S. and Myers, C.J. (1964), 'Evaluation of group and individual forms of the embedded-figures measures of field-independence', *Educational and Psychological Measurement*, vol. 24, pp. 177–92.

James, W.H. and Rotter, J.B. (1958), 'Partial and one hundred percent reinforcement under chance and skill conditions', *Journal of Experimental Psychology*, vol. 55, pp. 397–403.

Jensen, A. (1971), 'The race x sex x ability interaction', in R. Cancro (ed.), *Intelligence: Genetic and Environmental Influences*, New York, Grune and Stratton.

Johnson, T.J., Feigenbaum, R. and Weiby, M. (1964), 'Some determinants and consequences of the teacher's perception of causation', *Journal of Educational Psychology*, vol. 55, pp. 237–46.

Jones, E.E. and Davis, K.E. (1965), 'From acts to dispositions: The attribution process in person perception', in L. Berkowitz (ed.), *Advances in Experimental Social Psychology*, vol. 2, New York, Academic Press.

Jones, E.E. and Nisbett, R.E. (1971), 'The actor and the observer: Divergent perceptions of the causes of behaviour', in E.E. Jones *et al.* (eds), *Attribution: Perceiving the Causes of Behaviour*, Morristown, New Jersey, General Learning Press.

Jung, C.G. (1921), *Psychologische Typen*, Zürich, Rascher.

Kagan, J. and Moss, H.A. (1962), *Birth to Maturity: A Study in Psychological Development*, New York, Wiley.

Kahneman, D. and Tversky, A. (1973), 'On the psychology of prediction', *Psychological Review*, vol. 80, pp. 237–51.

Karabenick, S.A. and Srull, T.K. (1978), 'Effects of personality and situational variation in locus of control of cheating: determinants of the "congruence effect"', *Journal of Personality*, vol. 46, pp. 72–95.

Karp, S.A. (1977), 'Psychological differentiation', in T. Blass (ed.), *Personality Variables in Social Behaviour*, Hillsdale, New Jersey, Lawrence Erlbaum Associates.

Kelley, H.H. (1967), 'Attribution in social interaction', in D. Levine (ed.), *Nebraska Symposium on Motivation*, vol. 15, Lincoln, University of Nebraska Press.

Kelly, E.L. (1955), 'Consistency of the adult personality', *American Psychologist*, vol. 10, pp. 659–81.

Kelly, G.A. (1955), *The Psychology of Personal Constructs*, vols. I and II, New York, Norton.

Kline, P. (1969), 'The anal character: a cross-cultural study in Ghana', *British Journal of Social and Clinical Psychology*, vol. 8, pp. 201–10.

Kline, P. (1972), *Fact and Fantasy in Freudian Theory*, London, Methuen.

Kline, P. and Storey, R. (1977), 'A factor analytic study of the oral character', *British Journal of Social and Clinical Psychology*, vol. 16, pp. 317–28.

Kline, P. and Storey, R. (1980), 'The etiology of the oral character', *Journal of Genetic Psychology*, vol. 136, pp. 85–94.

Kogan, N. and Wallach, M.A. (1964), *Risk Taking: A Study in Cognition and Personality*, New York, Holt, Rinehart & Winston.

Kohlberg, L. (1964), 'The development of moral character', in M.L. Hoffman *et al.* (eds), *Child Development*, vol. 1, New York, Russell Sage Foundation.

Kohlberg, L. (1969), 'State and sequence: the cognitive developmental approach to socialisation', in D.A. Gosler (ed.), *Handbook of Socialization Theory and Research*, New York, Rand McNally.

Kohlberg, L. (1976), 'Moral stages and moralization: The cognitive developmental approach', in T. Lickona (ed.), *Moral Development and Behaviour: Theory, Research and Social Issues*, New York, Holt, Rinehart & Winston.

Kretschmer, E. (1948), *Körperbau und Charakter*, Berlin, Springer.

Lader, M. (1977), *Psychiatry on Trial*, Harmondsworth, Penguin Books.

Latané, B. and Darley, J.M. (1970), *The Unresponsive Bystander: Why Doesn't He Help?*, New York, Appleton-Century-Crofts.

Lawson, A. (1976), 'Formal operations and field independence in a heterogeneous sample', *Perceptual and Motor Skills*, vol. 42, pp. 981–2.

Lay, C.H. and Jackson, D.N. (1969), 'Analysis of the generality of trait-inferential relationships', *Journal of Personality and Social Psychology*, vol. 12, pp. 12–21.

Lemert, E. (1972), *Human Deviance: Social Problems and Social Control*, 2nd edn, Englewood-Cliffs, Prentice Hall.

Levinson, D.J. (1978), *The Seasons of a Man's Life*, New York, Knopf.

Lewin, K. (1935), *A Dynamic Theory of Personality*, New York, McGraw-Hill.

Lewis, M. and Brooks, J. (1975), 'Infants' social perception: A constructivist view', in L.B. Cohen and P. Salapatek (eds), *Infant Perception: From Sensation to Cognition*, vol. II, *Perception of Space, Speech and Sound*, New York, Academic Press.

Lingle, J.H., Geva, N., Ostrom, T.M., Leippe, M.R. and Baumgardner, M.H. (1979), 'Thematic effects of person judgments on impression organisation', *Journal of Personality and Social Psychology*, vol. 37, pp. 674–87.

Linton, M. (1978), 'Real-world memory after six years: An in vivo study of very long-term memory', in M.M. Gruneberg, P.E. Morris and R.N. Sykes (eds), *Practical Aspects of Memory*, London, Academic Press.

Livesley, W.J. and Bromley, D.B. (1973), *Person Perception in Childhood and Adolescence*, London, Wiley.

Livson, N. (1973), 'Developmental dimensions of personality: A lifespan formulation', in P.B. Baltes and K.W. Schaie (eds), *Life-Span Developmental Psychology: Personality and Socialisation*, New York, Academic Press.

Loehlin, J.C. (1977), 'Psychological genetics from the study of human behaviour', in R.B. Cattell and R.M. Dreger (eds), *Handbook of Modern Personality Theory*, New York, Halsted.

London, H. and Exner, J.E. (eds) (1978), *Dimensions of Personality*, New York, Wiley.

Luria, A.R. (1976), *Cognitive Development: Its Cultural and Social Development*, Cambridge, Massachusetts, Harvard University Press.

McBain, E. (1978), *Doors*, London, Pan.

McClelland, D.C., Atkinson, J.W., Clark, R.A. and Lowell, E.L. (1953), *The Achievement Motive*, New York, Appleton-Century-Crofts.

Maccoby, E. and Jacklin, C. (1974), *The Psychology of Sex Differences*, Stanford University Press.

McCord, W. and McCord, J. (1964), *The Psychopath: An Essay on the Criminal Mind*, Princeton, New Jersey, Nostrand.

Mackintosh, N.J. (1974), *The Psychology of Animal Learning*, New York, Academic Press.

Maclean, C. (1979), *The Wolf Children*, Harmondsworth, Penguin Books.

McVicar, J. (1979), *McVicar By Himself*, London, Arrow.

Magnusson, D. and Endler, N.S. (eds), (1977), *Personality at the Crossroads: Current Issues in Interactional Psychology*, Hillsdale, New Jersey, Lawrence Erlbaum Associates.

Mann, R.D. (1959), 'The relation between personality characteristics and individual performance in small groups', Unpublished PhD dissertation, University of Michigan.

Marcus, B. (1960), 'A dimensional study of a prison population', *British Journal of Criminology*, vol. 1, pp. 130-53.

Markus, H. (1977), 'Self-schemata and processing information about the self', *Journal of Personality and Social Psychology*, vol. 35, pp. 63-78.

Marsh, P. (1978), *Aggro: The Illusion of Violence*, London, Dent.

Marsh, P., Rosser, E. and Harré, R. (1978), *The Rules of Disorder*, London, Routledge & Kegan Paul.

Matza, D. (1969), *Becoming Deviant*, Englewood Cliffs, New Jersey, Prentice Hall.

Mausner, B. and Graham, J. (1970), 'Field dependence and prior reinforcement as determinants of social interaction in judgment', *Journal of Personality and Social Psychology*, vol. 16, pp. 486-93.

Mead, G.H. (1934), *Mind, Self and Society*, University of Chicago Press.

Megargee, E.I. (1966), 'Undercontrolled and overcontrolled personality types in extreme antisocial aggression', *Psychological Monographs*, vol. 80, whole no. 611.

Miller, D.T. and Ross, M. (1975), 'Self-serving biases in the attribution of causality: Fact or fiction?', *Psychological Bulletin*, vol. 82, pp. 213-5.

Millham, J. and Jacobson, L.I. (1978), 'The need for approval', in H. London and J.E. Exner (eds), *Dimensions of Personality*, New York, Wiley.

Mirels, H.L. (1970), 'Dimensions of internal versus external control', *Journal of Consulting and Clinical Psychology*, vol. 34, pp. 226-8.

Mirels, H.L. (1976), 'Implicit personality theory and inferential illusions', *Journal of Personality*, vol. 44, pp. 467-87.

Mischel, W. (1968), *Personality and Assessment*, New York, Wiley.

Mischel, W. (1973), 'Toward a cognitive social learning reconceptualisation of personality', *Psychological Review*, vol. 80, pp. 252-83.

Mischel, W. (1977a), 'On the future of personality measurement', *American Psychologist*, vol. 32, pp. 246-54.

Mischel, W. (1977b), 'The interaction of person and situation', in D. Magnusson and N.S. Endler (eds), *Personality at the Crossroads: Current Issues in Interactional Psychology*, Hillsdale, New Jersey, Lawrence Erlbaum Associates.

Moos, R.H. (1969), 'Sources of variance in responses to questionnaires and behaviour', *Journal of Abnormal Psychology*, vol. 74, pp. 405-12.

Morris, S. and Messer, S.B. (1978), 'The effect of locus of control and locus of reinforcement on academic task persistence', *Journal of Genetic Psychology*, vol. 132, pp. 3-9.

Mosher, D.L. (1965), 'Approval motive and acceptance of "fake" personality test interpretations which differ in favourability', *Psychological Reports*, vol. 17, pp. 395-402.

Mower White, C. (in press), *Social Psychology*, London, Routledge & Kegan Paul.

Mulaik, S. (1964), 'Are personality factors raters' conceptual factors?', *Journal of Consulting Psychology*, vol. 28, pp. 506-11.

Munro, D.J. (1977), *The Concept of Man in Contemporary China*, Ann Arbor, Michigan, University of Michigan Press.

Nagpal, M. and Gupta, B.S. (1979), 'Personality, reinforcement and verbal operant conditioning', *British Journal of Psychology*, vol. 70, pp. 471-76.

Nebelkopf, E.B. and Dreyer, A.S. (1973), 'Continuous-discontinuous concept attainment as a function of individual differences in cognitive style', *Perceptual and Motor Skills*, vol. 36, pp. 655-62.

Newell, A. and Simon, H.A. (1972), *Human Problem Solving*, Englewood Cliffs, New Jersey, Prentice Hall.

Newcomb, T.M. (1929), 'The consistency of certain introvert–extravert behaviour patterns in 51 problem boys', Teachers' College, Columbia University, Contributions to Education, no. 382.

Nisbett, R.E. and Wilson, T.D. (1977), 'Telling more than we can know: Verbal reports on mental processes', *Psychological Review*, vol. 84, pp. 231--59.

Nisbett, R.E., Caputo, C.G., Legant, P. and Maracek, J. (1973), 'Behaviour as seen by the actor and as seen by the observer', *Journal of Personality and Social Psychology*, vol. 27, pp. 154-64.

Norman, W.T. (1963), 'Toward an adequate taxonomy of personality attributes: Replicated factor structure in peer nomination personality ratings', *Journal of Abnormal Social Psychology*, vol. 66, pp. 574-88.

Nowicki, S. and Duke, M.P. (1974), 'A locus of control scale for non-college as well as college adults', *Journal of Personality Assessment*, vol. 38, pp. 136-7.

Nunnally, J.C. (1973), 'Research strategies and measurement methods for investigating human development', in J.R. Nesselroade and H.W. Reese (eds), *Life-span Developmental Psychology: Methodological Issues*, New York, Academic Press.

Olshan, K. (1970), 'The multidimensional structure of person perception in children', Unpublished PhD dissertation, Rutgers University.

Olweus, D. (1977), 'A critical analysis of the "modern" interactionist position', in D. Magnusson and N.S. Endler (eds), *Personality at the Crossroads: Current Issues in Interactional Psychology*, Hillsdale, New Jersey, Lawrence Erlbaum Associates.

Orpen, R.B. and Jamotte, A. (1975), 'The acceptance of generalised personality interpretations', *Journal of Social Psychology*, vol. 96, pp. 147-8.

Osgood, C.E. (1962), 'Studies on the generality of affective meaning systems', *American Psychologist*, vol. 17, pp. 10-28.

Overton, W.F. and Reese, H.W. (1973), 'Models of development: methodological implications', in J.R. Nesselroade and H.W. Reese (eds), *Life-span Developmental Psychology: Methodological Issues*, New York, Academic Press.

Passingham, R.E. (1972), 'Crime and personality: a review of Eysenck's theory', in V.D. Nebylitsyn and J.A. Gray (eds), *Biological Bases of Individual Behaviour*, New York, Academic Press.

Passini, F.T. and Norman, W.T. (1966), 'A universal conception of personality structure?', *Journal of Personality and Social Psychology*, vol. 4, pp. 44-9.

Pearson, J. (1972), *The Profession of Violence*, London, Panther.

Peevers, B. and Secord, P. (1973), 'Developmental changes in attributions of descriptive concepts to persons', *Journal of Personality and Social Psychology*, vol. 27, pp. 120–8.

Pervin, L.A. and Lewis, M. (eds) (1978), *Perspectives in Interactional Psychology*, New York, Plenum Press.

Phares, E.J. (1957), 'Expectancy changes in skill and chance situations', *Journal of Abnormal and Social Psychology*, vol. 54, pp. 339–42.

Phares, E.J. (1976), *Locus of Control in Personality*, Morristown, New Jersey, General Learning Press.

Phares, E.J. (1978), 'Locus of control', in H. London and J.E. Exner (eds), *Dimensions of Personality*, New York, Wiley.

Piaget, J. (1932), *The Moral Judgement of the Child*, London, Routledge & Kegan Paul.

Popper, K. (1959), *The Logic of Scientific Discovery*, New York, Basic Books.

Price, R.H. (1974), 'The taxonomic classification of behaviours and situations and the problem of behaviour-environment congruence', *Human Relations*, vol. 27, pp. 567–85.

Price, R.H. and Bouffard, D.L. (1974), 'Behavioural appropriateness and situational constraint as dimensions of social behaviour', *Journal of Personality and Social Psychology*, vol. 30, pp. 579–86.

Quinney, R. (1970), *The Social Reality of Crime*, Boston, Little, Brown.

Rachman, S. (1969), 'Extraversion and neuroticism in childhood', in H.J. Eysenck and S.B.G. Eysenck (eds), *Personality Structure and Measurement*, San Diego, California, Knapp.

Radzinowicz, L. and King, J. (1977), *The Growth of Crime*, London, Hamish Hamilton.

Rest, J. (1974), 'Manual for the defining issues test: An objective test of moral judgement', University of Minnesota, Minneapolis.

Rich, M.C. (1979), 'Verbal reports on mental processes: Issues of accuracy and awareness', *Journal for the Theory of Social Behaviour*, vol. 9, pp. 29–37.

Rock, P. (1973), *Deviant Behaviour*, London, Hutchinson.

Rogers, C.R. (1959), 'A theory of therapy, personality, and interpersonal relationships, as developed in the client-centered framework', in S. Koch (ed.), *Psychology: A Study of Science*, vol. 3, New York, McGraw-Hill.

Rogers, C.R. (1961), *On Becoming a Person*, London, Constable.

Rosch, E. (1975), 'Cognitive representations of semantic categories', *Journal of Experimental Psychology: General*, vol. 104, pp. 192–223.

Rosch, E. (1978), 'Principles of categorisation', in E. Rosch and B.B. Lloyd (eds), *Cognition and Categorisation*, Hillsdale, New Jersey, Lawrence Erlbaum Associates.

Rosch, E. and Mervis, C.B. (1975), 'Family resemblances: Studies in the internal structure of categories', *Cognitive Psychology*, vol. 7, pp. 573-605.

Rosch, E.M., Mervis, C.B., Gray, W.D., Johnson, D. and Boyes-Braem, P. (1976), 'Basic objects in natural categories', *Cognitive Psychology*, vol. 8, pp. 382-439.

Rosenberg, S. and Olshan, K. (1970), 'Evaluative and descriptive aspects in personality perception', *Journal of Personality and Social Psychology*, vol. 16, pp. 619-26.

Rosenberg, S. and Sedlak, A. (1972a), 'Structural representations of implicit personality theory', in L. Berkowitz (ed.), *Advances in Experimental Social Psychology*, vol. 6, pp. 235-97, New York, Academic Press.

Rosenberg, S. and Sedlak, A. (1972b), 'Structural representations of perceived personality trait relationships', in A.K. Romney, R.N. Shepard and S. Nerlove (eds), *Multidimensional Scaling: Theory and Applications in the Behavioural Sciences*, vol. II, *Applications*, New York, Seminar Press.

Rosenberg, S., Nelson, C. and Vivekananthan, P.S. (1968), 'A multidimensional approach to the structure of personality impressions', *Journal of Personality and Social Psychology*, vol. 9, pp. 283-94.

Ross, L. (1977), 'The intuitive psychologist and his shortcomings: Distortions in the attribution process', in L. Berkowitz (ed.), *Advances in Experimental Social Psychology*, vol. 10, pp. 173-220, New York, Academic Press.

Ross, L., Amabile, T.M. and Steinmetz, J.L. (1977), 'Social roles, social control, and biases in social-perception processes', *Journal of Personality and Social Psychology*, vol. 35, pp. 485-94.

Ross, L., Greene, D. and House, P. (1977), 'The false consensus phenomenon: An attributional bias in self-perception and social perception processes', *Journal of Experimental Social Psychology*, vol. 13, pp. 279-301.

Rotter, J.B. (1954), *Social Learning and Clinical Psychology*, Englewood Cliffs, New Jersey, Prentice-Hall.

Rotter, J.B. (1966), 'Generalised expectancies for internal versus external control of reinforcement', *Psychological Monographs*, vol. 80, whole no. 609.

Rotter, J.B. (1975), 'Some problems and misconceptions related to the construct of internal versus external control of reinforcement', *Journal of Consulting and Clinical Psychology*, vol. 43, pp. 56-67.

Rotter, J.B., Chance, J.E. and Phares, E.J. (eds) (1972), *Applications of a Social Learning Theory of Personality*, New York, Holt, Rinehart & Winston.

Rotter, J.B., Liverant, S. and Crowne, D.P. (1961), 'The growth and extinction of expectancies in chance, controlled, and skill tasks', *Journal of Psychology*, vol. 52, pp. 161–77.

Ruble, D.N. and Nakamura, C.Y. (1972), 'Task orientation versus social orientation in young children and their attention to relevant stimuli', *Child Development*, vol. 43, pp. 471–80.

Rudikoff, E.C. (1954), 'A comparative study of the changes in the concepts of the self, the ordinary person, and the ideal in eight cases', in C.R. Rogers and R.F. Dymond (eds), *Psychotherapy and Personality Change: Co-ordinated Studies in the Client-Centred Approach*, University of Chicago Press.

Sampson, E.E. (1977), 'Psychology and the American Ideal', *Journal of Personality and Social Psychology*, vol. 35, pp. 767–82.

Scarlett, H.H., Press, A.N. and Crockett, W.H. (1971), 'Children's descriptions of peers: a Wernerian developmental analysis', *Child Development*, vol. 42, pp. 439–53.

Schaie, K.W. (1965), 'A general model for the study of developmental problems', *Psychological Bulletin*, vol. 64, pp. 92–107.

Schaie, K.W. (1973), 'Methodological problems in descriptive developmental research on adulthood and old age', in J.R. Nesselroade and H.W. Reese (eds), *Life-span Developmental Psychology: Methodological Issues*, New York, Academic Press.

Schaie, K.W. (1974), 'Translations in gerontology – from lab to life: Intellectual functions', *American Psychologist*, vol. 29, pp. 802–7.

Schaie, K.W. and Parham, A. (1976), 'Stability of adult personality traits: fact or fable?', *Journal of Personality and Social Psychology*, vol. 34, pp. 146–58.

Schneider, D.J. (1973), 'Implicit personality theory: A review', *Psychological Bulletin*, vol. 79, pp. 294–309.

Schuessler, K.F. and Cressey, D.R. (1950), 'Personality characteristics of criminals', *American Journal of Sociology*, vol. 55, pp. 476–84.

Schur, E.M. (1971), *Labeling Deviant Behaviour. Its Sociological Implications*, New York, Harper & Row.

Sears, R.R., Maccoby, E.E. and Levin, H. (1957), *Patterns of Child Rearing*, New York, Harper & Row.

Seidenberg, M.S. and Petitto, L.A. (1979), 'Signing behaviour in apes: A critical review', *Cognition*, vol. 7, pp. 177–215.

Sells, S.B., Demaree, R.G. and Will, Jr D.P. (1970), 'Dimensions of personality. I. Conjoint factor structure in Guilford and Cattell trait markers', *Multivariate Behavioural Research*, vol. 5, pp. 391–422.

Sells, S.B., Demaree, R.G. and Will, Jr D.P. (1971), 'Dimensions of personality. II. Separate factor structure in Guilford and Cattell trait markers', *Multivariate Behavioural Research*, vol. 6, pp. 135–85.

Shapland, J. and Rushton, J.R. (1975), 'Crime and personality: further evidence', *Bulletin of the British Psychological Society*, vol. 28, pp. 66-8.

Sheehy, G. (1976), *Passages: Predictable Crises of Adult Life*, New York, Dutton.

Shepard, R.N. (1975), 'Form, formation, and transformation of internal representations', in R.L. Solso (ed.), *Information Processing and Cognition*, Hillsdale, New Jersey, Lawrence Erlbaum Associates.

Shields, J. (1976), 'Heredity and environment', in H.J. Eysenck and G.D. Wilson (eds), *A Textbook of Human Psychology*, Baltimore, University Park Press.

Shrauger, J.S. and Schoeneman, T.J. (1979), 'Symbolic interactionist view of self-concept: Through the looking glass darkly', *Psychological Bulletin*, vol. 86, pp. 549-73.

Shweder, R.A. (1975), 'How relevant is an individual difference theory of personality ratings?', *Journal of Personality*, vol. 43, pp. 455-85.

Siegler, I.C., George, L.K. and Okun, M.A. (1979), 'Cross-sequential analysis of adult personality', *Developmental Psychology*, vol. 15, pp. 350-1.

Sinclair, I. and Chapman, B. (1973), 'A typological and dimensional study of a sample of prisoners', *British Journal of Criminology*, vol. 13, pp. 341-53.

Singer, J.L. (1976), *Daydreaming and Fantasy*, London, Allen & Unwin.

Smith, E.E., Shoben, E.J. and Rips, L.J. (1974), 'Structure and process in semantic memory: a featural model for semantic decisions', *Psychological Review*, vol. 81, 214-41.

Smith, E.R. and Miller, F.D. (1978), 'Limits on perception of cognitive processes: A reply to Nisbett and Wilson', *Psychological Review*, vol. 85, pp. 355-62.

Snodgrass, S.R. (1976), 'The development of trait inference', *Journal of Genetic Psychology*, vol. 128, pp. 163-72.

Snow, R.E. (1977), 'Research on aptitudes: A progress report', in L.S. Shulman (ed.), *Review of Research in Education*, vol. 4, Itasca, Illinois, Peacock Press.

Snow, R.E. (1978), 'Aptitude-treatment interactions in educational research', in L.A. Pervin and M. Lewis (eds), *Perspectives in Interactional Psychology*, New York, Plenum Press.

Snyder, M. and Swann, W.B. (1978), 'Behavioural confirmation in social interaction; from social perception to social reality', *Journal of Experimental Social Psychology*, vol. 14, pp. 148-62.

Snyder, M. and Uranowitz, S.W. (1978), 'Reconstructing the past: Some cognitive consequences of person perception', *Journal of Personality and Social Psychology*, vol. 36, pp. 941-50.

Spearman, C. (1927), *The Abilities of Man*, New York, Macmillan.

Steele, C.M. (1975), 'Name-calling and compliance', *Journal of Personality and Social Psychology*, vol. 31, pp. 361-9.

Stephenson, W. (1953), *The Study of Behaviour: Q-technique and its Methodology*, University of Chicago Press.

Storms, M.D. and Nisbett, R.E. (1970), 'Insomnia and the attribution process', *Journal of Personality and Social Psychology*, vol. 2, pp. 319-28.

Stricker, L.J., Jacobs, P.I. and Kogan, N. (1974), 'Trait correlations in implicit personality theories and questionnaire data', *Journal of Personality and Social Psychology*, vol. 30, pp. 198-207.

Strickland, B.R. (1977), 'Internal-external control of reinforcement', in T. Blass (ed.), *Personality Variables in Social Behaviour*, Hillsdale, New Jersey, Lawrence Erlbaum Associates.

Sullivan, H.S. (1953), *The Interpersonal Theory of Psychiatry*, New York, Norton.

Sundberg, N.D. (1955), 'The acceptance of "fake" versus "bone fide" personality test interpretations', *Journal of Abnormal Social Psychology*, vol. 50, pp. 145-7.

Terman, L.H. and Oden, M.H. (1959), *The Gifted Group at Mid-life. Thirty-five Years' Follow-up of the Superior Child*, vol. 5 of L.M. Terman (ed.), *Genetic Studies of Genius*, Stanford University Press.

Thorne, F.C. (1961), *Clinical Judgement: A Study of Clinical Errors*, Brandon, Vermont, Journal of Clinical Psychology.

Thurstone, L.L. (1947), *Multiple Factor Analysis*, University of Chicago Press.

Tupes, E.C. and Christal, R.E. (1961), 'Recurrent personality factors based on trait ratings', *USAF ASD Technical Report*, No. 61-97.

Turner, R.G. (1978), 'Consistency, self-consciousness, and the predictive validity of typical and maximal personality measures', *Journal of Research in Personality*, vol. 12, pp. 117-32.

Tversky, A. and Kahneman, D. (1973), 'Availability: A heuristic for judging frequency and probability', *Cognitive Psychology*, vol. 5, pp. 207-32.

Tversky, A. and Kahneman, D. (1974), 'Judgment under uncertainty: Heuristics and biases', *Science*, vol. 184, pp. 1124-31.

Ulrich, R.D. Stachnik, T.J. and Stainton, R.N. (1963), 'Student acceptance of generalised personality interpretations', *Psychological Reports*, vol. 13, pp. 831-4.

Vagg, P.R. and Hammond, S.B. (1976), 'The number and kind of invariant personality (Q) factors: a partial replication of Eysenck and Eysenck', *British Journal of Social and Clinical Psychology*, vol. 15, pp. 121-9.

Vaillant, G.E. (1977), *Adaptation to Life*, Waltham, Massachusetts, Little, Brown.

Valins, S. and Ray, A.A. (1967), 'Effects of cognitive desensitization on avoidance behaviour', *Journal of Personality and Social Psychology*, vol. 1, pp. 345-50.

Vernon, P.E. (1972), 'The distinctiveness of field independence', *Journal of Personality*, vol. 40, pp. 366-91.

Vestewig, R. (1978), 'Cross-response mode consistency in risk-taking as a function of self-reported strategy and self-perceived consistency', *Journal of Research in Personality*, vol. 12, pp. 152-63.

Wadsworth, M.E.J. (1975), 'Delinquency in a national sample of children', *British Journal of Criminology*, vol. 15, pp. 167-80.

Wadsworth, M.E.J. (1979), *Roots of Delinquency*, Oxford, Martin Robertson.

Waldo, G.P. and Dinitz, S. (1967), 'Personality attributes of the criminal; an analysis of research studies 1950-65', *Journal of Research in Crime and Delinquency*, vol. 4, pp. 185-202.

Wallerstein, J.S. and Wyle, C.J. (1947), 'Our law-abiding law breakers', *Probation*, April, pp. 107-12.

Warburton, F.W. (1965), 'Observations on a sample of psychopathic American criminals', *Behaviour Research and Therapy*, vol. 3, pp. 129-35.

Warr, P.B. (1974), 'Inference magnitude, range, and evaluative directions as factors affecting relative importance of cues in impression formation', *Journal of Personality and Social Psychology*, vol. 30, pp. 191-7.

Watts, A.F. (1944), *The Language and Mental Development of Children*, London, Harrap.

Weisberg, P. (1970), 'Student acceptance of bogus personality interpretations differing in level of social desirability', *Psychological Reports*, vol. 27, pp. 743-6.

Welford, C. (1975), 'Labelling theory and criminology: an assessment', *Special Problems*, vol. 22, p. 332.

Werner, H. (1957), *Comparative Psychology of Mental Development*, New York, International University Press.

West, D.J. (1963), *The Habitual Prisoner*, London, Macmillan.

West, D.J. and Farrington, D.P. (1973), *Who Becomes Delinquent?*, London, Heinemann.

West, D.J. and Farrington, D.P. (1977), *The Delinquent Way of Life*, London, Heinemann.

White, P. (1980), 'Limitations on verbal reports of internal events: A refutation of Nisbett and Wilson and of Bem', *Psychological Review*, vol. 87, pp. 105-12.

Wicklund, R.A. (1975), 'Objective self-awareness', in L. Berkowitz (ed.), *Advances in Experimental Social Psychology*, vol. 8, pp. 233-75, New York, Academic Press.

Wicklund, R.A. (1978), 'Three years later', in L. Berkowitz (ed.), *Cognitive Theories in Social Psychology*, New York, Academic Press.

Wiggins, J.S. (1973), *Personality and Prediction: Principles of Personality Assessment*, Reading, Massachusetts, Addison-Wesley.

Winslow, R.W. (1969), *Crime in a Free Society*, Belmont, California, Dickenson.

Wishner, J. (1960), 'Reanalysis of "impressions of personality"', *Psychological Review*, vol. 67, pp. 96-112.

Witkin, H.A. and Berry, J.W. (1975), 'Psychological differentiation in cross-cultural perspective', *Journal of Cross-cultural Psychology*, vol. 6, pp. 4-87.

Witkin, H.A. and Goodenough, D.R. (1977), 'Field dependence and interpersonal behaviour', *Psychological Bulletin*, vol. 84, pp. 661-89.

Witkin, H.A., Goodenough, D.R. and Karp, S.A. (1967), 'Stability of cognitive style from childhood to young adulthood', *Journal of Personality and Social Psychology*, vol. 7, pp. 291-300.

Witkin, H.A., Dyk, R.B., Faterson, H.F., Goodenough, D.R. and Karp, S.A. (1974), *'Psychological differentiation: Studies of development'*, Hillsdale, New Jersey, Lawrence Erlbaum Associates.

Witkin, H.A., Lewis, H.B., Hertzman, M., Machover, K., Meissner, P.B. and Wapner, S. (1972), *Personality Through Perception: An Experimental and Clinical Study*, Westwood, Connecticut, Greenwood Press.

Wohlwill, J.F. (1970), 'The age variable in psychological research', *Psychological Review*, vol. 77, pp. 49-64.

Wohlwill, J.F. (1973), *The Study of Behavioural Development*, New York, Academic Press.

Wolfgang, M.E., Figlio, R.M. and Sellin, T. (1972), *Delinquency in a Birth Cohort*, University of Chicago Press.

Woodruff, D.S. and Birren, J.E. (1972), 'Age changes and cohort differences in personality', *Developmental Psychology*, vol. 6, pp. 252-9.

Wootton, B. (1959), *Social Science and Social Pathology*, London, Allen & Unwin.

Wyer, R.S. (1970), 'Information redundancy, inconsistency, and novelty and their role in impression formation', *Journal of Experimental Social Psychology*, vol. 6, pp. 111-27.

Yarrow, M.R. and Campbell, J.D. (1963), 'Person perception in children', *Merrill-Palmer Quarterly of Behaviour and Development*, vol. 9, pp. 57-72.

Yochelson, S. and Samenow, S.E. (1976), *The Criminal Personality*, vols I & II, New York, Jason Aronson.

Zimbardo, P.G., Cohen, A., Weisenberg, M., Dworkin, L. and Firestone, I. (1969), 'The control of experimental pain', in P.G. Zimbardo (ed.), *The Cognitive Control of Motivation*, Glenview, Illinois, Scott Foresman.

Index

Achievement Motive, 10
adolescence, and life-span research, 233-8
Adorno, T.W., 10
ageing, 208, 210-11, 215
Alker, H.A., 78, 84, 87, 89
Allen, R.B., 91-2, 93, 117, 204-5
Allport, G.W., 1, 33, 51, 101
Amabile, T.M., 197
analysis of variance, 79-81, 87, 89
Anastasi, A., 22
Anderson, N.H., 111-13, 114-15, 117, 119, 123
anxiety, 40, 42, 47, 83, 87
Argyle, M., 78, 88
ascending reticular activating system (ARAS), 46, 49
Asch, S.E., 105-10, 112, 123
Atkinson, J.W., 10
attribution theory, 98
Authoritarianism, 10
autonomic nervous system (ANS), 46
Averill, J.R., 78

Baer, D.M., 230
Bales, R.F., 66, 147
Baltes, P.B., 208
Bandura, A., 187
Bannister, D., 132
Baumgardner, M.H., 167-8
Beattie, M., 26
Becker, H.S., 261
behaviour: age-differences as inherent characteristics of, 215; and Cattell's theory, 60; consistency in, 2-3, 63-96, 156-7; criminal, 249-50;
and data-base for multi-trait theories, 34-6; deviant, 246-9, ethogenic approach to, 284-5; FD-I and, 19; as function of both person and environment, 75; as function of reinforcement, 20-1; helping, 185-6; immediate behaviour ratings and implicit personality theory, 144-51; as product of interactive effects, 62; and re-attribution studies, 184; self-awareness and, 94-5; self-observations of, 188-92; and single-trait theories, 10; situationism and, 75-8; social, I-E and prediction of, 30-1; social, and personality theories, 5; and social labelling theory, 261-2
Belson, W., 262, 263
Bem, D.J., 78, 84, 88-9, 91-2, 93, 188-91, 204-5
Bem, S.L., 29
Bennett, T., 263
Berg, I.A., 23
Berman, J.S., 155-6
Berry, J.W., 16
Beunreuter Personality Inventory, 221
Billig, M., 284
Birren, J.E., 225-8
Blackburn, R., 258
Blass, T., 11
Block, J., 1, 72, 149, 155, 209, 219 220, 228-9, 231, 232-8, 244
Bloom, B.S., 221
Borgatta, E.F., 146
Bouffard, D.L., 88

Bowers, K.S., 75, 76-7, 78, 82, 83, 85, 89, 159
Box, S., 250, 261, 263, 264-5, 266
Boyes-Braem, P., 165
Boyle, M., 126, 127
Brand, E.S., 125
Bransford, J.D., 168
Bromley, D.B., 127, 128, 129, 133
Brooks, J., 181
Bruner, J.S., 5, 99, 110, 112, 113, 114, 120, 163
Burgess, P.K., 252
Buros, O.K., 202
Burton, R.V., 71
Butler, J.M., 201
Byrne, D., 10

California Test of Personality (CTP), 226-7
Campbell, J.D., 128
Cantor, N., 117, 164, 165-7, 168, 284
Caplan, N.S., 254
Caputo, C.G., 195
Carlson, K.A., 257
categories, traits as, 159-70
Cattell, R.B., 10, 33, 34, 35, 39, 44, 46, 138, 139-40, 158, 174, 207, 251; and consistency, 67; and criminal personality, 253-4; cf. Eysenck, 52, 53-4, 56; Personality Theory, 50-60, 221, 222-3
Chance, J.E., 20
Chapman, B., 257
Child, D., 38, 58
Child, I.L., 1
children: childhood experience and adult personality, 216-17, 218-19; consistency tests, 71; and factor analysis re. multi-trait theories, 36, 39; I-E tests on, 27-8; implicit personality theories in children over seven, 127-32; in children under seven, 125-7; study of gifted children, 217-18
Christal, R.E., 136-7, 140, 142
Claridge, G.S., 48
Clark, R.A., 10
Clark, T., 272
Cleckley, H., 258
Clinger, D.L., 175
Coates, S.W., 17
Cochrane, R., 252

cognitive psychology: 'cognitive algebra', 115; cognitive consequences of self-perception, 194-9; cognitive models of trait integration and inference, 115-24; and constructivist view of personality, 164-70; increasing influence on social psychology, 283-4; and social cognition, 133-4; Werner's theory of development, 133
Cohen, A., 184
cohorts, 208, 209, 210-14, 219, 223-4, 225, 226-8, 237-8
Collins, A.M., 116, 118
Collins, R.W., 175
Comrey, A.L., 33
conditioning, 47-8, 49
consistency, 2-3, 63-96; evidence for and against, 70-5; four types of, 64-6; interactionism and, 91-5; meaning of, 63-4; Mischel's attack on personality theorist's perspective, 68-9; personality concept, basis in, 67-8; situationism and, 75-8
constructivist position: and cognitive psychology, 164-70; and cross-situational consistency, 204-5; and life-span research, 207, 228-45; and traits as categories, 160-70
Cooley, C.H., 178
Cottrell, L.S., 146
Couch, A., 23
Cowie, J. and V., 250
Craft, M., 258
Craig, G., 126, 127
Crandall, V.C. and V.J., 25, 27
Cressey, D.R., 251
criminal personality, 246-78; Cattell and, 253-4; criminal subgroups, 256-60; criminal thinking patterns, 270, 272-7; criminals as scapegoats, 265; criminals vs. non-criminals, 251-6; defining deviance, 246-9; Eysenck's theory, 251-3; high psychoticism scores, 43; and intelligence, 254-5; lay and self perspectives, 261-9, 277-8; lay perspective and function of labelling, 264-5; Lombroso and, 7; and moral reasoning, 254-6; personality theorist's perspective, 249-60; psychopaths, 48; rehabilitation, 276-7; self perspective and effect

of labels, 266-8; social labelling theory, 261-4; Yochelson and Samenow's theory, 269-77
criterion analysis, 42
Crockett, W.H., 128
Cronbach, L.J., 90, 91, 96
Crowne, D.P., 21, 24
cultures, different: and concept of self, 202-3; cultural relativism and deviance, 247-8; culture-specificity of I-E, 29; and satisfaction of ergs, 58-9

D'Andrade, R.G., 73, 141, 142-3, 146, 147-50, 159, 167
Darley, J.M., 185
Demaree, R.G., 158
deviance: defining, 246-9; as nonconformity, 246-9; three perspectives on, 249; *see also* criminal personality
De Waele, J.-P., 285
Dinitz, S., 251
Dmitruk, V.M., 175
Doors (McBain), 275
Dreger, R.M., 222
Dreyer, A.S., 14
Dubin, R. and E.R., 125
Duke, M.P., 24
Duval, S., 193
Dworkin, L., 184

Eaves, L.J., 48
Ebbesen, E.B., 117
Eber, H.W., 55, 253, 275
Edwards, J., 78, 83
Eiser, J.R., 93, 283
Ekehammar, B., 75
electroencephalogram (EEG), 48
Embedded Figures Test (EFT), 13, 14, 70
Endler, N.S., 78, 83
Epstein, S., 156-7
ergs, 58-9, 60
Erikson, E.H., 207, 230-1, 238-9, 240, 242
Erikson, K.T., 264
Eskimos, 16 18
extraversion, *see* introversion/extraversion
Eysenck, H.J., 4, 10, 33, 34, 35, 139, 158, 174, 207, 222, 251, 256; cf. Cattell, 52, 53-4, 56, 60-2; and

consistency, 67; Personality Theory, 39-50, 221; theory of criminal personality, 251-3
Eysenck Personality Inventory (EPI), 43, 70, 205, 221, 222
Eysenck, S.B.G., 35, 40, 43, 54, 158, 222, 252, 256

factor analysis: criticism of, 62; and multi-trait theories, 36-9, 41, 42, 45, 50, 52-6, 60-2; and person by situation interaction, 87-8; of personality inventories, 158; and personality ratings, 137; solutions produced by, 9-10
false consensus bias, 195-7, 198
Farrington, D.P., 254
Feldman, M.P., 249, 250, 255, 262
Fels Institute, 218-20
Field Dependence-Independence (FD-I), 10, 11-19; criticism of concept, 19; differences between FD and FI individuals, 14-16; distinguishing between FD-I and intelligence, 17-19; origin of concept, 11-14; relevance, 11; sex difference in, 17; and type B consistency, 71
Figlio, R.M., 263
Firestone, I., 184
Flavell, J.H., 133
Fodor, E.M., 180, 255
Forer, B.R., 173
Forrest, A.R., 252
Franks, C.M., 47
Frederikson, N., 87
Frenkel-Brunswick, E., 10
Freud, S., 4, 7, 32, 69, 216, 217, 229, 230, 231
fundamental attribution error, 162, 195
Funder, D.C., 88-9

Gale, A., 48
Gallup, G.G., 181
Gardner, R.A. and B.T., 180
Garrity, D.L., 257
generalised expectancies, 20-1
George, L.K., 225
Gergen, K.J., 91, 215, 229
Gestalt models, 106-7, 109-10, 112
Geva, N., 167-8
Gibbons, D.C., 257
Gibbons, F.X., 93-4

Gilmour, R., 175, 176
Goffmann, E., 266
Gold, M., 263
Golding, S., 85
Gollin, E.S., 127-8, 129, 133
Goodenough, D.R., 15, 16
Gray, J.A., 49
Gray, W.D., 165
Greek philosophy, and personality
    types, 39-41
Griffore, R.J., 255
group interaction, 66, 144, 147-9
Guardian, 246
Guilford, J.P., 33, 158
gullibility studies, 174-7
Gupta, B.S., 49
Gurin, P. and G., 26
Gurwitz, S.B., 267-8

Haigh, G.V., 201
Hall, C.S., 4
Hammond, S.B., 158
Hampson, S.E., 117, 175, 176, 259,
    285
Harman, H.H., 9, 53
Harré, R., 187, 284, 285
Harris, P.L., 117, 175, 176, 285
Hartshorne, H., 71-2
Hayner, N.S., 257
Hays, W.L., 101
Heider, F., 193, 195
Herrnstein, R.J., 8
Hidden Picture Test, 14
hierarchies: hierarchical nature of
    personality, 44-6; and trait organ-
    isation, 132
Hoghughi, M.S., 252
Hollan, J.D., 117
Honess, T., 130-1, 132, 133-4
Honzik, M., 219
House, P., 196
hysteria, 40, 42, 47

Immergluck, L., 17
implicit personality theory: acquisition
    of, 124-34; in children over seven,
    127-32; in children under seven,
    125-7; cognitive models of trait
    integration and inference, 115-24;
    epistemological status of, 144-59;
    generality of, 98-9; methods of
    studying, 99-100; personality des-

cription, 100-1; quantitative models
    of trait integration, 110-15; social
    cognition and intellectual develop-
    ment, 132-4; structural represent-
    ation of, 102-4; trait sorting and
    rating, 100-1; traits as categories,
    159-70; using to form impressions,
    104-10
insomniacs, 184-5, 187-8
Institute for Human Development, 232
Intellectual Achievement Responsi-
    bility Questionnaire, 25, 27
intelligence: and criminal personality,
    254-5; distinguishing between FD-I
    and, 17-19; measurement of, 8-9;
    testing, and measurement of per-
    sonality, 9-10
interactionism, 78-95; analysis of
    variance, 79-81, 87, 89; and
    consistency, 91-5; criticisms of
    interactionist research, 85-91; evalu-
    ation of, 84-95; person by situation
    interactions, 82-4, 85-9
Internal versus External Locus of
    Control (I-E), 19-32; acquiescence
    response set, 23; culture-specificity,
    29; and generalised expectancies,
    20-1; investigation of, 26-7; meas-
    urement of, 21-6; and political
    activism, 27; and prediction of
    social behaviour, 30; Rotter's I-E
    scale, 21, 22-5, 26; social desir-
    ability response bias, 23-5; and
    social learning theory, 20; test
    validity, 25-6; theoretical back-
    ground, 19-21
internality, 2
introversion/extraversion: and analysis
    of variance, 79-81; criminality and,
    252; lifespan research, 222; and
    multi-trait theories, 40, 41-3, 45-6,
    47, 48-9, 54, 61; and traits as
    categories, 166-7

Jacklin, C., 17
Jackson, D.N., 14, 152, 153
James, W.H., 21
Jamotte, A., 174
Jensen, A., 17
Johnson, M.K., 165, 168
Johnson, T.J., 193-4
Jones, E.E., 193, 195
Jung, C.G., 40

Kagan, J., 209, 218, 219, 233
Kahneman, D., 186
Karabenick, S.A., 30, 31, 83
Karp, S.A., 11 14
Katkovsky, W., 25, 27
Kelley, H.H., 193
Kelly, E.L., 220
Kelly, G.A., 163
Keniston, K., 23
Kenny, D.A., 155-6
King, J., 250, 262
Kline, P., 51, 53, 56, 57, 216-17, 223, 259
Kogan, N., 84
Kohlberg, L., 71, 254-5, 256
Kray, Reginald, 272, 273, 274
Kray, Ronald, 272, 273, 274
Kretschmer, E., 40

Lader, M., 247
language, 115-17; acquisition of, 124; set-theoretic and network accounts, 116, 117; use of knowledge encoded in, 116-17; *see also* semantic similarity
Lao, R.C., 26
Latané, B., 185
Lawson, A., 14
Lay, C.H., 152, 153
lay perspective, 97-171; and criminal personality, 261-9, 277-8; implicit personality theory, 97-134; interpretation of personality ratings, 136-46; vs. personality theorists perspective, 136-58; and reality, 135-71; and social labelling theory, 264-5; *see also* implicit personality theory
Legant, P., 195
Leippe, M.R., 167-8
Lemert, E., 248, 261
Levinson, D.J., 10, 229, 231, 240-4, 245, 285
Lewin, K., 75
Lewis, N., 78, 90, 181
lifespan psychology: change model, 229-32; and constructivist approach, 207, 228-45; cross-sectional designs, 211-12, 221-3; lifespan research designs, 207-15; longitudinal designs, 209-11, 217-21, 232-44; and personality theorist's perspective, 215-28,

245; purpose of, 208-9; sequential designs, 212-15, 223-8; stability mode, 215-17
Lindzey, G., 4
Lingle, J.H., 167-8
Linton, M., 227
Lipsitt, L.P., 208
Little, B.R., 78
Liverant, S., 21
Lives Through Time (Block), 232
Livesley, W.J., 127, 128, 129, 133
Livson, N., 221
Locus of Control, 10; and interactionism studies, 83-4; *see also* Internal versus External Locus of Control
Loehlin, J. C., 48
Loftus, E.F., 116, 118
Lombroso, C., 7
London, H., 11
Lowell, E.L., 10
Luria, A.R., 202-3

McBain, E., 275
McClelland, D.C., 10
Maccoby, E., 17
McCord, W. and J., 258
Mackay, Patrick, 272, 275
Mackintosh, N.J., 50
Maclean, C., 179
McVicar, John, 272, 273, 274, 276-7
Magnusson, D., 78
Mair, J.M.M., 132
manic depression, 40
Mann, J.H., 146
Maracek, J., 195
Marcus, B., 257
Markus, H., 198-9
Marlowe, D., 24
Marlowe–Crowne Social Desirability Scale, 24, 175
Marsh, P., 284
Matza, D., 266, 269
May, M.A., 71-2
Mead, G.H., 6, 178-9, 180
Mearini, M.C., 17
Megargee, E.I., 257-8
Mervis, C.B., 165
Messer, S.B., 27-8
Messick, S., 14
Miller, D.T., 187, 188
Miller, F.D., 194
Mirels, H.L., 26, 152

Mischel, W., 68-9, 70-5, 76, 77-8, 89, 117, 139, 156, 164, 165-7, 168, 284
Moos, R.H., 82, 87
Morris, S., 27-8
Mosher, D.L., 175
Moss, H.A., 209, 218, 219, 233
motivation, 57-60
Mower White, C., 283, 284
Mulaik, S., 73, 141, 143
multi-trait theories, 33-62; Cattell's personality theory, 50-60; and consistency, 67, 68; data-base for, 34-6; dimension concept, 40, 45; Eysenck's Personality Theory, 39-50; and factor analysis, 36-9; genetic factor in personality, 48; hierarchical nature of personality, 44-6; motivation, 57-60; 'personality sphere', 51-2; physiological basis of personality, 46-50; purpose, 33; cf. single-trait approach, 34
Munro, D.J., 203, 247
Myers, C.J., 14

Nagpal, M., 49
Nakamura, C.Y., 15
Nebelkopf, E.B., 14
Nelson, C., 100
neuroticism: criminality and, 252; and lifespan research, 222; and multi-trait theories, 40, 41-3, 45-6, 47, 48, 49, 54, 56, 61
Newcomb, T.M., 149, 150
Newell, A., 187
Nisbett, R.E., 184-5, 186-8, 195, 227, 285
Norman, W.T., 73, 137, 138, 139, 140, 142
Nowicki, S., 24
Nunnally, J.C., 207, 208

Odbert, H.S., 51, 101
Oden, M.H., 217-18
Okun, M.A., 225
Olweus, D., 82
Orpen, R.B., 174
Osgood, C.E., 103, 104, 143
Ostrom, T.M., 167-8
Overton, W.F., 90, 229-30

Padilla, A.M., 125
parental ratings, 204-5
Parham, A., 223-4, 225
Passingham, R.E., 252
Passini, F.T., 73, 137, 138, 139, 142
Pearson, J., 272
peer nomination techniques, 137-40
peer ratings, 204-5
Peevers, B., 129-31, 133
Penycate, J., 272
personality: Cattell's theory of, 50-60, 221, 222-3; definition of, 1-2; development, 4; dynamics, 4; Eysenck's theory, 39-50, 221; Freud's theory, 4; hierarchical nature of, 44-6; see also consistency; constructivist position; criminal personality; deviance; factor analysis; Field Dependence-Independence; implicit personality theory; Internal vs. External Locus of Control; introversion/extraversion; lay perspective; lifespan psychology; multi-trait theories; neuroticism; personality ratings; personality theorists; self-perspective; single-trait theories; traits
Personality and Assessment (Mischel), 68-9
personality ratings, 136-59; measures of implicit beliefs, 137-41; of personality, 136-7; of semantic similarity, 141-3; self-report questionnaires, 152-4
personality theorists: and criminality, 249-60; importance of consistency issue, 63, 66; vs. lay perspective, 136-58; and lifespan research, 207, 215-28; multi-trait theories, 33-62; origins of personality measurement, 8-10; significance of outward signs, 7; single-trait theories 7-32; 'trait' and 'dimension', 10; see also *individual psychologists*
Pervin, L.A., 78, 90
Pettito, L.A., 180
Phares, E.J., 20, 21, 27, 28
Piaget, J., 14, 133, 230, 254
Popper, K., 76
Press, A.N., 128
Price, R.H., 88
prototypicality, 165-7
psychopathy, 47-8, 247, 253, 258

psychosexual personality syndromes, 216-17
psychoticism, 40, 43, 45-6, 47, 54, 56, 61, 222, 252

Q factor analysis, 257 259
Q sorts, 89, 201, 234-6
questionnaires: Cattell and, 54-5; and false consensus bias, 196; and hierarchical model, 45; and multi-trait theories, 34; and self-esteem, 202; self-report, 152-4; Sixteen Personality Factor questionnaire (16PF), 55-6, 221, 222-3, 225
Quinney, R., 264, 265

Rachman, S., 222
Radzinowicz, L., 250, 262
Ranney, J.T., 175
Ray, A.A., 184
Reese, H.W., 90, 208, 229-30
reinforcement, 20-1, 30, 31
Repression versus Sensitisation, 10
Rest, J., 255
Rich, M.C., 187
Rips, L.J., 116
risk-taking, 93
Rod and Frame Test (RFT), 12, 13, 17, 18, 70
Rogers, C.R., 6, 200-1
role bias, 195, 197-8
Rosch, E., 165
Rosenberg, S., 100, 102, 104, 140
Ross, L., 162, 194, 195-6, 197, 244
Rotating Room Test (RRT), 12, 13, 18
rotation, 53, 61-2
Rotter, J.B., 20, 21-5, 26, 30, 32, 67
Ruble, D.N., 15
Rudikoff, E.C., 201
Ruiz, R.A., 125
Rushton. J.R., 252-3
Rust, J., 256

Samenow, S.E., 269-78
Sampson, E.E., 29
Samuels, D.D., 255
Sanford, R.N., 10
scapegoats, 265
Scarlett, H.H., 128
Schaie, K.W., 207, 208, 210, 223-4, 225
Scheier, I.H., 59

schizophrenia, 40, 43
Schneider, D.J., 99
Schoenemann, T.J., 182-3, 191
Schuessler, K.F., 251
Schur, E.M., 261
Secord, P.F., 129-31, 133, 187, 284
Sedlak, A., 100, 102, 104, 140
Seidenberg, M.S., 180
self-awareness, 94
self-perception: cognitive consequences of, 194-9; individual differences in self-concept, 199-203; motivational consequences of, 193-4, 198; theory, 189-91
self perspective, 172-205; anti-introspectionist view, 186-7; consequences of self-perception, 192-203; do we know ourselves?, 173-7; guillibility studies, 174-7; privileged information, 183-8; self-observations of behaviour, 188-92; sources of information about self, 177-92; symbolic interactionism, 177-83
self-schemata, 198-9
Sellin, T., 263
Sells, S.B., 158
semantic similarity: and co-endorsement, 152; measures of, 141-3, 147-8, 150
sex differences: in FD-I, 17; in I-E, 28; and lifespan research, 218-19; risk-taking, 93
sexual stereotypes, 169
Shapiro, D., 110
Shapland, J., 252-3
Sheehy, G., 232
Shepard, R.N., 187, 188
Shields, J., 48
Shoben, E.J., 116
Shrauger, J.S., 182-3, 191
Shuttleworth, F.K., 71
Shweder, R.A., 149-51, 152-3, 159, 167
Siegler, I.C., 225
Simon, H.A., 187
Sinclair, I., 257
Singer, J.L., 274
single-trait theories, 7-32; advantages and disadvantages of approach, 32; and consistency, 67, 68; Field Dependence-Independence, 10, 11-19; influential examples, 10-11

situationism, 75-8
Sixteen Personality Factor question-
naire (16PF), 55-6, 221, 222-3,
225
Skinner, B.F., 188-9
Slater, E., 250
Smith, E.E., 116
Smith, E.R., 187, 188
Snodgrass, S.R., 125-6
Snow, R.E., 90
Snyder, M., 169, 266-7
social desirability response bias, 23-6,
175
social labelling theory, 261-2
social learning theory, 76, 77-8
Spearman, C., 9
Srull, T.K., 30, 31, 83
Stachnik, T.J., 174
Stainton, R.N., 174
Steele, C.M., 267
Steinmetz, J.L., 197
Stephenson, W., 89, 201, 235
Storey, R., 217
Storms, M.D., 184-5, 187
Stricker, L.J., 152
Strickland, B.R., 28
Sullivan, H.S., 201
Sundberg, N.D., 175
Swann, W.B., 266-7
symbolic interactionism, 177-83

Tagiuri, R., 5, 99, 110
Tatsuoka, M.M., 55, 253, 275
Temne, 16, 17, 18
Tennessee Self Concept Scale, 202
Terman, L.H., 217-18, 239
Thorne, A., 1, 149
Thorne, F.C., 175
Thurstone, L.L., 9
time of measurement, 208-9, 210,
211, 212, 213, 223-4, 225
Topol, B., 267-8
traits: as categories, 159-70, 171;
in Cattell's theory, 51, 55; cognitive
models of trait integration and
inference, 115-24; constructivist
position, 160-70; co-occurrence
likelihood of traits, 138-9, 140-1,
142-6, 152, 161; given traits,
110-15, 118-23; hierarchical
aspect of trait organisation, 132; in
hierarchical model, 45; implicit
personality theory, 98-9; impressions assessed by trait choices,
105-10; and interactionist research,
91-2; probe traits, 110-15, 118-23;
trait integration, quantitative
models of, 110-15; trait position,
interactionism and, 82-3; trait
ratings, 135-6; trait relations,
102-4; trait sorting/rating, 100-1;
trait theories attacked, 69; trait
vocabulary in children, 125-6,
128-9, 132-3; see also multi-
trait theories; single-trait theories
Tupes, E.C., 136-7, 140, 142
Turner, R.G., 94-5
Tversky, A., 186

Ulrich, R.D., 174
Uranowitz, S.W., 169

Vagg, P.R., 158
Vaillant, G.E., 229, 231, 238-40,
242, 243-4, 245
Valins, S., 184
Vernon, P.E., 17
verticality, 12-13
Vestewig, R., 93
Vivekananthan, P.S., 100

Wadsworth, M.E.J., 250, 263
Waldo, G.P., 251
Wallach, M.A., 84
Wallerstein, J.S., 262
Warburton, E.W., 57, 253
Warr, P.B., 111-12, 113, 114-15,
117, 119, 123
Watts, A.F., 127, 128, 133
Weisberg, P., 175
Weisenberg, M., 184
Weiss, D.S., 1, 149
Welford, C., 261
Werner, H., 133
West, D.J., 254, 257
White, P., 187
Wicklund, R.A., 193
Wiggins, J.S., 7
Will, Jr D.P., 158
Wilson, T.D., 184, 186-8, 227, 285
Winslow, R.W., 262
Wishner, J., 107-10, 112, 123, 134
Witkin, H.A., 11, 12-13, 14, 15, 16, 17
Wohlwill, J.F., 215
Wolfgang, M.E., 263
Woodruff, D.S., 225-8

Wootton, B., 250, 258
Wyer, R.S., 114
Wyle, C.J., 262

Yarrow, M.R., 128

Yochelson, S., 269-78

Zimbardo, P.G., 184
Zimmerman, W.S., 33